# AMERICAN WAGS AND ECCENTRICS
## *from Colonial Times to the Civil War*

GENERAL STORE AT WIGGIN'S OLD TAVERN, NORTHAMPTON, MASS.
*Courtesy House & Garden*

# AMERICAN CLASSICS

# AMERICAN WAGS AND ECCENTRICS
## from Colonial Times to the Civil War

ILLUSTRATED

## RICHARDSON WRIGHT

FREDERICK UNGAR PUBLISHING CO.
*NEW YORK*

*For*

MARSHALL R. KERNOCHAN

# INTRODUCTION

## *"Grandfather Was Queer"*

### WAGS AND ECCENTRICS IN GENERAL AND OF A
### CERTAIN ONE IN PARTICULAR

On a sunny June day, at the turn of the last century, a very old man and a very little boy were walking down Chestnut Street in Philadelphia. The very little boy had a tight grip on the very old man's hand. In the other hand the very old man carried a blackthorn cane, with which he thumped the pavement. He also shuffled his feet and he panted as he walked, puffing out his cheeks.

People glanced at the very old man and smiled. He had a funny fringe of white whiskers on his chin and his hair was long, and he wore a broad-brimmed soft straw hat, a choker collar on which his chin whiskers rested, an old-fashioned white stock and a swallow-tailed coat. There were spots, too, on his waistcoat, for the very old man was unsteady at table.

In the middle of a square, before a long, brick building, he halted, straightened up, took off his hat and said, "Remove your cap, my boy; this is the birthplace of our liberty." And, imitating his grandfather, the very little boy made a profound bow toward the front door. Then, hand in hand again, they mounted the steps into Independence Hall.

Inside, the very old man said something to a guard, who then spoke to another, and finally a third and more dignified person appeared. The small boy was introduced by the very old man as his grandson and namesake, and the dignified person shook his hand and asked them to wait a moment.

7

When he again appeared, he said, "We are ready, sir," and led the way.

The march ultimately ended in a large room. There were chairs on each side, and in front of them guards stood stiffly. At the end, on a platform, was a desk. The very old gentleman, his hat over his wrist, his head thrown back, and the boy's hand in his, walked through the line of guards to the platform. There the dignified man untied a ribbon, and the very old gentleman sat down in the chair behind the desk. The small boy was left standing alone before it.

After a silence, during which the very old gentleman passed his hands over the desk as if caressing it, he bowed forward and said, "My grandson and gentlemen; I am the last man who sat officially in this chair. It was John Hancock's chair. And this, as you know, is the anniversary of the day I last sat in it as an officer of this commonwealth. Thank you for the privilege of recalling pleasant memories and old friends."

Then the very old man thumped down the steps, grasped the small boy's hand again and, as he passed the guards, bowed to them right and left. The dignified person allowed the small boy to touch the Liberty Bell, and on the way home the very old man stopped at a shop and bought for himself a Pittsburgh stogie, and for the very small boy, a bag of all-day suckers.

That was one of the idiosyncrasies he pursued. The last man in Philadelphia to wear a swallow-tailed coat, stock and choker collar, he observed this private anniversary year after year, until too feeble to go to town. When, eventually, he passed away, the newspapers printed long tales about him. They mentioned that in the legislature at Harrisburg before the stormy years of the Civil War, he had sat in John Hancock's chair. But none of them knew that—usually alone—

he came on this certain day in June to Independence Hall, to claim the privilege of sitting in that chair again.

He displayed other eccentricities. If while walking down the street he saw an attractive woman approach with a child in leading, he would halt, raise his hat, gaze at the child, then at the mother, and address her with, "Ma'am, I can tell from the resemblance that you are the mother of this beautiful child." A pleasant conversation invariably ensued.

Another gallantry, followed to his latest tottering days, was in punctiliously offering his seat in a train or horse-car to a woman—any woman. With grave ceremony he would install her in the seat, and then explain, "Ma'am, perhaps you would care to know who it was that gave you his place. . . . I am Richardson L. Wright."

In those days we, being young and unthinking, used to say that "Grandfather was queer." Now that time has sobered us, we hold his eccentricities as precious marks of the man. Since some of us have ourselves reached the status of grandfathers, granduncles, or grandaunts, we realize the weight of Leslie Stephen's pronouncement, "We always think our grandfathers fools, because we value inordinately the changes which have been effected in our own time. For our great-grandfathers we can make allowance, for they are at a distance which levels all petty jealousy." [1]

From the remembrance of those gallantries, and especially that ceremony in Independence Hall, has stemmed, after these many years, this study of eccentrics and wags.

This book will have no social significance. Not by the widest stretch of the imagination can it be interpreted as showing that the race has gone—or isn't going—to the dogs. And still it has an excuse for being.

An age that can count among its highly-publicized citizens such outstanding men and women as flag-pole sitters,

champion hog-hollerers, lady vaudeville preachers, candi-
dates who attain gubernatorial office with a hill-billy band,
debutantes who pursue sweet charity to get their photo-
graphs in newspapers, and yokels who reap national notoriety
by spitting tobacco juice the admirable distance of eighteen
feet six inches—such an age would seem likely to produce
enough queer bits and pieces to make its own crazy quilt
without dipping into the scrap-bag of the past. It might
appear pointless, then, to speak of grandfather being queer,
when the present generation of potential grandfathers is
producing its own race of odd sticks that could easily over-
shadow those eccentrics who strutted their feeble, obscure
little days through the early history of this country.

Yet from that obscurity the succeeding pages will drag
them forth, for they are the veritable ancestors, many of
them unpublicized and unsung, of our present breed. Their
simple annals are hid away in dusty local town histories,
in broadsides, cartoons, and in the cracking and yellowed
sheets of the rural press. One doesn't go out casually and dig
them up the way a research worker might accumulate the
facts and anecdotes, say, on Shays' Rebellion, or the Campaign in the Wilderness, or that dreariest of all subjects, the
ecclesiastical history of New England. They crop up when
you least expect them—when you are searching for something else. You go up into the attic to find a spinning-wheel
—and come down with a handful of crazy-looking puppets.

It might be possible, did the mood and time conspire, to
make a profound-appearing study of these Early American
eccentrics—something tricked out with Freudian *clichés* and
the professional argot of those who poke their bug-lights
across the uneven terrain of border-line cases. Let someone
else prove *why* grandfather was queer, while we satisfy ourselves with discovering why he *seems* queer to us. This may
involve, as we go along, excursions into the customs, habits

and thinking of eighteenth century America—an age that produced individuals—and into the early circumstances of this country which fostered this individualism. Our eccentrics and individuals are worthy of a setting.

Viewed in the light of our present state of regimentation, any rugged or unstandardized individualism appears to be a ludicrous deviation from what we consider the classic standard for human beings. The last seventy-five years have witnessed a general leveling off to a standard. Easy communications make for fewer individualities. Publicity and photography repress eccentricity, except where the person is eccentric through guile—in which case the eccentricity is merely the seeking of publicity.

Our purpose is not to poke fun at these dusky shades. Indeed, many who seemed ludicrous to their contemporaries have since acquired, through the appreciation of passing time, a nobility of stature and purpose. And in many an instance we will discover that Grandfather was simply wrong.

The wag is a horse of a different color. His wit and quixotic notions, nine times out of ten, are part of his racial inheritance. Waggery, in Early America, did not get under way until the Scotch-Irish and the Irish had infiltrated the ranks of those middle-class English who formed the bulk of the first arrivals. And before this mercurial element came to these shores, they themselves had been transformed.

Sprung from lowland Scotch and borderland English, the Scotch-Irish crossed the North Channel into counties Antrim and Down, abandoning their pastoral lands for flax fields and bleach greens and changing an isolated existence to living close together on small farms. New scenes quickened the mental processes of the transplanted Scots, and the more compact community life enlarged their social instincts. In this way the sternness of the Scotch covenanter was softened by a century of residence in Ireland amid persecution and trial, and gradually was tinctured there with the pathos and comic humor of the Irish.[2]

Captain Marryat, who came over in 1838 to observe and pass judgment on us, states in his diary, "The Americans themselves are often the cause of their being misrepresented: there is no country, perhaps, in which the habit of exceeding for what is termed hoaxing, is so common." Peddling, swapping and practical joking appeared to foreign visitors as our national preoccupations. Marryat found another cause for our being misrepresented in that "travelers are not aware of the jealousy existing between the inhabitants of the different states and cities. The eastern states pronounce the southerners to be choleric, reckless, regardless of law and indifferent to religion; while the southerners designate the eastern states as a nursery of over-reaching pedlars, selling clocks and wooden nutmegs." [3]

How that hoaxing and waggery developed and spread is woven into the tapestry of the American scene. It is a well-founded part of our legend. We can start our study of eccentrics and wags, then, with those three centers of American waggery—the general store, the tavern, and the barber shop.

In the first we encounter the evolution of retail merchandising, in the second the rise of public hospitality, in the third we will trace the style evolutions of one form of masculine vanity. Since the general store is so typically an American institution, let us begin, here and now, to consider it.

The progress of selling assorted merchandise in the United States went forward in three successive steps.

At the peak of this evolution proudly rests today's department store, a resplendent, complicated, complete and efficiently staffed organization, dedicated with voluble ardor to "Service"—presumably at a profit.

Midway in this progress stands the general store of the country town.

At the other end is a gaunt and shabbily dressed Yankee pedlar with a pack of assorted notions on his back and no exalted ideas of service in his head, apart from the service he might render himself in making a living by whatever profits his glib tongue or slick salesmanship might secure.

Somewhere in this evolution there disappeared, as though it were an unnecessary prehensile tail, the essential characteristic of picturesque selling and pronounced individualism in salesmen. Merchandising lost its sense of humor when business developed fixed prices, promoted commercial honesty to a major virtue, subjected its selling force to standardized intelligence tests, and began spinning auras of godliness around the retreating brows of department store owners.

For one hundred and fifty years the Yankee pedlar (and sometimes he wasn't a Yankee) served as the butt for the nation's jokes from Maine to California. His immediate descendant, the general store, served as a center of jokes and waggery. After this phase of the merchant's rise in the social scale, it was found convenient to forget lowly beginnings.

Only within the past few years, when some uncontrolled merry pen occasionally expresses itself in playful or sardonic advertising copy, does the department store show an inclination to regain that mirthful and gossip-provoking salesmanship which once made the Yankee pedlar symbolic of trade in America.

The best way to understand this Yankee pedlar is to watch him in action.

# CONTENTS

## Part I

### THREE CENTERS OF WAGGERY

## Part II

### WAGS AND ECCENTRICS

16                 Contents

# ILLUSTRATIONS

*Part I*

# THREE CENTERS OF WAGGERY

# I

## THE GENERAL STORE

### *Mr. Davis Buys Earrings*

Nightfall of a March day in 1802 found John Davis finally arrived at Frying-Pan Run.

A sailor, linear ancestor of the Conrads and McFees, he had left the sea to follow literary pursuits, and he took it as part of his calling to inspect the new United States. When obliged to, he traveled by horseback, stage coach and sloop, but ordinarily he journeyed on foot, for he prided himself on being a mighty pedestrian. He had walked through all fifteen states, had visited towns and cities and traversed a fair share of the countryside, and now was about to experience the backwoods hospitality of Virginia.

After much circuitous wandering, he stumbled up to the solitary log hut at Frying-Pan Run. There he found an honest, open-handed welcome and, on the importunities of the planter and his five children, Mary, Eliza, Wilmot, Bill and Jack, was persuaded to stay the night.

"We had breakfast the next morning," he says, "and the old man was gone to cultivate his tobacco, when a pedlar came to the door. The appearance of Sam Lace lighted up joy in the eyes of Mary and Eliza.

"The pedlar first exhibited his ballads. 'Here,' said he, 'is the whole trial, examination and condemnation of Jason Fairbanks, who was executed at Philadelphia for cutting off Peggy Placet's head under a hedge on the road to Frankford.'

23

" 'Lord,' said Eliza, 'what a wicked fellow: I would not live in one of those great big towns for all the world. But I wonder whether it is true.'

" 'True?' replied Mary. 'Certainly it is. Don't you see it in print?'

" 'And here,' cried the pedlar, 'is the account of a whale that was left ashore by the tide in the Bay of Chesapeak, with a ship of five thousand tons in his belly, called the *Merry Dane* of Dover. She was the largest ship ever known.'

" 'And is that true, too?' asked Eliza.

" 'True?' cried Mary. 'How can you ask such a question? Do you think they would print it if it was not true?'

" 'Come, pedlar,' said I, 'let us examine the contents of your box. Have you any earrings?'

"At this interrogation, I could perceive the bosom of Mary rise to her chin.

" 'Yes, Sir,' said the fellow. 'I have earrings that would be an ornament to the ears of the President's lady. I have them at all prices—from five dollars down to one and a half. My five dollar pairs are fit for the first tip top, quality breeding.'

" 'Let me see some,' said I, 'that are fit for the first tip top, quality breeding.'

" 'There,' said he, 'is a pair—and there is another, that a duchess need not be ashamed of. I sold the fellow pair last week to Squire Cartwright's lady in Gloucester County.'

"I thought the heart of Mary would have burst from its bondage. It made her little bosom heave up and down like a bird that was dying.

" 'Mary,' said I, 'do me the favour to accept that pair of earrings; and, Eliza, I beg you will take the other.'

"Eliza had put on her little straw bonnet to visit Miss M——, at the shrine of whose beauty Wilmot was offering his incense; and she now danced off with an accession of happiness from the present I had made her. The pedlar strung his box over his shoulder, and seizing his staff, pursued his journey through the woods." [1]

## Yankee Pedlars

So off into the woods he goes, a rangy, sprawling-gaited figure in butternut brown, weighted down with his box of wares—the Gypsy of American commerce, our most picturesque perambulating early institution. He was also the most energetic, the most courageous.

It took energy to carry heavy packs of merchandise interminable miles along Indian trails, or drive laden carts over rutted roads through all seasons. It took persistence and a quick wit to seek out and sell likely customers in isolated districts where sales resistance was built up by stern necessity. Yet even in the backwoods, "people would rather be shaved by a sharp razor than a dull one." [2] They easily succumbed to his "soft sawder."

It took courage to face the dangers of this solitary existence, to sleep under the stars with the howls of wild animals for lullaby, to travel alone through wilderness or thinly inhabited countryside. A pedlar with a pack of merchandisable notions or the cash from three months' sales was an easy mark for savage and highwayman. Many an inland trader met his death at their hands. [3]

It was also a particularly rigid brand of honesty that impelled these men to return the profits to their employers when an easy chance for a getaway appeared in every port and side road.

Many hands were against the pedlar, and not the least of these was the law, urged on by tax-paying shopkeepers who smarted under his competition.

Boston merchants, finding the hawkers' door-to-door selling had cut in on their trade, started complaining to the

General Court in 1713, saying the goods they sold were stolen in the fire of two years before that almost devastated the city. The court, heeding this pressure, forbade the traffic.

In 1714, New York required country chapmen to be licensed before they could trade from town to town. Connecticut, the spawning ground of a thousand pedlars, began worrying over the "Multitude of foreign or Peregrine Pedlars who flock to this Colony and travel up and Down in it with Packs of goods to sell." The bewailing merchants also feared that these chapmen would introduce into the Colony "many raging and contagious diseases" and they petitioned the Governor and House of Magistrates to come to their help. So in 1727 the authorities demanded a £5 license from them and a 4s. fee, which eventually rose to £20 and an 8s. fee, and forbade all peddling except in deerskins, beaver furs, and the produce and manufacture of Connecticut and neighboring colonies. In 1720, Philadelphia merchants, stating that these idle and vagrant persons "have greatly imposed upon many people as well in the quality as in the price of their goods," first required the pedlar to produce a warrant of good character before allowing him to apply for his license. In South Carolina, tax-paying town and country shopkeepers accused the pedlar of cut-throat competition, and of clandestine traffic with servants and slaves. The Assembly set his fee at £50 for land hawking and £100 by water, and in addition demanded that he post a bond not to trade with slaves or servants.

An irate merchant, writing to the *New York Gazette,* called pedlars "Idle and Lazy Strangers, who have no families to maintain, who pay neither Lot nor Scot nor do any duty in service of their King or Country, yet are suffered to wander from House to House and from Place to Place, to dispose of all manner of wares and Merchandize, to the ruin of trade." [4]

In short, about everything the law could do to restrain and inhibit the pedlar's business was set in motion by the middle of the eighteenth century. In spite of this, in spite of dangers of the road and arduous travel, the pedlar persisted. He may have been banished from towns, but in the backwoods and expanding frontiers of America he flourished.

The first pedlars—usually young men seeking profit and adventure—sold goods that they and their families had made at home. When they took to the road with them, they filled the triple role of manufacturer, salesman, and transportation agent. Later they were employed by manufacturers to distribute their wares. Such were the early tin pedlars of Connecticut, who were sent out by the tinware makers of Berlin in that colony, the catechism and broadside venders of Massachusetts, and the stocking sellers who hailed from Philadelphia.

As their own resources grew, they bought their stocks of a wholesale town merchant. Their silver buttons and cheap jewelry came from some such dealer as Charles Oliver Bruff, New York goldsmith and jeweler, whose sign of the Teapot, Tankard and Earring on Maiden Lane was familiar to country chapmen before the War of Independence, as he advertised that pedlars who favored him with their custom would be well used.[5] By the early years of the nineteenth century, many pedlars were thus financing their own stocks and buying them from town merchants. Thomas Danforth, pewterer of Rocky Hill, Connecticut, was also an outfitter of pedlars. Eventually he established a chain of stores down the Atlantic seaboard as far south as Savannah, stores that sold general merchandise and furnished the same to pedlar's packs and carts. Many an ancestor of our present-day proud and respectable owners of department stores at one time was a pedlar himself and later carried on a profitable backdoor trade with pedlars.

So long as travel from settlement to settlement was by blazed Indian trail, the pedlar was limited in the quantity and size of the goods he carried. James Gray, famous Boston book pedlar, who died in 1705, must have been restricted in the number of books and pamphlets he carried "up and down the country selling," and in the distances he could carry them even on horseback.

And yet the foot pedlar's tin trunk could hold an amazing assortment. When one of them was robbed in New Jersey in 1762, the highwaymen seized this miscellany: "Calicoes, Chintzes, printed linen, long, clear and flowered lawns, sundry sorts of silks and linen handkerchiefs, Satin, Pelong and solid silver buttons." [6] These foot and horseback pedlars in little merchandise also sold Yankee notions—combs and pewter and brass buttons, cheap jewelry such as John Davis bought the two Virginia backwoods girls, shoelaces, Jew's-harps, indigo and essences and perfumes, drugs and laces. At Williamstown, Mass., an early nineteenth century pedlar joshed the crowd and did a thriving trade with this assortment—lead pencils, steel pens, cakes of shaving soap, gilt finger rings, bracelets, clasps and other jewelry, cards of pearl buttons, bundles of wooden combs, boxes of matches and suspenders. [7]

How did he ever get so many things into his pack? Calicoes went in with tin pans, cotton checks and ginghams were stowed beneath tin cups and iron spoons, "shining coffee pots were crammed with spools of thread, papers of pins, cards of horn buttons and cakes of shaving soap—and bolts of gaudy riband could be drawn from the pepper-boxes and sausage-stuffers." The gradual unpacking of this assorted merchandise was part of his sales presentation.

With the Indian trails developed into "tote" roads and widened to cartways and new roads cut into the back country, the pedlar took to a wagon. By 1790, private companies and the nation began penetrating the wilderness with turnpikes and connecting rivers and lakes with canals. The pedlar could now offer bulkier merchandise in addition to his small wares. He could carry more of it and he could travel longer distances from his source of supplies. In that way he became the manufacturer's and wholesaler's country distributor.

Without the pedlar to carry his goods through forest and farmland and along the frontiers, the manufacturers and merchants of New England and the middle colonies would have had scant country distribution. Through the pedlar's efforts were brought to isolated farmhouses the clocks, tin-ware and brass of Connecticut, the pottery of Massachusetts, Vermont and New Jersey, the chairs, baskets, brooms, lad-ders, rakes, horsewhips, woollen goods, oysters and fish, cheese and horseradish, sheet music, tracts and cook-books, hats and plaited ware, and diverse other products from a hundred little factories. The pedlar brought the store in miniature to the consumer's door.

The pedlar's market expanded with the growth of the colonies and states, the pushing westward of the frontiers and improvements in the ways of travel. The day was to come when he would be as familiar a figure among the gold-dig-gers' camps of California as he had been in the settlements along the Atlantic seaboard and down the Ohio Valley.

As immigration to these shores increased, his nationality changed. The first two generations of pack pedlars were Yankees, Irish and Scotch-Irish. By 1836, German Jews had seriously invaded the trade. It is in this earlier race of pedlars that we find the rise of rustic waggery and sharp practices, although those who followed them were schooled in the same commercial cunning. Whether Yankee or Jew, the pedlar persisted as one of the brightest facets of the American scene up to the Civil War.

## Pedlars' Tricks

Tales of Yankee and Jewish pedlars' tricks are legion. He provided a source of laughter and furnished the butt for jokes in the theatre long before the first stage Irishman stepped out of the wings. An old description of a pedlar runs: "He wer hatched in a crack—in frosty rocks, whar nut-maigs am made outen maple, an whar wimmen paints clock faces an' pints shoe-paigs, an the men invents rat-traps, man-traps an' new-fangled doctrines for the aid ov the devil."

The hardy, rapscallion Yankee chapman continued to be a funny figure in American literature and on the stage and in taverns until the 1840's, when Sam Slick started out with his load of clocks. Then he grew into the stature of a folk hero. His witty remarks, wise saws and provincial eccentricities made him an important figure in American political and social satire.

He found satisfaction for all the contumely heaped on him by making good bargains out of his gullible customers. His sharpness was part of his aforesaid provincial eccentricities. Coming mostly from New England, both the climate and the unyielding soil—an existence bounded by "twenty acres of rock, a Bible and a cow"—had sharpened his wits. Also, as we have seen, in most places the law was against him; and he needed cunning either to evade it or to succeed in spite of it. He was instinctively an alert merchant. A ready answer and disarming flattery were essentials of his salesmanship.

There was the pedlar who used to visit Nantucket and Martha's Vineyard each Spring, selling straw hats to the women. He was their source of style news, a sort of perambulating *Vogue.* One year, when the hats were tiny, he announced that it was now the fashion to wear two hats—"one on the front of the head and the other over the bun at the back"—and he sold each of them a pair!

The differences in currencies between the colonies before the War of Independence and the confusion in currency that followed it made barter the only possible method for most rural sales. Now the principle of a deal in bartering in those days was to outwit the customer—to use such persuasive methods of what we call "salesmanship" that the pedlar almost invariably got the better end of the bargain. While in cities before the war some effort was made to arrive at dependable price lists for raw goods and manufactured articles, isolated country districts knew no such fixed prices. The pedlar could ask all the traffic would bear. He was like the medicine vendor in O. Henry's story: he respected his profession and was satisfied with 300 per cent profit!

From the town, where he had acquainted himself with current prices, the pedlar went into a thinly settled region and bartered his goods for farm produce and local wares. The straw-chewing yokels, having no notion of current town prices, could be persuaded to accept goods and pay for them in produce that, in town, had a marketable value far in excess of what they had received in exchange. The pedlar might swap dress goods for bees-wax and tinware for pelts. Many a time Eli Terry swapped a clock for a piece of pork.

He also had the genial habit of "accommodating" his customer. He took an old book or a chair or a good piece of pewter or old rags in exchange for their purchases. Of course, he always knew the value of these articles—which leads us to believe that the pedlar was the first dealer in Early American antiques.[8]

Many other were the tricks Yankee pedlars played in this Golden Age of countryside hawking, before chambers of commerce and better business methods discovered honesty and made it the criterion of success. They sold brass buttons for

gold, and $10 clocks for $30. Hawthorne encountered a pedlar who sold perfumes made at Ashfield, Mass., but bearing
foreign labels, which added authenticity to his glamorous
selling. This slick Yankee also sold essences—anise, cloves,
red cedar, wormwood and hair oil—which he blandly recommended for the complaints of both children and grownups! [9]
A drug pedlar would buy his pills in quantity lots, put them
up under his own label, fortified with his own self-concocted
recommendations, and sell them as his own make. The next
pedlar sold the same pills under a different fancy name, and
sometimes recommended them for quite a different illness.
As Captain Simon Suggs remarked, "It's good to be shifty in
a new country."

In the middle of the eighteenth century New Jersey, as
well as other colonies, was being flooded with counterfeit
paper money. It was discovered that pedlars were distribut-
ing it. At Princeton in 1757, two pedlars who said they hailed
from Lancaster, Pa., appeared on horseback with packs of
linen and other dry-goods, and were arrested for exchanging
counterfeit ten-shilling Pennsylvania bills. They claimed
these had been passed to them in Trenton and offered, with
all the indignation in their noble souls, to go right back there
and find the culprit. The judge, however, insisted that they
leave their packs for security. Of course, they never returned;
so their goods were sold for the benefit of the poor.[10]

During the Revolutionary War a number of Yankee pedlars, dressed in the uniform of Continental officers, complete
with swords and cockades, used to travel around New England. Their uniforms gave them free passage and practically
compelled sales. Another Yankee pedlar, a dealer in fifes,
always wore a military uniform, which provided the authentic "air" to his merchandise. One Connecticut pedlar, who,
by the way, was later found murdered, attracted his customers by "rolling" on a drum as he entered a village. It is

not recorded that his untimely demise followed an outburst
of wrath from a native who disliked drum-rolling.

The tin pedlar later became a tinker and the clock pedlar
a repairer of clocks, thus giving us the first faint indication
of that "Service" on which the reputation of department
stores today is so firmly established. With equal ease did
the hawker of nostrums add a sideline of simple doctoring
in order to gain a standing in those backwoods communities
where every housewife had her own set notions of *materia
medica*. Often they actually claimed to be doctors and carried
recommendations from grateful patients. Much of their doctoring was bluff and a lot of it crude superstition, but a
bright Yankee with a trunkful of patent medicines and a
smart head on his shoulders could be depended on to gain
a medical reputation in no time.

The clocks of Connecticut, which eventually appeared in
every American household, however humble, were marked,
with Yankee canniness, "Warranted if Well Used." The men
who sold them were often equally canny. From the large
body of clock pedlar tales and legends, let us pick the plum
of them. It has to do with a slick chapman from the middle
reaches of Connecticut who always sold a clock on the under-
standing that he would return in a few weeks, and if the
clock did not run satisfactorily, would replace it with another. It was also his rule to sell all the clocks in his stock
but one. When he reached the end of his route he turned
back with his one remaining clock. At the first house the
clock he had sold there had not run, so he replaced it with
the one that remained. At the second house he replaced the
unsatisfactory clock there with the one he had taken back
from the first house. And so on he went, selling and replac-
ing clocks that would never work!

Spring and Autumn country fairs, weekly and semi-weekly
markets, militia training days were the pedlar's happy hunt-

ing grounds. Here he opened his pack or displayed his goods on his cart and hawked them to those who gathered around. He always seems to have had a way with the ladies. John Dunton, the roving bookseller, states that a virtuous woman could be distinguished as one who did not go to the fair "in order to meet with the chapmen or pedlars." Even on ordinary days, when a pedlar appeared on the village green and opened his pack, women dropped their chores and men their work, to see his wares and hear his gossip. And if he were welcome in towns, imagine how cordial the welcome by isolated farm wives and country girls. When Dr. Alexander Hamilton traveled along the Atlantic seaboard in 1744, he set down in his diary an encounter with a gossipy Scotch-Irish pedlar at Stonington, Conn. Having sold some "dear bargains" to the host and "smoothed her with palaver," the pedlar offered a tidbit of scandal to Dr. Hamilton—how that when Paul Ruiz, the Portuguese, and N—y H—y were in Philadelphia and the neighborhood of that city, they passed for man and wife, which they certainly weren't.[11]

After many solitary days and hours on the road, was it any wonder that the pedlar's tongue began wagging both ways when he got his feet inside a door? In "Mr. Higginbotham's Catastrophe," Hawthorne relates how the pedlar's gossip, taken for gospel truth, rolled up a countryside crisis. The tobacco pedlar, Dominicus Pike, having been met by a stranger who informed him that the rich and crusty Mr. H. of a nearby town had been murdered in his orchard the night before, so spread the news that it had the whole neighborhood agitated.

Genial, gay, at times obscene, the pedlar delighted country wenches with gossip, news and ribald balladry. Many a lad among them displayed a light-hearted contempt for respectability, especially for that branch of respectability supported by the Seventh Commandment. And many a country wench,

it would seem, shared his contempt. To the numskulls and
lack-wits in little towns and on distant frontiers, this traveled
stranger was a God-sent boon.

He had many virtues withal. He lightened the burden of
domestic manufacturing: whereas frontier women had to
make their own goods and household utensils, the pedlar
now brought them to her door. His Yankee notions were
luxuries. The possession of these trinkets bolstered the vanity of women and thereby helped them over many a weari-
some passage in their hard lives.

He knew the Indian trails and the white man's roads as
well, and he could help stranger and native alike to find the
way and locate kin and shelter. In times of national stress
he helped rally the farm folk to the country's support.
Politicians used him for an election tout. From house to
house he carried good news and bad, gossip, scandal, droll
stories, and love messages that set many a maiden's heart
aflutter.

## The General Store

It is quite easy to trace the course of the pedlar from his
pack carried on foot to his load carried on horseback, to his
cart with the bigger load—and then to the general store. A
well-traveled man, he observed the opportunities of the
countryside. He was the first to make a merchandise survey. He saw embryo cities in cross-roads hamlets. Often he
found a girl there whom he married and with whom he
would settle down. He chose the likeliest town—and his cart-
load of assorted merchandise came to rest in a general store.
And, just as he had been a carrier of waggery when on the
road, so did his general store in the country town become its
local center when he settled there.

These general stores were literal emporiums. Ancestors
of our department stores, they offered an amazing array of

merchandise. Samuel Temple, who harried the youth of his
day by writing "Temple's Arithmetic," was also a rhymster
of sorts. When he went into storekeeping, at Dedham, Mass.,
he set forth his stock in verse—and saw that it was printed
in the local paper:

> Salt Pork and Powder, Shot and Flints,
> Cheese, Sugar, Rum and Peppermints,
>
> Tobacco, Raisins, Flour and Spice,
> Flax, Wool, Cotton and sometimes Rice,
>
> Old Holland Gin and Gingerbread,
> Brandy and Wine, all sorts of Thread,
>
> Segars I keep, sometimes on bunch;
> Materials all for making Punch,
>
> Biscuit and Butter, Eggs and Fishes.
> Molasses, Beer and Earthen Dishes.
>
> Books on such subjects as you'll find
> A proper food to feast the mind.
>
> Hard Soap and Candles, Tea and Snuff,
> Tobacco Pipes—perhaps enough,
>
> Shells, Chocolate, Stetson's Hoes
> As good as can be (I suppose),
>
> Straw Hats, Oats, Baskets, Oxen Muzzles,
> A thing which many people puzzles,
>
> Knives, Forks, Spoons, Plates, Mugs, Pitchers, Platters,
> A Gun with shot wild geese bespatters,
>
> Spades, Shovels, Whetstones, Scythes and Rakes,
> As good as any person makes,
>
> Shirts, Frocks, Shoes, Mittens, also Hose,
> And many other kinds of Clothes,
>
> Shears, Scissors, Awls, Wire, Bonnet Paper,
> Old Violin and Cat Gut Scraper,

Tubs, Buckets, Pails and Pudding Pans,
Bandana Handkerchiefs and Fans,

Shagbarks and Almonds, Wooden Boxes,
Steel Traps (not stout enough for Foxes,

But excellent for holding Rats
When they elude the Paws of Cats),

I've more than Forty kinds of Drugs,
Some good for Worms and some for Bugs,
Lee's, Anderson's and Dexter's Pills,
Which cure at least a hundred ills,

Astringents, Laxatives, Emetics,
Cathartics, Cordials, Diuretics,

Narcotics, Stimulants and Pungents,
With half a dozen kinds of Unguents.

Perfume most grateful to the Nose
When mixed with Snuff or dropped on clothes,

One Medicine more (not much in fame),
Prevention is its real name,
An ounce of which, an author says
Outweighs a Ton of Remedies.

The many things I shall not mention
To sell them cheap is my intention.
Lay out a dollar when you come
And you shall have a glass of Rum.

N.B. Since man to man is so unjust,
'Tis hard to say whom I can trust.
I've trusted many to my sorrow:
Pay me today: I'll trust tomorrow.[12]

With such a storekeeper at its head, imagine what humor
ran through the ordinary day as country purchasers came
and went and loiterers leaned against the counter or sat
enthroned on the cracker box!

The cracker box, to the contents of which general store

habitués helped themselves, has long stood as the symbol of folk disquisition in rural America. The general store ranked next to the town meeting as a home of free expression and discussion, where local counselors sat in judgment upon all men who were not within reach of their voices and upon all crying evils of the time which were too mighty for them to struggle against,[13] whatever went on in national and local politics, major and minor events of the town and countryside, rural practices, husbandry, farming, family life and theology. With equal ease these loiterers discussed foreordination and the duties of the pound-keeper.

> They met, made speeches full long winded,
> Resolved, protested and rescinded.

Here they gathered "to gratify their gregarious propensities. Here amid characteristic odors of brown sugar, plug tobacco, vinegar, whiskey, molasses and the dressed leather of boots and shoes, social intercourse was carried on by a group seated on top of nail kegs, the protruding ends of shoe boxes and the counter. . . . Here were related again all those stock anecdotes which have come down from an antiquity inconceivably remote." [14]

It is impossible to write a tale of a New England village or a frontier town without this institution, where everything was sold from hoe-handles up to cambric needles, where the post office was kept and where was a general exchange of news, gossip and good stories, as the different farm wagons stood hitched around the door and their owners spent a leisurely moment discussing politics, the weather or theology from the top of codfish and cracker barrels while their wives and daughters were shopping among the dress goods and ribbons on the other side of the store.

Here also were hatched practical jokes and extra-legal punishments and waggery untold. The tight-fisted, the hen-

pecked, the local dandy, the outrager of public morals, the
pompous and the dolt all came in for their share of read-
justment and public pillorying by members of the Supreme
Court of the Cracker Box.

Their humor was generally of the hand-hewn, earthy type.
It was the product of a coarse-grained class of men and it
had the sanity of coarseness. Often it bordered on the obscene. In its production and application the storekeeper had
a hand; although, because of his position in the town, his
hand could not be shown. During the councils of his habitués, he was apt to speak a word of warning from behind
the counter or drop a suggestion.

Rarely was any record made of these pranks, although
occasionally, in the time-browned pages of country newspapers, hints of them can be sensed. However, old men in
little country towns can still dig down into their memories
and bring forth gems of cracker barrel wit. Consider as
typical this little touch of correction administered by a
storekeeper and his circle in Marion, Mass. Hadley's General Store stood in a prominent place opposite the Congregational Church. One of its customers was known throughout
the town for his habit of counting the pennies. A persistent
materialist, there was scarcely anything he wouldn't do to
save a cent. He came into the store one fine Summer day
with an order from his wife for two necessary household
items—a broom and a chamber pot. The "boys" had been
waiting for just this chance and they hinted to the storekeeper that he might suggest a bargain: that he throw in the
broom on condition that the local tight-wad carry the pot
slung over his shoulder on the broom. While this was being
agreed to, one of the "boys" slipped out of the store and
spread the news, so that when the pinch-penny yokel
marched down Main Street with his intimate purchases
openly displayed, he was accorded an enthusiastic reception.

## Local Munchausens

The general store, too, furnished an audience for local Munchausens who were given to the characteristic American humor of exaggeration. Any visit away from town, any extraordinary experience, was related in all the realistic color the narrators could command. These town liars were like that Coonskin hero who stated, "I'm that same David Crockett, fresh from the backwoods, half-horse, half-alligator, a little touched with the snapping-turtle; can wade the Mississippi, leap the Ohio, ride upon a streak of lightning, and slip without a scratch down a honey-locust, can whip my weight in wild cats—and if any gentleman pleases, for a ten-dollar bill he may throw in a panther." [15]

Often the town liar and general butt for practical jokes was the village half-wit. A panegyric should be written on these poor, cloudy-brained but harmless dolts whom the small country towns of America tolerated and often helped maintain with a charity beyond praise. The wags of the general store may have made his public life miserable—they were always inducing him to smoke loaded cigars!—but, privately, they put their hands into their pockets and their larders when he and his family were hard pressed.

Burlington, N. J., had its extravagant narrator in John Wood, who used to delight small boys and even some adults in the first quarter of the last century with tall tales, which he invariably claimed to have witnessed or experienced. One was about some dogs he saw that would eat fire until it blazed out of their mouths. In another he related how once he had ridden through a field of rye which had grown so high that, even though he was on a large horse, he had to part the grain with his whip as he galloped across the field at full speed. Another of Burlington's vivid characters was savage-faced Jonathan Grimage, a tall, stout pedlar, crier of vendues and constable, who proved a terror to children. Still another terror to Burlington's younger generation was Old Joany, a little, black-visaged female, who always carried a bag into which she put the food she begged, but told children it was full of "sabble rats." [16]

A magnificent town-bragger was Captain Lemuel Gulliver, who once lived at Algerine Corner, Milton, Mass. In 1723 he returned to his native Ireland, where he described New England and its resources to his neighbor, Jonathan Swift —told of frogs so large that they reached to a man's knees and had musical voices that sounded like the twang of guitars; of mosquitoes with bills as large as darning needles. It is believed that from these and similar exaggerations related by Captain Gulliver, Swift first caught the idea and the name for "Gulliver's Travels." [17]

Among those who were natural liars, "just as some horses are natural pacers and some dogs natural setters," was the local adventurer in the West who, on returning home, told this yarn of the soil's fertility there to a gaping audience: "Just before I left Muskingum, one day, horseback, having taken some pumpkin seeds into my hand at the door of a house, several of which I dropped, turning about to speak to a person then passing, so instantaneous was their growth, so surprisingly rapid their extension and spread, that before I turned back the seed had taken root in the earth to such a degree that I was dangerously encompassed about with enormous serpentine vines, which threatened keeping pace with my utmost exertions to escape being tied in; so I immediately clapped spurs to my horse and with difficulty was disentangled." [18]

## The "Regulators"

Loiterers in the general store and local tavern were as capable of cooking up condign and salutary punishments as they were of concocting practical jokes. It seems almost certain that the ruddy sense of justice which guided the thinking of such countrymen was responsible for that marital K. K. K. of upper New Jersey in the middle of the eighteenth century.

In this neighborhood appeared a group of men who called themselves "Regulators." If they heard of a man who had beaten his wife, they dressed in women's clothes, painted their faces and, going to the man's house at night, dragged him out of bed, stripped him and "thrashed him across his posteriors, shouting, 'Woe to the men who beat their wives!' " [19]

A local commentator suggested that another sect might be called "Regulatrixes" and be composed of women who would dress in men's clothes and "flagellate the Posteriors of Scolds and Termagants." After the visit of the "Regulators" to her home (or was this letter the creation of a local wag?), Prudence Goodwife wrote to the *New York Gazette* that her husband had often been in liquor and smashed all her cups and saucers, but that after having been beaten by the "Regulators" he left off whipping her, and now "there never was a better harmony subsisting between Man and Wife. . . . We are as happy as we were in our Courting Days." [20]

Another time the blacked-face gang went to beat a husband for his excessive jealousy of his wife, but when they found the woman and her gallant together, they whipped them both. [21]

Finally these punishers of matrimonial trespassers went to a house intending to make a man ride "Skimmington," i.e., on a pole carried on their shoulders. In the scuffle he

THE CAT INSPECTOR OF LITTLE REST

killed one of them and wounded two others, which caused the association to disband for a time. Their activity broke out again five years later when, near Bound Brook, they went to punish a William Daniels for beating his wife. The next morning William was found dead in bed. Of the three men concerned in this affair, one fled and the other two surrendered to the authorities and were confined in Brunswick jail.[22]

## The Cat Inspector of Little Rest

Often out of these groups of loiterers in general store and tavern sprang social clubs. The names of many of them are written in water. Others, surviving their salad days, grew into substantial institutions, such as the American Philosophical Society, which stemmed from Franklin's gatherings of the leather-apron boys of the Junto at the Indian King in Philadelphia. Hell Fire Clubs of rowdy youths, if we are to believe that Connecticut arch-counterfeiter, William Stuart,[23] were common in New England. Boston had a Tippling Club, the members of which devoted themselves to drinking for drinking's sake, and might be dubbed the ancestors of the Hub's present Club des Arts Gastronomique, which goes in for "selective drinking."

Others of these clubs left only a vague history. Among them would be classed the Hornet's Nest, which stands apart for waggery. In 1806 Charles Comstock published its record in a little volume with the tantalizing title: "A History of South Kingston . . . With a particular description of the Hornet's Nest and the Cat Let out of the Bag." This club appears to have been a water-front organization at Little Rest, R. I., as Kingston was then called, given to playing merry pranks. Especially did its members focus their activities on a local dolt, by name Elisha B. Gardiner. They sent forth the ultimatum that no cats were to be sold in near-by

Newport unless they were branded "E.B.G." under their
tails. They supplied Br. Gardiner with an elaborate gold-
laced uniform and cockaded hat and a silver branding iron,
which was the official mark of the Hornet's Nest Cat Inspector. It was Br. Gardiner's duty to go about picking up
stray cats, and to see that they bore the proper posterior
marks, and to enter houses where such felines were kept as
pets and give them his stamp of their authenticity.

# II

## THE TAVERN

### *Loitering and the Do-nothing*

THE SECOND CENTER OF TOWN HUMOR AND MERRY PRANKS TO consider is the tavern or pothouse, but before we plunge into that picturesque history and meet those who foregathered there, we should contemplate the subject of loitering. The waggery in general store and tavern was a product of the loiterer, a type of individual which scarcely fits in with the legendary notion of our forebears being always brisk, busy and purposeful.

In Atlantic coast towns that grew into cities, doubtless ambitious citizens could afford little time for loitering; but, if we lean on the testimony of travelers, we find that life there and in the frontier and country villages as well, even though the farmer and backwoodsman were supposed to work from dawn to dusk, bred an occasional type that lacked ambition—men who were congenitally inclined to take life less strenuously. Odd job men, ne'er-do-wells, gossipers and jacks-of-all-trades—when they needed or wanted a trade they accepted employment—helped cut hay or shock corn or dig gardens or pull stumps; but they never worked for long and then no more than was necessary. Their wives always told them they'd wind up in the poorhouse, which, perhaps many of them did, but this did not deter them from loitering. In "Oldtown Folks" Harriet Beecher Stowe created the perfect character of the village do-nothing, Sam Lawson. "Every New

England village," she explains, "must have its do-nothing
as it has its school-house or meeting house. Nature is always
wide awake in the matter of compensation. Work, thrift and
industry are such an incessant steam-power in Yankee life,
that society would burn itself out with intense friction were
there not interposed here and there the lubricating power
of a decided do-nothing—a man who won't be hurried, and
won't work, and will take his ease in his own way, in spite
of the whole protest of his neighborhood to the contrary.
And there is on the face of the whole earth no do-nothing
whose softness, idleness, general inaptitude to labor and ever-
lasting universal shiftlessness can compare with that of this
worthy, as found in a brisk Yankee village." [1]

Such men found occasion to hang around the tavern, pass
the time of day with the shoemaker, the blacksmith, the
barber and to sit enthroned for hours on the barrels of the
general store amid its heterogeneous collection of merchandise.

Loitering was evidently accounted among the anti-social
habits by our earliest forebears. Massachusetts early imposed
a fine of 2s. 6d. "for sitting idle and continuing drinking
above half an hour." In 1646, complaints were made to the
General Court against the games of shuffleboard and bowling
"in and about Houses of Common entertainment," because
thereby "much precious time is spent unprofitably and much
waste of beer and wine occasioned." To put an end to this,
the court prohibited shuffleboard and "any other play or
game in or about any such houses" under a penalty of 20s.
for the tavern keeper, and 5s. for each person who "played
at the same game." Twenty-four years later, indicating that
idleness was still a serious problem even among the alert
Yankees, the fine for the keeper was jacked up to £5. A
previous law had forbidden dancing at taverns, another waste
of time, under a 5s. fine for each offense. Cotton Mather,

who was naturally opposed to enjoyment, also objected to smoking and drinking in Boston's taverns. He supported the edict which forbade smoking in public. Those who insisted on indulging in this time-wasting, filthy habit had to do so either at home or in a special room at the tavern.[2] Even as late as 1808 the staid town of Salem, Mass., forbade street smoking under fine of $1 per person.

Charleston, S. C., faced the same problem. One of the earliest acts of the Assembly there took steps "to drive the class of diverse careless persons who frequent Church Street to work, instead of allowing them to congregate on street corners or to hang around the Punch Houses." Evidently too many citizens were wasting precious time at the Sign of the Two Brewers, or The Pig and Whistle.[3]

Obviously, there was some sustenance, yes, stimulant, in the crackers that general store loiterers munched—but there was even more in rum. When Daniel Webster declared that the tavern was the headquarters of the Revolution, he must have taken into account the fact that men are rarely stirred into either bold or quixotic action by bread alone. Those who gathered in the Red Sabin Tavern at Providence to plot the capture of the British naval schooner *Gaspee* (which was lying offshore to snatch rum and molasses runners), could scarcely be expected to have ventured on so brave an undertaking with merely the stimulus of patriotism—and crackers. Nor those who left the Green Dragon to embark on the Boston Tea Party. Nor even Thomas Jefferson sitting down in the Indian Queen at Philadelphia to pen the immortal words of the Declaration of Independence. The story of what rum contributed to the Revolution still remains to be written and the story of how it roused the risibilities of country tavern loiterers can be inferred, we hope, from these paragraphs.

What part did the small country town tavern play in maintaining democracy and in developing those rugged individuals who contribute to our store of merry legends? The answer to these questions is written in the history of the tavern.

### Suspicion, Curiosity, Hospitality

When first established in New England, and it was established there as early as 1634, the tavern served two purposes: it afforded shelter to strangers and it housed them in a place where the authorities could keep an eye on them. Make no mistake about it—in early New England, strangers were suspects. If a householder took one of them into his home, he was required to give security for the good conduct of the newcomer. There was a definite length of time strangers were allowed to stay. Moreover, New England domestic hospitality was "constrained by formality and preciseness." In 1688 each town in New Jersey was required by law to maintain an ordinary for the relief and entertainment of strangers under penalty of 40s. for each month's neglect, and the same suspicions as that demonstrated in New England is implied. Newbury, Mass., was twice fined by the county for being destitute of an ordinary. Just as Connecticut merchants feared that pedlars would introduce "raging and contagious diseases," so did the early authorities in the northern colonies fear that strangers would introduce raging and contagious doctrines.

In the South the hospitality offered strangers differed from that in the North. Towns were few and far between, so strangers stayed at private homes or in primitive inns. In the plantation houses hospitality was offered without guile or stint. Some planters were given to "a chronic excess of hospitality." Some would post slaves along roads to invite strangers into their homes, not only from motives of hospitality but because they yearned for company—company to talk with, company whose presence gave justification and a chance for extended eating and drinking. For the sort of midday meal that would be accompanied by the staggering succession of brandy, claret, cider, Madeira, punch and sangaree, after which host and guest alike went to sleep with a vain hope of clearing their befuddled heads. Many a planter seemed always prepared to offer such a generous board. In 1686 William Fitzhugh of Bedford, near to Chotank in Virginia, hung up a record for open-handed entertainment when he housed and dispensed hospitality to a party of twenty horsemen at Christmas. Not only did he offer them good wines and other things to drink, but he called in three fiddlers, a clown, a tight-rope dancer and an acrobatic tumbler to amuse them. His main room fireplace was so large that he never put less than a tree trunk on it.[4]

In poorer homes the welcome might be a little less warm, and certainly the fare was meagre. A traveler in 1790 describes a North Carolina ordinary as being a log or frameboarded house consisting of one room furnished with some benches and chairs in the last stages of palsy, a miserable bed and a long pine chest in which were kept the family's belongings. In one corner, a rum keg and tumbler served for bar. Before the front door, the only entrance, stood a clay oven. Travelers slept on the floor, using their saddles for pillows. In Winter they slept indoors, in Summer, outdoors under a blanket stretched over four sticks to keep off dew and damp and to avoid fleas. Bacon and eggs, hoe cake and peach brandy were the usual fare. If there was a bed, it usually consisted of a mattress stuffed with shavings and set on a frame that rocked like a cradle. The room was usually so well ventilated that the traveler had difficulty keeping his umbrella erect to find shelter from the rain while sleeping. John Bernard, who gives this description, says that on emerging from the woods "you might always know an ordinary by an earthenware jug suspended by the handle from a pole." [5] These out-of-the-way Southern taverns were generally kept by poor whites.

Except in the Southern backwoods and on the frontier, the tavern soon assumed a dignity both of location and architecture, albeit sometimes its customers did not grace this dignity. Before it usually stood a horse trough and a sign on a tall post that creaked and flapped in the winds "with a leisurely, rich, easy note of invitation." A broad verandah ranged in front, too, with benches. Inside was an open taproom where great barrels of beer and cider were kept on draft and a bar where the various bottled goods proscribed by the temperance fanatics were allowed an open and respectable standing.

From the inhospitable New England attitude of suspicion, the stranger at the tavern eventually took on the semblance of a curiosity. In the days before newspapers were common, and for some time afterwards, let a stranger ride up to the tavern and soon the local worthies, including the constable, would drop in to hear the news he brought of other towns and what fresh ideas he had on politics and the affairs of the colony. Many a traveler testifies to this Yankee trait of being inquisitive and credulous. Who are you? Whence came you? What is your business? What is your religion? When the stranger had satisfied their curiosity, then they treated him with all the hospitality at their command.

A Virginia officer found he could never procure refreshment for himself or horse till after he had answered questions and those at the tavern had compared the answers with their own information. So when he alighted at an ordinary and the master or mistress met him at the door, he began, "Worthy people, I am Mr. —— of Virginia: by trade, a tobacco planter and a bachelor; have some friends in Boston

whom I am going to visit: my stay will be short, when I shall
return and follow my business as a prudent man ought to.
This is all I know of myself and all I can possibly inform
you. I have no news. And now, having told you everything,
have compassion upon me and my horse and give us some
refreshment." [6]

When Lord Napier was quartered in a private house in
New England, the women of the neighborhood, with characteristic impertinence and curiosity, crowded into his room
demanding to see him, because they wanted to see what a
lord looked like. He was stained with the dust of travel and
his boots were caked with mud. After surveying him from
head to foot, one of the women exclaimed: "If that be a
lord, I never desire to see any other lord than the Lord
Jehovah," whereon she and the rest flounced out of the
room.[7]

Thus the tavern became not only a news center, but also
a center of expectation. Even as today, men who loitered in
taverns always were figuring on what might happen next,
or who would turn up.

Since its long room was usually the largest room in the
village, the tavern was the obvious place to hold meetings.
In many a village outside of New England—where the church
served for town assemblies—the town meeting and the
tavern were inseparable. There also dances—many of them
lasting until dawn—and other social affairs were given.
Masonic Lodges held their communications, dining clubs
thrived, and public sales were held.

On the tavern's bulletin board were posted the lists of
jurors, notices of vendues, advertisements for lost and found
dogs, cats, cattle and slaves, and legal notices of all kinds.
Lotteries, too, were drawn in the tavern.[8] Theatricals, caucuses and military drills were equally welcome and, as a

haven between long church services, it was a necessity. Church and tavern were often close together. An old poem runs:

I knew by the pole that's so gracefully crown'd
Beyond the old church, that a tavern was near.

Between these various excitements came hours and days when life dragged on with laggard pace. If there was to be any excitement, it had to be made—and the service of the wag is to provide excitement. He it was who enlivened conversation, who uttered the merry jest, who plotted with his fellow tosspots those crude pranks that set the town a-laughing.

## Conversations at Taverns

As in the general store, so in the tavern, the conversation ranged through a wide list of topics, led by the keeper, who usually was an assertive and opinionated person. John Davis says Americans discussed politics and government, and Englishmen talked about themselves.[9] In the taverns of the South the gentry were accustomed to talk literary, dramatic and political gossip of England and the Continent, since many of them were educated there—a practice which ceased with the Revolution. Dr. Alexander Hamilton describes an inn where the landlord's sole topic of discussion was religion. At a Philadelphia tavern they talked politics, religion and trade, "some tolerably well but most of them ignorantly, displaying, however, that curiosity which was one of the characteristics of the American rustic everywhere."[10] At Trenton he overheard politics, religion and physics being discussed and, farther north in New Jersey, two Irishmen, a French Jew and a Scot argued about sacred history. At Saybrook Ferry, Conn., a country rabble came in and fell to talking theology. In that colony, he says, the lower classes talked "so pointedly about justification, sanctification, adoption, regeneration, repentance, free grace, original sin and a thousand other such pretty chimerical knick-knacks as if they had done nothing but study divinity all their lives . . . and yet the fellows look as much, or rather more like clowns than the very riff-raff of our Maryland planters."

John Adams, who wielded a fairly caustic pen and was violently allergic to taverns, describes them as "full of people drinking drams, toddy, carousing, swearing; but especially plotting with the landlord to get him, at the next town meeting, elected selectman or representative." [11] He also wrote, "Here the time, the money, the health and the modesty of most that are young and of many old, are wasted: here diseases, vicious habits, bastards and legislators are frequently begotten." Often the "Victualler and Tapper of Strong Drink," as Delaware called its early innkeepers, was the postmaster, captain of the trained band, and generally holder of some important community office. After the Revolution many officers took to tavern-keeping—an ex-colonel would be host and an ex-captain, hostler. Since such pronounced individuals guided the hospitality of taverns, there was no such standardization of hopitality as we find it even in the small town hotel today; each inn took its character and color from the proprietor. He was the leader in conversation and, according to his sentiments and to his piety or lack of it, steered tap-room discussions.

## Early American Tipples

What did these Bacchic worthies of Early America drink? The gentry might prefer wines on occasions, Madeira and French wines, but for the farmer and laborer there were beer, cider, black-strap and metheglin made from fermented honey and rum. The last became the exchange medium for

New England's slave trade and it was an essential ingredient in the punches and other drinks of the age. Black-strap seems to have been a combination of rum, molasses and other ingredients. Casks of it were found in every country store and tavern. In the middle colonies and the South, beer and home-made wines and brandies were popular. The peach brandy of Virginia was especially notorious. Those who imbibed too freely of it were prone to fight duels.

West Indian rum from Barbados and Jamaica—"a hot, hellish and terrible liquor" commonly called "Kill Devil"— began appearing on these shores about 1640. Sixty years later New England was making its own. Both these rums were flooding the country in no time. Drinkers either tossed them off neat or mingled them with various drinks. Mumbo, for example, was a concoction of rum, water and loaf sugar. When the water was hot it was called toddy and was stirred with a toddy stick which had a knob on one end for crushing the lump sugar. With the sugar left out—plain rum and water—it was called grog. In New Jersey local tipplers consumed their home-made applejack either straight or as Scotchem—apple jack, boiling water and a dash of mustard.

Another favorite and not too potent libation was Creaming Flip, which was compounded of strong beer, New England rum, sugar or molasses and dried pumpkin, into which a red-hot poker or logger-head was thrust to make it foam and bubble, and to impart a burnt taste which was the joy of connoisseurs. The tavern host at Canton, Mass., gained a reputation for his flip by adding four great spoonfuls of mixed cream, eggs and sugar. When a fresh egg was beaten into the flip so that the froth poured over the rim of the mug, the drink was called a "bellow's-top." Flip was generally served in large glass tumblers.

A colonial recipe for flip reads as follows: "Keep grated Ginger and Nutmeg with a fine dried Lemon Peel rubbed

together in a Mortar. To make a quart of Flip: Put the Ale
on the fire to warm, and beat up three or four eggs with four
ounces of moist sugar, a teaspoonful of grated Nutmeg or
Ginger, and a Quartern of good old Rum or Brandy. When
the Ale is near to a boil, put it into one pitcher and the Rum
and Eggs, etc., into another; turn it from one Pitcher to
another till it is as smooth as cream. To heat, plunge in the
red-hot Logger-head or Poker. This quantity is styled One
Yard of Flannel."

Another eighteenth century drink was Negus, named for
Lt. Col. Francis Negus of the 25th (Suffolk) Regiment of
Foot. Pour half a bottle of port into a jug. Rub ten lumps of
sugar on the rind of lemons. Then squeeze out the lemon
juice and add it and the sugar to the port. A quart of boiling
water and a dash of nutmeg finished this drink, which was
taken hot. In fact, our great-great-grandfathers were given to
taking hot drinks: mulled wine was consumed in large quantities.

Punch was almost as popular as flip. Tea, rum, sugar and
lemons together with water were the ingredients. It was
often served before dinner as we serve cocktails. A tavern
keeper of any repute usually had his own punch mixtures,
bearing either his name or the tavern's. In Philadelphia the
Fish House Punch, produce of the State in Schuylkill, a
sporting club that still flourishes, is held in almost the same
regard as the Liberty Bell.

The ladies, being polite, might indulge in Madeira or one
of the light home-made wines. Some country women entertained their friends with "whiskey made palatable with sugar,
milk and spices," which would be equivalent to our present-
day milk punch. Morning bitters were quite commonly
taken.

The consumption of malted and spirituous liquors and

wines was prodigious and it cut through all classes. "In matters of drunkenness there was no difference observable between the classes or colonies and not seldom as much liquor was consumed in the ordination of a New England minister as at a barbecue in the South, while the velvet-coated dandy slipped under the table no more readily than the leather-jerkined plowman." [12]

> For he that drinks till all things reel
> Sees double, and that's twice as well.[13]

More than one tavern loiterer distempered himself by an excess of drink, and his prodigious thirst brought him to no good end. The annals of New Amsterdam are rich in recollections of stout drinking and its consequences. Philadelphia, too, for all its Quaker atmosphere, rolled up an enviable reputation for public tippling. There, at the Red Lion on Elbow Lane, in 1736, a mighty drinker, Thomas Apty, "laid a wager of Half a Crown that he could drink within the space of one hour and a half, a Gallon of Cyder Royall; which he had no sooner accomplished and said I have finished, but he fell down and then expired." [14]

Some tavern keepers acquired a colony-wide reputation for their drinks. One of the most famous in the South was Henry Wetherburn of the Raleigh Tavern, Williamsburg. In 1738 Thomas Jefferson's father bought the plantation, Tuckahoe, in return for "Henry Wetherburn's biggest bowl of Arrack punch."

Evidently in the Old Dominion a barkeep had to be free to work at all hours and long hours at that, without being worried by family ties. The *Virginia Gazette* once printed an advertisement for a bachelor, "a single man, well recommended, who understands the Business of Bar."

Soon enough the South took to whiskey—the "corn" of Prohibition—and its taste for the subtleties of wines and punches, of cider and cider royal, sadly degenerated. The local wag became a fellow "full of fun, foolery and mean whiskey."

### Prices of Drinks and Drink Control

The prices that could be charged for drinks as well as for provender for horses at taverns were soon fixed by the authorities. In Philadelphia the town crier proclaimed them at the end of the session of the court and then posted them on the courthouse door. In 1731 they ran: Wine per quart, 2s.; Rum per gill, 2d.; Rum punch made of double refined sugar, per quart, 1s. 4d.; Flip, per quart, 8s.; Beer, per quart, 3d.; Best beer, 5d.; Cider, per quart, 3d. In 1748 a New Jersey tavern was charging 10d. for a hot meat meal; 7d. for a cold one; 4d. for lodgings per night; rum and brandy, by quart, 4d. and 6d. respectively; wine, by quart, 2s. 8d.; Metheglin, 1s. 6d.; punch, 1s. 2d.

Of course the authorities saw that some control was exercised over the drinking habits of the people. Connecticut levied stiff fines as early as 1708—10s. for drunkenness and 5s. for tippling after 9 P.M. The master or mistress where post-curfew drinking went on was fined 40s., and for want of payment of any of these fines, the offender must sit in the stocks not more than three hours nor less than one. Later it was decreed that no tavern keeper should be allowed a license who in the preceding year had sued anyone for the price of drinks. Massachusetts' law of 1721 forbade an innkeeper to trust a customer for more than 10s. By 1720 the Connecticut bond for sellers of strong drink soared to £20 and three years later if any inhabitants were found in the tavern on the eve of the Lord's Day or the night after, or after 9 P.M. any day, they should be fined £5. Constables were required to search taverns and even break open locks and doors, if necessary to warn tipplers to depart or be arrested. In Philadelphia at the Indian King in 1755, the closing hour was 11 P.M., as befitted a sophisticated city, and a servant civilly acquainted visitors with the time, after which no more liquor would be served to anyone.

Tavern keepers were required to post the names of local habitual drunkards. Only 17 names, however, appeared on Boston's list of inebriates for 1727, which didn't necessarily indicate that the people were universally sober. At Newport, R. I., a fine of 20s. was exacted from the innkeeper who sold to "Common Tipplers."

On the other hand, a landlord was subject to a fine if he refused to permit a guest to drink all that could legally be consumed on the premises, provided that the guest could take care of himself and the constable had no objection. This officer, if he thought a guest was exceeding bounds, would pour out the libation himself. The test for exceeding bounds in New England was set forth in realistic terms: "any person who either lisps or faulters in his speech by reason of over much drink, or that staggers in his going, or that vomits by reason of excessive drinking, or that cannot follow his calling."

## Games at the Tavern

Besides beer there was skittles. The tavern was a natural center for games. As we have already seen, shuffleboard was early played in New England ordinaries. By 1700, billiard tables appeared in taverns there, and by 1721 Thomas Amory of Boston was shipping these tables to southern ports to equip plantation homes and city taverns as well. Boston set its face sternly against cards and dice, but the South was more lenient. Horseshoe pitching, skittles or nine pins, and bowling on the green were all played near the tavern, so that thirsts so honestly come by might be easily quenched. In Virginia the tavern was also the starting place for quarter races, and cock-fights were often held in its assembly room. At night and in Winter cards, dice and backgammon were the diversions.

When traveling showmen put up at taverns they generally gave performances in the long room, or, where acting was forbidden, they disguised it under the name of "lectures."

Warmed with rum punch, or with any other liquor for that matter, the provincial gave way to song. Madrigals and rounds were commonly sung in taverns more or less spontaneously by both citizenry and traveling musicians. Pedlars who sold musical instruments were apt to give concerts at the local inn to show how the instruments were played, thereby anticipating by several generations those "demonstrations" of new gadgets we see in department stores today.

This close harmony at taverns was apt to accompany words so libidinous as to defy printing. However, from the body of Colonial drinking verse we can choose a few.

Perhaps the first of the tosspot rhyming pranksters was. Thomas Morton, who in 1634 scandalized pious New England by raising a Maypole at Merrymount—Mount Wolaston—brewing a barrel of beer and shouting such Bacchanalian verses to his fellow roisterers as:

> Drink and be merry, merry, merry boys,
> Let all your delight be in Hymen's toys.

Benjamin Franklin's *Gazette* of Philadelphia once opened its columns to a drinking jingle that answered a local temperance drive put on by Quakers:

> There's but one Reason I can think
> Why People never cease to drink.
> Sobriety the cause is not,
> Nor fear of being deemed a Sot,
> But if the Liquor can't be got.

> If on my Theme I rightly think,
> There are Five Reasons why men drink:
> Good Wine, a Friend, because I'm dry,
> Or else I should be by and by;
> Or any other reason why.[15]

It remained for the Rev. Mather Byles, Boston's salty old parson rhymster of the end of the eighteenth century, to picture the sodden drinking of his time at inns and ale-houses:

> From cruel thoughts and conscience free,
> From dram to dram we pass,
> Our cheeks like apples ruddy be,
> Our eyeballs look like glass.

> Thus lost in deep tranquility,
> We sit supine and sot,
> Till we two moons distinctly see,
> Come, give us t'other pot.

It might be gathered from these carousing rhymes that no good end came to the men who sang them. Consider, then, the story of that priceless eccentric and tosspot of Suffield, Conn., Timothy Swan. A merchant by calling and a composer of music by avocation, he patronized the ale shops whenever his throat felt dry, which apparently happened at increasing intervals. When in his cups, the sordid affairs of business fled from his mind and music became uppermost. It is said that he wrote one of his best known musical compositions in the sand, while lying drunk by the roadside.[16]

Not all taverns were the scenes of endless riotous drinking and discussion, but to find one that was not was an exception so rare as to cause comment on it. When William Ellery in 1777 discovered domestic industry at a tavern in Fishkill, N. Y., he made a special note of it: "We were ushered into a room where there was a good fire, drank a

dish of tea and were entertained during a greater part of the
evening with the music of the Spinning Wheel, Wool Cards
and the sound of the Shoemaker's Hammer. For Adriance
(the innkeeper) had his Shoemaker's bench, his wife her
great wheel, and the girl her wool cards in the room where
we sat. By elevating our voices a little we could find and
did keep up a conversation during the music." [17]

At one inn the Marquis de Chastellux, who traveled here
at the end of the Revolution, found the works of Milton,
Addison and Richardson, which the tavern keeper and his
two younger sisters read when not waiting on travelers.[18]
In Hartford, Conn., Hawthorne found an innkeeper reading a Hebrew Bible in the bar by means of a lexicon and an
English version.[19] One would not expect much waggery from
such taverns as these proper examples.

## Tavern to Hotel

Whereas the tavern in growing cities and country centers
gradually took on the semblance of a hotel, in the back
country it remained primitive for a long time. The Indian
Queen of Baltimore might offer the magnificent accommodation of 200 bed chambers, and the Fountain Inn of the
same city a ballroom, stables for eighty horses and a hair-
dresser's parlor; but in little villages the layout was simplicity itself—a large public assembly room, with tables and
chairs, a wide fireplace and a bar in one corner, occupied
most of the bottom floor. Off this was the dining-room, to
which guests were called by the ringing of a bell or the
sounding of a cow's horn by the proprietor. Above were the
bedrooms which might range from a mere open loft to a
few separate chambers. When these upstairs rooms were
filled—usually every bed having its three occupants—travelers unrolled their blankets on the assembly room floor and

characteristics and customs were lost. It ceased being a public forum, except when, as today, it provides public banquets. In the old tavern the neighborhood wits and wise men and tellers of tall tales regularly came together to scan the national horizon. Neighbors met to spit, talk, smoke cigars, drink, read the news and bring topics home for local commentary. There they yarned and gossiped. There they helped popular opinion to be born.

"As the tavern disappeared before Prohibition and the corner grocery before the mail-order catalog, the wits and wise men find new lounging places, in clubs, in the smoking rooms of railway trains, in all the minor caucuses of ordinary life. But the channels of folk disquisition, though thus widened, have not greatly shifted." [21]

Today the drugstore in the small town—the drugstore that is 75 per cent restaurant and 25 per cent pharmacy dealing out packaged medicines and patented nostrums—has become the center of village gossip, news and waggery. The crackerbox philosopher and tavern argufier have been supplanted somewhat by the local paper's "colyumist," by the drugstore smart aleck and the moocher whose conversations are stimulated by nothing stronger, *hinc illae lacrimae,* than chocolate sundaes or four bottles daily of Coca-Cola.

## Rum and Waggery

Waggery that sprang from the pothouse bar in old times found as few recorders as did the pranks of loiterers in general stores. Even the merriest of old gentlemen, when they come to set down their recollections, were apt to gloss over these youthful indiscretions. We can only judge from internal evidence that rum and waggery mixed easily.

Consider those young men in Newark, N. J. It was March, 1749. The newspaper account says they were "minded to make themselves merry with dancing." What "minded" them is not stated, whether it was New England rum or the native applejack. Anyhow, they were "minded," and in this mood for merriment dressed one of their number in women's clothes. Then they were "minded" to invite one of the town's most pompous individuals to join them.

At the sight of "her" he was smitten (so the account says), and fell to hugging and kissing the "woman" in a dark corner, until the only way she could rid herself of his amorous importunities was to suggest that he dance with her. This he refused to do, so she asked another, and when the dance was over, retired with him to a dark corner and fell to giving a realistic demonstration of hugging and kissing the new partner. At this, the pompous individual flew into a rage, called her a strumpet, swore that he would beat out her brains for leading him on—he who had an honest wife at home. This was too much for the harpy. Even in those primitive times there were some things that even a flirtatious dancing girl wouldn't stand. "She" stepped out of the room and changed his clothes and . . . well, sometime afterward, the great person had "her" arrested for assault and battery, and actually recovered 13s. 4d.[22] It was cheap at the price.

Soldiers in barracks, as Kipling assures us, seldom grow into plaster saints. They are even less inclined to tread the narrow way when the weather is cold and the near-by tavern is warm and time hangs heavy on their hands. So we can understand why certain officers in barracks in Philadelphia in 1768, after they "had drunk as hard as they could to keep out the cold," would sally forth at midnight, "attended by the band, which consists of ten musicians—clarinets, hautboys, and bassoons, and march through the streets and play under the window of any lady" they wished to distinguish.

This may have angered the sleeping Quakers, but, we are assured, the lady esteemed it a high compliment. "In about an hour all the blackguards who sleep upon bulks, with gentlemen of a certain profession who sweeten the streets at night, are collected round, drawn by that charm which soothes a savage breast, and altogether make it extremely agreeable to be out on a fine frosty morning." [23]

American fiction of the early nineteenth century is fairly replete with tavern waggery. We can start with "The Legend of Sleepy Hollow" and learn that Tarrytown got its name from the housewives of the adjacent countryside, whose husbands lingered there on market days. Again, Rip Van Winkle escaped from a termagant wife to join his cronies in "a kind of perpetual club of the sages, philosophers and other idle personages" which held its sessions on a bench before a small tavern in the Catskills. "Here they used to sit in the shade through a long, lazy Summer's day, talking listlessly over village gossip or telling endless sleepy stories about nothing." [24]

From these respectable characters we can pass to that small Southern town ne'er-do-well who took more than his share of mean whiskey at the tavern and then was ready for any prank. Sut Lovingood was his name and, on one occasion, being well primed, he tried to break up a camp meeting—a favorite diversion among rustic roughnecks—by putting an open bag full of lizards under the bottom of the parson's trouser leg. The worthy evangelist was so startled that he stopped preaching "rite in the middle ove the word damnation." [25]

There was also that Southern small town tavern where loungers and local gossips assembled "to pick their teeth in company, whittle the backs of the split-bottom chairs and discuss the topics of the day—the price of cotton, the corn crop and the weather." These hotel loungers were once startled out of their lethargy by the rattling noise of a buggy, drawn by a jaded horse and driven by two heavily veiled women. Since the travelers did not stop, but drove furiously through the town, the tavern idlers believed the women to be bank robbers who, thus disguised, were making away with the booty. The loafers gave chase, caught the strangers and brought them before the judge. The veiled women proved to be two of their own townsmen who were playing a joke on their gullible fellow citizens! [26]

# III

## THE BARBER SHOP

*Shoemaker and Blacksmith*

It was probably fortunate for the shoemaker that he inherited the reputation of being a philosopher, else his shop would have been crowded with frivolous chatterers. An indication of the attitude the public held toward the sons of St. Crispin is found in one of the earliest books of New England, "The Simple Cobler of Aggawam" (as Ipswich was once called). Writing under this character the local pastor, Rev. Nathaniel Ward, launched his attacks against this and that in his world, especially the vanity of women's clothes—the "foole-fangles of Unguiferous Gentledames." No, one did not expect frivolous gossip in the shoemaker's shop. Old men, rather than young, were apt to drop in there.

The blacksmith's shop, with its doors invitingly open in Summer and its fire comfortably warm in Winter, offered a more receptive atmosphere for the conversation of countrymen. But blacksmiths are taciturn men. When the buzz of voices became too thick or the gossip dull, the smith could always beat it out of hearing by pounding on his anvil. The cigar store, with its resplendent wooden Indian, became another gathering-place, especially for younger men, but it also acquired a shady reputation, especially if card games or pool were played in the "back room."

These three we shall pass by as scarcely suitable for centers of rural conversation that led to hoaxing and waggery and

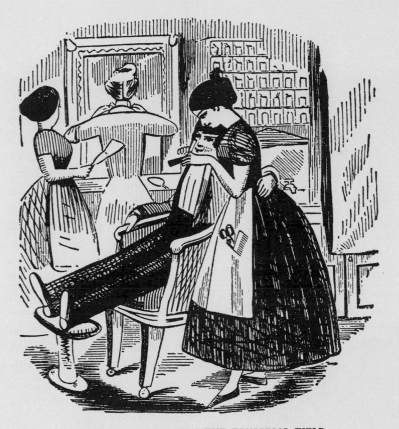

LADY BARBERS INVADE THE TONSORIAL FIELD

go on to the barber shop, which, somehow, has been neg-
lected by chroniclers of the Early American scene. Since it
often contained waiting customers, it became a committee
room for discussion, innocent plot and counterplot, practical jokes and rustic hoaxes. And here, we can be fairly
certain, the barber himself was leader—in the conversation
at least, for when has a barber not been garrulous?

Although the conversation there was often one-sided and
consequently lacked the complete ease and untrammeled
fervor of discussion in the general store and tavern forums,
yet the barber shop well deserves to be accounted another
Early American institution of free speech and democracy.
The annals of our past reveal that occasionally the small
town Figaro was a character of such local stature as to be
worthy of remembrance. All too often he appears to have
been a heedless person and certainly an individualist.

## Colonial Barbers

The earliest reference we have to barbers is brought to
light through their misdeeds. In 1702, so the Archives of
Pennsylvania reveal, four barbers—John Furnis, Thomas
McCarthy, Thomas Anderson and Henry Flower—were
fined "for Trimming people on the first Days of the week." [1]

Full twenty-two years later, barbers in Boston encountered
the same opposition. There the numbers in their craft, and
evidently the price-cutting by some of them, caused a Barbers' Union to be formed. On December 7, 1724, the thirty-
two principal barbers of Boston (which indicates how flour-
ishing was their trade) assembled at the Golden Ball and,
with a trumpeter attending them (perhaps to lend dignity,
perhaps as a symbol of their universal and unending talka-
tiveness), began to debate regulations for their trade. Thereafter, none should shave or dress wigs on Sunday morning

under a penalty of £10. One gathers from the size of this
penalty that Sunday business had been prevalent, and that
the strict Sabbatarians were determined to stop it. The price
of shaving would be advanced from 8s. to 10s. a quarter and
the dressing of common wigs to 5s. and tie wigs to 10s.[2] But
it was Sunday barbering for which they rolled up disrepute.
As the New England satire on the Sabbath ran:

> No barber, foreign or domestic bred,
> Shall e'er presume to dress a lady's head.[3]

In 1759 came a piquant announcement—a barber shop in
the country is advertised for sale, complete with all equip-
ment. It is located in a pleasant country town on the Post
Road from Boston to Portsmouth, hinting that its location
promised good trade. Indeed there is enough business, so
the advertisement states, to keep two hands employed.[4]

The following year the *New England Weekly Journal*
carries the advertisement: "If any Person has a Jersey, English or Irish Boy's Time to dispose of, that can Shave or
Cook, may hear of a purchaser by Enquiring of the Printer
hereof." [5] Since a pious divine had propounded the theory
that God imposed the duty of shaving on men to compen-
sate for the pains of childbirth imposed upon women, this
young indentured servant might well have considered himself an arm of God's avenging force in New England.

It was not to be expected that hairdressers should be considered an essential trade in Early America. When a member
of the General Court of Massachusetts made up a list of
what he called "unprofitable labourers" he lumped together
in one general useless group, "artists, hairdressers, tavern
keepers, musicians, stage players, buffoons, and exhibitors
of birds and puppets."

However, there was some justification for taking the
barber seriously. In the beginning the barber was also a

surgeon, as his blood-red and white-bandaged pole indicates. This put him one or two notches above the peruke-
or wig-maker, who only pandered to the vanity of mankind.
Later, when physicians in this country began to assert themselves and formed medical societies, the barber became less
and less a surgeon, and more and more a shaver of faces and
a dresser of wigs. Readers of the *New York Gazette* in 1750
learned that the two callings were combined by an advertisement which read: "This is to acquaint the Publick that
there is lately arrived from London the Wonder of the
World, an honest Barber and Peruke-maker, who might
have worked for the King if his Majesty would have employed him." He thereupon acquaints Ladies and Gentlemen that he, John Still (what a name for a barber!) is that
aforesaid Wonder of the World, that he lives near Rosemary
Lane and that he can supply "Tyes, Full-bottoms, Majors,
Spencers, Foxtails, Ramalies, Tucks, cuts and bob Perukes,
also Ladies Tatematongues and Towers after the manner
that is now worn at Court." [6]

Six years pass and a Frenchman (or was it just a barber
wag?) inserted the following advertisement in the *New York
Gazette:* "Me gives de Avertisement to every Body of New-
York. . . . Yes, dammee, me advertisee for makes de Vig,
Cuttee and curlee de Hair, dressee and shavee de Bard of the
Ghentlemen, selle de Pomate, and de Powdre, so sweet for
de Hair, and de Vig for makee de bon Approach to de
Madam-moselle. . . . Me makes all in de Bon Taste, Ala-
mode de Paris; and me no charges above three Hundred
per cent. more dan all de Workmans in Town.

For dressee de Hair............ o   6 6
For curlee de Hair............. o   4 o
For Cuttee de Hair............ o   6 6
For Makee de Bag............. o  10 6
For Makee de Ramilee......... de Half de Pistole

For Makee de Toupee . . . . . . . . .   de Half of de Pistole
For Von Stick de Pomat . . . . . . . .        2 6
For Von Bottle de Lavender . . . .            4 0
And so in de Proportion." [7]

Against this background of pomades and wigs, perukes, shaves and witticisms, we can propound our theory that the barber shop not alone was a gathering place for local worthies, but also a forum for discussing national and local issues and events and that on more than one occasion waggery was hatched within its walls.

## Knight of the Comb

The outstanding wag among the tonsorial artists of old New York was John Richard Desborus Huggins, K.C., who styled himself "Empereur du Frisseurs and Roi du Barbieres." He published his witty and impudent advertisements in New York newspapers of the early nineteenth century. These "literary productions" he gathered together in 1808 and reproduced in a little book bearing the title, "Hugginsiana or Huggins's Fantasy." [8]

A professional hair-dresser and wig-maker, he attracted a wealthy clientele—mostly, it can be believed, from the Federalists or aristocrats. Consequently his attacks on Jefferson and his democratic notions and on Tammany Hall with its warm espousal of Jeffersonian principles both pleased Huggins's customers and brought down on his pomaded head the wrath of Tammany followers. On one occasion Brom Martling, an early Sachem of the Wigwam, thrashed Huggins with a rope. Huggins also found time to sell political cartoons and commissioned "some of the best draughtsmen of his day to make graphic comment on the politico-tonsorial situation." [9]

One of the cartoons is labeled "The African Frisseurs

THE BARBER IS JOHN RICHARD DESBORUS HUGGINS, K.C.

Commemorating the Birth Day of Desborus the 1st Emp'r."
To the sound of a fiddle the darky barbers and their ladies
are dancing and their chief, Cuffey, is greeting the Knight
of the Comb (who wears an elaborate over-sized crown) with
the words, "May our Enemies have the Itch without the
benefit of Scratching." Behind Huggins stands the "President of 17 Shaving Societies," who is so overcome with the
*bouquet d'Afrique* that he holds his nose.

When trouble with Great Britain threatened further to
complicate the political situation, Huggins offered the fantastic suggestion that the British fleet might be sunk in the
Narrows and on top of the boats be piled the 120 barber
shops of New York!

This K.C. (Knight of the Comb) claimed to be an artist,
whereas others were mere "jaw scavengers." He called his
establishment a "Dressing Academy." So widespread became
his reputation that he journeyed to Philadelphia, Boston
and New Haven to attend to the wants of ladies and gentlemen there on special occasions. As his own poem states:

> At home, abroad, at school or on the stage
> Still Huggins shines the wonder of the age.

and

> Besides he convinces the most careless gazers
> That the Phiz is improved by his tongs and his Razors.

His shop, which was decorated with cartoons and land-
scapes for the amusement of visitors, also sold combs, razors,
soap, wash balls, pocket knives, shoe blacking, toothbrushes
and "a fresh assortment of odoriferous perfumery." As a
side line he ran an intelligence office, which certainly must
have proved a boon to his lady customers. His shop sign
was a "Skiagraphic Cat" which, he claimed, fed on canaries
—swallowed them song and all—"so that its bowels have all
the musical tones of a perfect orchestra."

Among his many poetic advertisements were these lines:

> Then stranger turn, thy beard forego,
> Rough beards and queues are wrong,
> Man wants but little hair just now,
> Nor wants that little long.

### Artist and Barber Too

While Mr. Huggins was merely a patron of the arts, the tonsorial annals of America disclose a barber who was also an artist, or, to put it more exactly, an artist who was a barber too. John Christian Rauchner pursued an obscure but charming branch of portraiture—he made wax pictures. For a time he worked in New York and Philadelphia, scraping chins when sitters were scarce. Then, having saved enough to live on for a while, he would wander over the country seeking out sitters and, en route, picking up an odd job of hairdressing. History does not record if his tonsorial accomplishments were of a superior order, but we do know that his wax portraits, made in a most painstaking manner, so that the colors penetrated the wax all the way through, have won him a niche among the minor artists of the early nineteenth century.

One New England barber, Peter Choice, was evidently both an artist and a lady's man besides. In 1807 he advertised that there was no room in his shop for "by-standers, lazy ones and smokers." His was more a beauty parlor than a barber shop for he not only dressed the hair of ladies but also cut their profiles in paper.

In 1808 a barber-wag of Salem, Mass., feeling both the urge for literary expression and the need for reading matter with which to amuse his patrons, produced a little pamphlet of tonsorial jokes, poems and witty sayings. It bore the title, "The Barber's Shop, kept by Sir David Razor,

NEGRO BARBERS CELEBRATE HUGGINS' BIRTHDAY

Grand Secretary to the Worshipful Association of Free and Accepted Barbers." From the few scant numbers available we can cull this choice rhyme, under the name, "The Wig Gallery":

> Walk in, walk in, each beau and belle
> Here wisdom, virtue, truth I sell. . . .
>
> I deal in wigs, a curious ware
> In which grey, red, black, brown and fair
> May suit their features to a hair
> In this our gay wig gallery
>
> The wig's the thing, the wig, the wig, etc.

## Barber's Shop as Museum

It will be gathered from these few references that the tonsorial parlor of the past was also one of our earliest forms of museum. The barber was careful to provide amusement and entertainment, apart from his conversation, to hold the attention of waiting customers and to furnish interest for his visiting friends. Philadelphia had its barber shop which, like Huggins's, displayed cartoons on its walls. In his boyhood recollections of Cambridge, James Russell Lowell keeps a warm spot in his heart for Mr. R's barber shop, which was only one degree less than the New England Museum opened in Boston in 1818 by E. A. Greenwood:

"The barber's shop was a museum, scarce second to the larger one of Greenwood in the metropolis. The boy who was to be clipped there was always accompanied to the sacrifice by troops of friends, who thus inspected the curiosities *gratis*. While the watchful eye of R. wandered to keep in check these rather unscrupulous explorers, the unpausing shears would sometimes overstep the boundaries of strict tonsorial prescription, and make a notch through which the

phrenological developments could be distinctly seen. As
Michael Angelo's design was modified by the shape of his
block, so R., rigid in artistic proprieties, would contrive
to give an appearance of design to this aberration, by making it the keynote to his work, and reducing the whole head
to an appearance of premature baldness. What a charming
place it was—how full of wonder and delight! The sunny
little room, fronting southwest upon the Common, rang
with canaries and Java sparrows, nor were the familiar notes
of robin, thrush, and bobolink wanting. A large white cocka-
too harangued vaguely, at intervals, in what we believed
(on R.'s authority) to be the Hottentot language. He had
an unveracious air, but in what inventions of former
grandeur he was indulging, what sweet South African Argos
he was remembering, what tropical heats and giant trees
by unconjectured rivers, known only to the wallowing hip-
popotamus, we could only guess at. The walls were covered
with curious old Dutch prints, beaks of albatross and pen-
guin, and whales' teeth fantastically engraved. There was
Frederick the Great, with head drooped plottingly, and keen
sidelong glance from under the three-cornered hat. There
hung Bonaparte, too, the long-haired, haggard general of
Italy, his eyes sombre with prefigured destiny; and there
was his island grave; the dream and the fulfilment. Good
store of sea-fights there was also; above all, Paul Jones in the
*Bonhomme Richard:* the smoke rolling courteously to lee-
ward, that we might see him dealing thunderous wreck to
the two hostile vessels, each twice as large as his own, and
the reality of the scene corroborated by streaks of red paint
leaping from the mouth of every gun. Suspended over the
fireplace, with the curling-tongs, were an Indian bow and
arrow, and in the corners of the room stood New Zealand
paddles and war-clubs, quaintly carved. The model of a
ship in glass we variously estimated to be worth from a

hundred to a thousand dollars, R. rather favoring the higher valuation, though never distinctly committing himself. Among these wonders, the only suspicious one was an Indian tomahawk, which had too much the peaceful look of a shingling-hatchet. Did any rarity enter the town, it gravitated naturally to these walls, to the very nail that waited to receive it, and where, the day after its accession, it seemed to have hung a lifetime. We always had a theory that R. was immensely rich (how could he possess so much and be otherwise?) and that he pursued his calling from an amiable eccentricity. He was a conscientious artist, and never submitted it to the choice of his victim whether he would be perfumed or not. Faithfully was the bottle shaken and the odoriferous mixture rubbed in, a fact redolent to the whole school-room in the afternoon. Sometimes the persuasive tonsor would impress one of the attendant volunteers, and reduce his poll to shoe-brush crispness, at cost of the reluctant ninepence hoarded for Fresh Pond and the next half-holiday. So purely indigenous was our population then, that R. had a certain exotic charm, a kind of game flavor, by being a Dutchman." [10]

### Shaving Mugs and Social Caste

Lowell's boyhood absorption in the wonders displayed at Mr. R.'s barber shop probably caused him to neglect its commonplace equipments and furnishings. What of the barber's chair? The shaving mugs?

One of Mr. Huggins's cartoons shows the chair of 1800 to be an ordinary armless affair, without a stool and with waiting customers accommodated on a plain bench. The usual curiosities hang from the ceiling, a stuffed frog among them. Later illustrations from *Yankee Notions,* one of the amusing weeklies of the '50s, reveal a substantial armchair, not unlike a French bergère, with a separate stool for the feet. Children were raised by placing a board over the arms of the chair.

Before the days of running hot and cold water, hot water for shaving was heated on the stove in a tea kettle or in a small brass or copper tank.

In these pre-Civil War days the shop provided one dressing table at which gentlemen fixed their cravats after being shaved and trimmed. This consisted of a long mirror with a shelf for brushes and combs. Eventually each barber in the shop had his own niche, his own altar to Tonsoria—a pier glass with a marble shelf and drawers beneath. On the shelf stood two bottles, one for bay rum, the other for witch hazel—usually blue and white, shaped long and narrow like Rhine wine bottles, and often elaborately hand-painted with scenes. Around the mirror the best of gingerbread-work set it off.

Equally decorative were the shelves of shaving mugs. Kept in orderly array and always washed and polished, these mugs presented a shining face to the world. They also marked grades in the tonsorial social caste. Each bore the name of its owner in old English or Gothic letters in gold leaf, sometimes his fraternal emblem (Masons vying with Odd Fellows) and others were embellished with bands, circlets of flowers, flags, eagles, rural scenes and signs of professions. One undertaker's mug proudly showed a hearse! These were of the upper caste. The ordinary customer hid under the anonymity of a number. At a glance you could tell the social standing or commercial rating of a customer by his mug. It also furnished the barber with evidence of his own standing in the community: the mugs he displayed (and they could easily be seen from the street over the low curtain that ranged along the bottom of his front window) were a vivid advertisement of his popularity.

Whereas in Colonial times the barber also dressed the hair of ladies, for the full century that succeeded these charming creatures were banished from the shop. It remained a stag parlor. Ladies were attended at home or served by women. It is during this purely masculine era that the barber shop reveals itself as a center of waggery.

## Styles in Haircuts and Beards

Barbers such as John Richard Desborus Huggins, K.C., and even the meanest of his followers had to be alert to changes in styles—men of the world, with their ears to the ground, delicately sensitive to whimsies in the tonsorial mode as they cropped up here and there in the centers of fashion. They had to be like James Mitchell of Boston, who advertised that he had "lately visited and work'd at the most noted centers in Europe" and consequently could cut and dress hair "after the London, French, Spanish or Italian Fashion." [11]

In one of Huggins's cartoons he is shown with his hair cut short and curly, and he wears a long apron and carries his comb over one ear. Some of the figures in the cartoon wear their hair in a pig-tail, others cropped close and curled. This was the "Brutus" crop, a French taste brought in by French refugees. Another style of the end of the eighteenth century was to have the hair brushed from the crown of the head toward the forehead "as if he had been fighting an old-fashioned hurricane backward." These were radical changes in the mode.

The decline of wigs and consequently of the wig-maker and dresser began when soldiers of Braddock's broken army began returning home. They wore their natural hair. As soon as wigs were abandoned, it became the style to dress one's hair by plaiting it, queuing and clubbing it and wear-

ing it in a black silk sack or bag adorned with a large black
rose. All this time, of course, the hair was dressed with
powder. Our own George Washington, whenever he was in
Williamsburg, went to his favorite French barber, although
only once do his expense accounts show that he had his hair
cut. Often, however, he bought powder, bags and puffs,
which were occasionally perfumed, and ribbons for his hair.[12]
This custom of "dressing" the hair didn't run out until
about 1810-20, when Brutus heads came in. The tied-back
powdered hair was the mark of a Federalist; cropped hair
of a Republican or follower of Jefferson. As the latter rose
in power, frizzle work disappeared and heads became round
by cropping off all pendent graces of tie, bob, club and
queues.[13]

During President Jackson's administration the prevailing
style followed that national hero—the hair combed back
from the forehead without parting. This was followed by
"soap locks," the hair being cut short on the back of the
head up to the crown, leaving it long in front of the ears
and letting it grow long down each side of the face. Some
boys used to let their side hair grow so long that they could
tie it under their chins. This was the prevailing mode in the
'40s.

The style then changed to the half-shingle—the hair was
allowed to grow quite long all around, then was cut short
on top and curled all over the head. This mode was adopted
by both men and women. After that the style was to part
the hair on both sides of the head and then roll it the whole
length of the head over the finger or curling iron. This
"top-knot" required the use of pomade to keep the curls
"set." In addition to the top-knot the hair all around the
back of the head was rolled under, although it usually was
long enough to fall to the coat collar.

In 1850 came another half-shingle, when the hair was

worn quite long, parted behind and then combed up over
the ears. It was followed by a revival of the Jackson style
of brushing the hair straight back, with the variation that it
was so cut and brushed as to form a front pompadour. After
this, it seems that eclecticism entered into the hair-cutting
art. Every man and barber became a law unto himself.
Today we have reached the apex of cutting hair to suit
individual craniums or casts of features.[14]

The rise, evolution and decline of the beard in America
seems still to be awaiting its official chronicler. The early
Fathers of New England chose to wear beards in the Old
Testament style. "Venerable beards, the mien and counte-
nance of authority, made it easy to distinguish the gentlemen of worship at that period from the tradesman with his
plodding air or the laborer in his leathern jerkin." [15]

So long as men wore wigs, they did not cherish beards.
Like many another masculine style, the beard habit of the
nineteenth century was imported from abroad. Sideburns
appeared even before Waterloo, but rarely moustaches, except in the case of military officers. In 1837 Hawthorne
found young officers at the Charlestown Navy Yard following the modern fashion of moustaches.[16] By the middle of
the century men from the trenches of the Crimean War came
back wearing beards—called Piccadilly Weepers—and openly
smoking cigars. George Augustus Sala, writing in 1861, states
that the beard worn *au naturel* had long been the accepted
mode in America.[17] We might say, then, that the beard in
America slightly antedates the Civil War, came into full
flowering during that four-year conflict (*vide* Jeb Stuart's
full and bushy appendage and the facial landscaping of
Samuel F. B. Morse of telegraph fame) and did not enter on
its decline until General Grant was finally entombed with
full military honors in the mausoleum on Riverside Drive
and that structure completed.

Regard some of our nineteenth century worthies as they stare at us from the pages of any encyclopedia of biography: Rev. John N. Scott (1848) wore a squarish full beard clipped short: Rev. James Thomas Ward (1846) shaved all his face except the chin, which remained adorned with a goatee of medium length; Charles A. Dana (1846) had a full beard trimmed short at the sides and tapered to a medium long tip; Joseph Medill of the same year let his full beard grow *au naturel*. By 1851 Theodore Winthrop was sporting a moustache, but shaved his cheeks and left an outer beard rimming his face from ear to ear. Benjamin Harrison (1864) had a moustache and a full beard trimmed square. Of his cabinet in 1889, five of the eight wore full beards; three medium long, one quite long, and one very long. Stephen J. Field (1869) had a close-clipped moustache and a full-shaped beard. James G. Blaine (1880) trimmed his full beard to a rounded point. The celebrated college president, Atticus Hapgood (1884) shaved only his cheeks, leaving a very large and full beard shaped to a dense round bush. Judge Morrison R. Waite (1886) had a chin beard which grew high, nearly covering the cheeks, while his upper lip was shaved clean. Oliver Ames, Governer of Massachusetts (1886), appears to have been content with mutton-chop sideboards. Of the same date is Lucius Quintus Cincinnatus Lamar, who adorned his features with a heavy moustache and a half-long beard trimmed square at the tip, the cheeks being shaved to the line of the jaws. Henry Cabot Lodge had a full short beard trimmed to a point. And finally we come to a worthy of our own day, one Valentine Tapley of Frankford, Mo., whose claim to fame rested substantially on a beard twelve feet long which, to keep it from trailing, he wore wound around his waist.

These fluctuations of tonsorial styles evidently produced their little effects on specialized business. Razors and razor

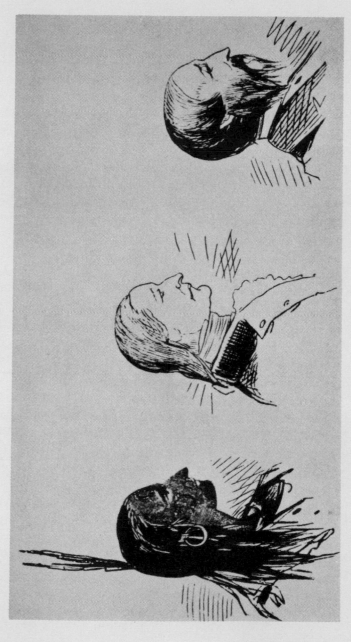

LATEST STYLE

IN 1859

IN 1740

IN 1620

strops were once essential items in the trunk of the Yankee
pedlar, indicating that the shaving habit was customary even
in the backwoods and countryside. When William Marshe
journeyed from Virginia to Lancaster, Pa., in 1744, he
seemed bothered by the fact that he couldn't get a shave
in a hamlet on the Susquehanna where he stopped. That
Thomas Hughes, who kept the ordinary there, offered to
shave him and did it satisfactorily was an act of hospitality
so unusual as to cause him to set it down in his diary.[18]
With the coming of beards the demand for razors and shaving must have dropped off to an alarming degree.

In 1877, when that wandering barber M. J. Vieira of
Indianapolis sat down to write his tonsorial recollections,
he added appreciably to our knowledge of the old-time
barber and his methods. Six towels were considered sufficient for a week's trade, and the customer often preferred
to wash his own face. The barber's chair, lacking all those
mechanical adjuncts to comfort for the customer and ease
of operation now enjoyed, was covered with red carpet. The
average size of the small town shop was 10' x 12', and $20
was enough capital to open one. Until 1820 Negroes practically controlled the trade, after which a few German barbers appeared. From this time on white barbers became
numerous, Italians especially falling into the trade. During
the "Bloomer" days of the '50s, when women were quiver-
ing under the urge for emancipation, several bold hussies
set themselves up as barbers and took to fancifying the
shops, but this invasion was stopped on the grounds that it
might be conducive to immorality.

Before 1860 the price for a shave was 5¢, for haircut 10¢
and for curling 15¢ to 20¢. These charges went up respectively to 6¢, 12¢, 25¢ and 25¢ for a shampoo. At least these
were the charges at Tony Delight's in Chicago, whom Mr.
Vieira dubs the "Prince of Barbers."

The really great step forward was in 1845 when Edward
Phalon opened his barber shop in New York and didn't
hesitate to explain to all and sundry that his glittering
tonsorial palace cost him no less than $20,000 to decorate
and equip.[19]

## A Pious and Learned Shaver

Even so short a study of tonsorial characters as this cannot
be brought to a close without giving mention to one who
left his own record behind him. Moreover, he carries us
up to the very threshold of our own times and his long
range of service with razor and scissors bridges the years
from the small town barber shop of the 1850s to the present
bright and shining city "parlors," whose most ardent claim
to reputation is that they are sanitary.

When John M. Todd of Portland, Maine, ceased being
a blacksmith, which business had followed a boyhood passed
mostly at sea, he stepped out of the production of "heavy"
goods to the lighter and finer art of haircuts and shaves.
For sixty-two years thereafter he pursued his tonsorial course,
as he describes it in his autobiography. No pomaded and
Frenchified dandy was John M. Todd. His portrait shows
him to have been a bald and full-bearded Yankee. He might
have passed for an Old Testament prophet; indeed, there
was much about his beliefs, sentiments, enthusiasms and
mode of life to indicate that he was a lineal descendant of
those ancient men of God.

From the very first Mr. Todd turned a stern face against
drink in all its forms. One of his fondest boasts was that, in
1906, he remained the only man in Maine whose name was
on all three of the temperance pledges of 1829, 1840 and
the Sons of Temperance, through whose activities the historic "Maine Law" set the example for the arid era into

which the nation was fatally plunged many years later. Mr.
Todd was also a spiritualist, having caught that inspiration
in 1842 when people in Maine were attracted by mesmerism
and six years later when the Rochester rappings caused
country and city dwellers alike to imagine vain things. He
likewise assumed a profound respect for the Shaker Testimony as he learned it from the lips of Elder John B. Vance
of the Shaker community at Alfred, Maine.

Mr. Todd's autobiography includes recollections and
anecdotes of the famous worthies he shaved, including Jefferson Davis, who once visited Portland and with whom he
argued abolition while that gentleman was under the razor.
It also contains poems he collected and learned by heart
between serving customers, conversations he had with the
great and near-great, and a gorgeous collection of barbers'
stories. On its pages are also found poetry of his own composing, which, considering the source and the saccharine
sentiment of the times, was no better nor no worse than the
general run of verse over which those mid-century generations thrilled and wept.

His barbers' stories should not be passed by with a mere
mention. Here we read of Charles C. Haskann, "the king of
left-handed barbers"; of J. J. Sullivan, who pushed the steel
over a man's face in the record time of a minute and a half;
of George N. Rich, who could prove that he had shaved
ninety men in one day; of A. O. Kenny, who successfully
shaved a man while riding on a tandem at Bar Harbor; of
W. A. Orr, who shaved and cut a man's hair in seven minutes; of that "razorial connoisseur," J. C. Morey, who was
in the business forty-five years and estimated he had chased
his blade over the human face an aggregate of 718 miles;
of A. Murphy, who kept canaries to amuse and soothe his
customers; of H. P. Newton, the barber-ornithologist-poli-
tician; and finally of J. Williams, the wag barber of Quebec,

who advertised himself as "Professor of Crinicultural Abscis-
sion and Cranilogical Tripsis, Tonsorial Artist, Physiognom-
ical Hair Dresser, Facial Operator, Cranium Manipulator
and Capillary Abridger."

That "things" were started in Mr. Todd's tonsorial parlor
is proven by the Log Cabin Club of Portland. As a young
man, he was an ardent supporter of the homely and rustic
political principles of William Henry Harrison. In those
far-off days of 1840, enthusiastic Whigs banded together
into Log Cabin Clubs. The Democrats pictured Harrison,
even though he had been a hero of 1812, "as a dotard, a
granny, one who should be content with a log cabin and a
barrel of hard cider" without aspiring to the White House.
The attack rebounded in Harrison's favor, the lads of the
nation sang:

> Hurrah for Harrison and Tyler!
> Beat the Dutch or bust your b'iler!

and Log Cabin Clubs of his followers sprang up like mush-
rooms. Most of them disappeared after the campaign was
over and were wellnigh a memory by the time Harrison's
administration had finished. Not so Portland—John M. Todd
kept it alive for over twenty-six years, "ruling the political
situation in Portland" and having much to do with keeping
that city in the Whig fold.[20] Its highest conception of merriment was to hold occasional mock trials, after which, if the
prisoner at the bar was convicted, he paid for the supper
of all who attended. These trials were on quite a higher
order than the ribaldry of the Hornet's Nest of Little Rest,
R. I., but then, times had changed, and, as Portlanders
would have said, Portland was *not* Little Rest!

The conversation in Mr. Todd's shop must have been
of a superior moral and intellectual order, for, whereas in
the other barber shops the only available reading matter

JOHN M. TODD, SIXTY YEARS A BARBER

would be the *Police Gazette* and such flashy and unsavory papers, Mr. Todd's customers were offered the substantial pabulum found in the *North American Review, Littell's Living Age,* the *Nation* and *Scribner's.* Those who patronized his shop knew they were coming to a fount of profound and comprehensive information: he had ancient history at his tongue's end, could quote Shakespeare by the yard, and could talk a man dumb on Greenbackism, protoplasm, transcendentalism and the Darwin theory.[21] He also seems to have been blessed with a gift for friendship; he kept two customers whose whiskers he removed and cranial adornment curtailed for over fifty years.

Leader in the community, poet, philosopher, skilled barber (did he not take in $15.50 in one day?), Mr. Todd often carried the measure of his friendship to the farthest limit any barber can carry it—he performed the "last service" by shaving the cold, placid faces of his deceased patrons when in their winding sheets.

## The Fall of Tonsorial Individuality

Those far-off days when six towels sufficed for a week's trade seem the veriest dark ages compared with our modern, sanitary tonsorial customs. And meantime man has made many inventions. In Asa Greene's "Travels in America, by George Fibbleton, Esq., Ex-Barber to His Majesty, the King of England," this superior person after several social rebuffs was finally driven to taking up his old trade. On opening a barber shop in New York, he invented a shaving machine. Since it cut more than it shaved, Mr. Fibbleton's career was short. This merry fiction was dated 1833. A shaving machine for mass work was the subject of a cartoon in *Yankee Notions.* Constantly men and barbers alike strove to free themselves from the thralldom of the razor blade.

The invention of the safety razor was one step towards liberty, yet it did not seem to lessen the number of barbers and barber shops. The electric razor has now struck off another link of the chain. With its coming, individuality seems to be slipping away from the barber. We now read in shops the sign, "If requested, will use electric razor." Farewell, soap and lather and shaving mug! Farewell, singing strop!

We might grow sad, too, over the disappearance of bay rum and the present-day effort to deliver shaven and shorn customers to their fellow men without those compelling perfumes that revealed to the world whence a man had just come. The old individual bottles of smelly hair tonic are fast disappearing: the barber now gets a tube of tonic—just enough for one application—from the cashier or a central bureau of supplies, and throws away the tube when it is emptied. He no longer has his own bottles, for bottles are no longer necessary.

Tonsorial decoration has gone modern. Lighting is "artistic." We weep for the old gingerbread woodwork that caught the dust of a century or more. The barber's chair is now on a par with dentist's and surgeon's. Complete sanitation reigns. Women invade the sacred masculine precincts and manicure girls loll about. With the coming of these improvements, the age of barber shop waggery was definitely over.

*Part II*

# WAGS AND ECCENTRICS

# I

## DREAMERS OF GRANDEUR

### *The Margin of Eccentricity*

JUST WHAT MAKES AN ECCENTRIC? TO WHAT EXTENT CAN A man or woman pursue idiosyncrasies and still be considered normal? The answer changes with the times.

At the beginning of our history, "regularity of conduct and conformity even in small particulars were regarded as moral essentials." The eccentric was given short shrift, "A slight measure of non-conformity was enough to earn the appellation of witch or wizard." In 1665, for instance, the widow of Hibbins, wife of a former magistrate, was hanged at Boston, poor thing, for "having more wit than her neighbors." [1]

Conformity or non-conformity depended on what passage of Scripture you were quoting at the time. The witches of Salem were sent to the gallows because their conduct matched a certain passage in Exodus. Those who committed unspeakable perjury against them, on the authority of the same page—but with complete disregard for the Ninth Commandment—went scotfree.

As liberal thought began to spread and the economic, social and religious habits of the community took on new forms, the margin for eccentricity widened. The eccentric found himself safe from persecution. Under these more tolerant circumstances, so long as a man or woman appeared to act normally 75 per cent of the time, his or her eccen-

tricity was called "singular." A man could afford to be
"singular," if he had something else with which to back it
up. Dr. Lemuel Hopkins of the famous Connecticut Wits,
that coterie of Hartford intelligentsia who foregathered at
the end of the eighteenth century to discuss topics of the
day, exchange puns and write execrable poetry, was classed
as "singular"! There wasn't another like him. A physician
of outstanding merit, he was also given to composing verse.
Long-legged and staring-eyed, he would stalk into a house,
sprawl on the floor, take a log out of the fireplace for pillow
and proceed to dictate poems.[2] His rhymes were more than
passing bad—but his diagnoses were more than passing good.
Nevertheless, had he acted thus a century before, he would
have sent the ministers scrabbling through Scriptures for
the apt text under which to punish him.

Sometimes the idiosyncrasy proved to be a breach of what
the people considered morality. The early days of Massachusetts Bay Colony produced two such eccentrics—Thomas
Morton and Sir Christopher Gardiner. Both showed a brazen
contempt for the contemporary code. Their idiosyncrasies
were anti-social, and earned them condign punishments.

Morton, an unscrupulous and crafty soldier, settled at
Merry-Mount, the present Mount Wollaston, where he succeeded his captain and set about to seduce others of the
company. Under his leadership they lived free and reckless,
"quaffing and drinking," "dancing and frisking" and sometimes even worse, to the annoyance of neighbors and the
scandal of all good people. Morton, so the Pilgrims decided,
feared neither man nor God. He sold guns and firewater to
the Indians. He and his merry fellows and their wenches
danced round a pagan Maypole. These outrages discredited
the whites and made the Indians forward and dangerous.
Governor Endicott chopped down the Maypole and administered a sharp rebuke, but it had no effect. Then Cap-

tain Miles Standish, tired of the nuisance, seized Morton,
burned down his house in the presence of the Indians and
packed him off to England to answer for his misdeeds. Morton retaliated by writing a scurrilous book on New England
and its worthies.[3]

Sir Christopher Gardiner's idiosyncrasies consisted in
being a Papist and in having loose notions of conjugal affairs.
Agent for Sir Ferdinando Gorges, he was sent over to look
after that nobleman's grants. He claimed to be a Knight of
the Sepulcher, but the Pilgrims considered his sepulcher
definitely whited. Sir Christopher already had two wives
living in England, "both of whom had written the governor,
one desiring his return and amendment, the other his destruction." At the time he had for companion an alleged
kinswoman, who was believed to be anything but what she
should be, "living with him after the Italian method." He
passed her off as his cousin, but those who spied in the
windows knew better. When the authorities came to arrest
him, he disappeared into the woods until eventually fer-
reted out. As for his "cousin," she refused to confess any
more than she saw fit. The authorities were nonplussed
what to do with her and finally decided that the way to
punish her would be to send her back to England to the two
wives![4] On just what they said to her and she to them history keeps silent.

The rise and popular acceptance of singular people towards the end of the seventeenth and through the eighteenth centuries may have been a normal reaction to the
rigid conformity of the previous age. Local history and
American literature began to be fairly peppered with men
who took pride in their idiosyncrasies. Some stayed at home
and practiced them; others were wanderers, such as Sam
Patch, the falls jumper, and David Gamut, the roaming
Yankee eccentric in "The Last of the Mohicans."

98 GRANDFATHER WAS QUEER

Not the least of these individuals worthy of consideration and remembrance were those who cherished dreams of grandeur.

## Chinoiserie on the Delaware

Any pleasant day in 1797 loiterers on the banks of the Delaware at sedate Burlington, or across at the point where Neshaminy Creek emptied its green water, would see a strange barge come down the river. Aft, on soft yellow cushions, sat a choleric-looking Dutchman of sizable paunch, surrounded by numerous small children and a coffee-skinned servant or two in the native costume of Malaysia; and the barge was rowed by eight lean, rangy Chinamen wearing white. Besides his girth, this man was otherwise encumbered with the name of Andreas Everardus van Braam-Houckgeest.

At the time, the infant Republic was fairly used to romantic strangers. The French Revolution had cast on these shores a brilliant flotsam of renowned and legendary figures —Prince Talleyrand, Médéric Louis Elie Moreau de Saint-author, Duc de la Rochefoucauld-Liancourt, a dandy with a knowing eye, St. Mémin the portraitist, Brillat-Savarin, prince of gourmets—but behind none of them stretched so exotic a career as was in the backwash of Andreas van Braam. Even Talleyrand, walking the streets of Quaker Philadelphia with a Negro mistress leaning on his arm, could not cause as much public wonder as this Dutchman and his Malaysian bodyservants and Chinese coolies.

Born at Workhoven in the Netherlands, November 1, 1739, he entered the service of the Dutch Republic as a midshipman; then, a year later, shifted over to the Dutch East India Company and was sent to China as supercargo. From 1758 to 1773 he ran the stations at Macao and Canton, fifteen years' service broken only by two trips back home to the Netherlands. On one of these voyages, he stopped off at the Cape of Good Hope and married. His eldest child, Everarda Catharina Sophia was born at Amsterdam in 1765.

His term with the company over, van Braam settled in the Netherlands and took up farming in the Province of Guelderland. Thirteen years later he was appointed consul to the Carolinas and Georgia, and he moved to Charleston. There he bought property, engaged in shipping and had interests in a rice plantation on the Ashley. He appeared to like this new country well, wanted to throw his life in with hers, so in 1784 he was naturalized an American citizen.

The country wasn't kind to him at first. The diphtheria epidemic of 1784 swept away his four youngest children. In January of the following year, his eldest daughter, Everarda, married Captain Richard Brooke Roberts of the American Navy. Van Braam and his wife were left alone, but not for long—a child, twenty years younger than Everarda, was born in October.

Either van Braam's business ventures did not turn out as he had hoped or his peppery temper made him unpopular among the Charlestonians, for in 1788 he returned to the Netherlands and settled in Utrecht. Five years later he was offered the post of resident director of the Dutch East India Company at Canton. While stationed there, he journeyed to Pekin with a large embassy to congratulate Emperor Ch'ien Lung on his sixty years' reign and to promote trade relations. It was an incredibly long hegira of thirty boats filled with Dutch notables and soldiers and servants and a drummer and a fifer to make impressive noises. When the rivers froze, the whole company took to sedan chairs—a forced day-and-night march to reach the capital for Chinese New Year's which cost the lives of eight coolie bearers and reduced van Braam's girth five inches!

His position in the Orient gave him a chance to better himself by mercantile ventures, so that by December, 1795, having amassed a substantial fortune, he was able to leave China for the United States. There was to be nothing small or obscure in his manner of traveling. He chartered a boat, the *Lady Louisa,* and its crew, loaded it with his collections of Chinese furniture, porcelains, fabrics, paintings and curios, including a set of Chinese Lowestoft especially made for Martha Washington, took aboard native Chinese servants, a comely Malay woman for housekeeper and a young Malay boy. At the Cape of Good Hope, where he stopped to see his wife's relations, he picked up her niece, Johanna van Schuler, a girl of eighteen, to whom he took a fancy and promised to give an education in the States. In April, 1796, this astounding cargo of Chinoiserie and humans docked at Philadelphia. The Chinese servants were said to be the first of this race ever to land in America.

For a while he took temporary quarters in the city, where he displayed his Chinese treasures to all and sundry who called. He also sent a coach the long distance to Goshen, N. Y., to bring back his daughter, Everarda, and her four young sons. During the six months' voyage from Canton van Braam had not been idle: he had written an account of that embassy to the Chinese Imperial Court. This book, in two volumes, was published by Moreau De Saint-Méry, who at the time was running a French newspaper in Philadelphia. Van Braam had also been looking around for a country place to accommodate his numerous family, exotic servants and collection of orientalia. In June, 1796, he bought a property in Bucks County on the Delaware just above the mouth of Neshaminy Creek, and proceeded to build a large mansion there. He called it "China's Retreat."

It was "an Elegant House upon a splendid situation," with a stable for eighteen horses, a coach house to hold a dozen carriages, a barn, cattle stables, cider press, poultry houses, ice house, orchards and gardens. The house itself was built in the grand manner: the ground floor rooms had ceilings over 17 feet high. Windows slid back like Chinese screens into the walls. The roof was sheeted with copper and topped by a pagoda, hung at its corners with small tinkling bells in the best Chinese tradition. The ballroom, used also for music, of which van Braam was passionately fond, reached the full length of forty-seven feet, had gilded walls and paintings of the four seasons. Even the basement, with its kitchens, servants' quarters, dairy, wine cellars, pantry and storerooms, was luxuriously furnished and equipped. Its entire floor was paved with blue marble flags.

"China's Retreat" attracted the smart French colony and other notables of Philadelphia. Washington is said to have planted a tree near the house. In this colorful ménage, surrounded by his Chinese and Malay servants in native costumes, van Braam lorded it over his family—disciplined his grandsons, lived "after the Italian method" with that niece of his wife whom he had picked up at the Cape and brought here to educate, and sang in loud and raucous voice to the strumming of his guitar. Madame van Braam, evidently unable to condone what was going on under her nose, departed for the Netherlands and there divorced him. Another break in their lives came when their daughter, Everarda, lost her husband. A year later she found relief from sorrow by marrying her former husband's best friend, Captain Staats Morris, of the famous manorial New York family of Morrisania. The marriage festivities were carried on with all the Oriental splendor and extravagance van Braam could command. The February before this brilliant affair, he had married his wife's niece, Johanna van Schuler, thus completing her "education," although she was thirty years younger than he.

Stormy and impetuous and open-handed as this old Dutchman might be, one could never predict what course his

choleric temperament would take next. Moreover, in spite
of all the exotic grandeur in which he lived, he had worries
aplenty. Some whom he believed to be friends turned out
enemies. The loss of a boat coming from China dealt his
available funds a body blow. As it was, he probably lived
and spent far beyond his income. Besides, the staid farming
people in the neighborhood of "China's Retreat" grew more
and more shocked at the heathen Chinese and the goings-on
in the big house down by the river. His own wedding in
February, 1798, and his daughter's the following June
marked the apex of the old man's attainments. He was
seventy now.

Scarcely had the guests departed from his daughter's wedding than he sold "China's Retreat." He packed up and
departed for England, where he lived a while, then to Ger-
many, which also didn't seem to please him, and finally
settled down in Amsterdam. There he died on June 8, 1801.[5]

What became of those Chinese servants and that pretty
Malaysian housekeeper is the stuff from which any romancer
could spin a tale. And the barge? . . . For years afterwards,
old country wives along the Delaware told of a ghostly boat
silently rowed by eight yellow-faced heathen Chinamen
dressed in white, which, when the mists rose from the river,
dissolved into thin air.

### Baron in Blown Glass

Whereas Andreas Everardus van Braam-Houckgeest wore
only the title of "Honorable," as befits an erstwhile consul of
a sovereign state, Henry William Stiegel, to whom we now
turn our attention, was given the title of "Baron" by popular
acclaim, nor with any false modesty did he refuse the crown.
Besides, it fitted well the sort of man he thought himself to
be. He was to furnish material for one of America's earliest

"success" stories and to demonstrate another Americanism—
that even one generation is enough to see a family pass from
shirt-tail to shirt-tail.

As Heinrich Wilhelm Stiegel, he arrived in Philadelphia
from his native city of Cologne in August, 1750, and, being
industrious, immediately found work in a near-by foundry.
Five years later, determined that this would be the land of
his fortunes, he became a British subject. After a period of
obscurity, he married Elizabeth, daughter of Jacob Huber,
an ironmaster of Brickerville, a hamlet near Lancaster. There
he began his meteoric climb to fame and fortune by forming
a partnership to operate this Elizabeth Furnace. It made six
and ten-plate stoves and a wide range of domestic and commercial iron castings. By 1760 he was the most prosperous
ironmaster in the country. He bought upwards of 11,000
acres of woodland, from which to cut the wood to feed his
furnaces, built a town of tenant houses for his workers, and,
as the town grew, built for himself three mansions, each
more magnificent than the previous one. The last, finished
in 1763, contained, among other amenities, a private chapel
and a roof platform, from which a band he had organized
among the workmen dispensed his favorite airs.

So successful did he become and on so grand a scale did
he live that the local provincial folks spoke of him as the
"Baron." [6] He accepted the title good-naturedly and began
casting stove plates on which was the inscription:

> Baron Stiegel ist der Mann
> Der die Oefen giessen kann.

Not content with being a follower of Tubal Cain, Stiegel
began experiments with glass-making at his Elizabeth Furnace—window glass and bottles. The results evidently satisfied his versatile tastes, for in 1763 he went to England and
brought back skilled glassworkers. The next year he opened

a glass house at Mannheim, Pennsylvania, and by 1767 the plant was in full operation. Two years later he opened another. Both his iron and his glass businesses were booming. Agents in Philadelphia, New York, Boston and other towns were glad to sell his wares.

He is remembered for his iron, especially for his decorative stove plates, but more especially does his reputation rest upon his glassware. He made a wide assortment—bottles, funnels, retorts, scent flasks, drinking glasses, toys and sheet and window glass. He attained the peak of artistic taste in those fragile, lovely glasses and bottles, some engraved, others engraved and enameled in white, green, emerald, olive, amethyst and blue, which are now the heart's desire of many a collector of Americana.

In addition to these manufacturing facilities, Stiegel had a German's passion for music and an equally Teutonic fealty to the Lutheran Church. Also, often on borrowed money, he pursued an extravagant building campaign that fairly dazzled his contemporaries.

He was open-handed, too. In 1770, when the Mannheim glass works were in full swing, he set aside a lot and built on it a Lutheran church. In those days it was usual to make return for such a free gift by an offering so insignificant that it threw the gift into the highest proportions. It might be a grain of wheat or a peppercorn or a rose. When, in 1695, Jeremiah Basse of Burlington, N. J., rented to John Reeves 200 acres, he required a yearly rental of two fat hens to be paid on Christmas Day. Later this was changed to an ear of Indian corn.[7] In his deed to this church, Stiegel placed the requirement that "the rent of one Red Rose in the month of June shall forever after be lawfully demanded." To this day, the payment is kept up by the Mannheim church. On the second day in June at the annual Feast of Roses, "Baron" Stiegel's requirement is solemnly met.

Through the course of the years and the continuance of this festival, the generous ironmaster and glassmaker has almost acquired the halo of a saint.

In a study of Stiegel and his glass, W. C. Hunter sums up his character:

"He had been dowered by nature with really fine abilities. He was a passionate lover of music. He was a discriminating connoisseur of beauty. He had an aptitude for science. He had a keen eye for business possibilities; was possessed of both energy and initiative; was a persuasive promoter and had a talent for organization. But some disgruntled fairy had endowed him at birth with the ironic gift of a too great facility. So that while he was brilliantly destined to do many things well without effort, he was doomed never, until too late, to learn his own limitations. And since, in the beginning, he knew no need to focus his ambitions and concentrate his endeavors, so to the end he found it more congenial to dazzle his inferiors than to retain the confidence of his equals.

"It would be but a superficial statement of the truth to say that Stiegel was the victim of his own vanity. His vainness was only the smoke that showed what fires of self-confidence burned in his heart. He was so supremely certain of his own potentialities and of the favor of which Fate held him in consequence, that he was not only led into dissipating his talents as freely as he squandered his substance, but actually, later on, came to regard as his own enemies, and as the enemies of God, those of his creditors who dared question the validity of his good intentions.

"He ran his many-sided life in very much the same happy-go-lucky, borrow-from-Peter-to-pay-Paul way that he ran his many-sided business. And he kept his conscience quite as naïvely as he kept his books. The truth of this lies in that astounding trial balance which he submitted to heaven in the prayer written during his imprisonment." [8]

By 1772 his extravagances and a current business depression began piling up trouble for him. Creditors crowded his heels. As he had been successful in inaugurating a lottery two years before, he tried the same device to extricate himself from his difficulties. In March, 1773, he advertised that the American Flint Glass Manufactory, as he called his Mannheim plant, would hold a lottery "to enable him to carry on a manufactory of public advantage" and he invited other "Gentlemen who incline to become Adventurers" to apply for tickets. The total sum paid out in prizes was £638, 12s. 11d. and the American Flint Glass Manufactory received only the miserly sum of £83, 3s. 10d., far too little to save Stiegel from going to the wall. He was forced to sell all his property and, since most of it was heavily mortgaged, he had no other course than to declare himself bankrupt.

After the manner of the times, he was promptly thrown into jail and kept there from November until Christmas, when a private act of the Assembly released him. While here he composed a prayer on a leaf in his prayer book, in which he expressed himself as being innocent of any wrong which might have contributed to his insolvency, told God in no uncertain terms what he thought of his enemies, begged that his slanderers be smitten and their evil mouths stopped, and then, with thorough Christian charity, asked God to forgive them. It is one of the most remarkable revelations of a man's heart and mind in the whole range of Early American literature.[9]

After those weeks in jail the way down to obscurity was swift. Like Mordecai who returned to the king's gate and his beggar's bowl after the king had honored him, so Baron Stiegel returned a beggar to his original Elizabeth Furnace

—and was given a job as caretaker. Later he turned school-master and music teacher. A final blow came in 1782, when his wife died. He lived on in obscurity and poverty until in 1785 death released his expansive spirit. He was only fifty-six, this Baron in Blown Glass, who had dreamed his dreams of grandeur and lived them too. So few remembered his generosity and accomplishments that his body was laid in an unmarked grave.

## Merry Masqueraders

It would seem that, having climbed these two foothills of grandeur, the only logical path ahead for us would lead to that summit whereon sits, crowned in his cocked hat and with his mangy mongrel at his side and resting in bleary peace, that most fantastic of Early American dreamers, Lord Timothy Dexter. Eventually we shall reach that eminence. For the present let us rest here and survey less romantic dreamers. Surely those who found grandeur in clothes are deserving of record among notable eccentrics.

It might be simpler to set down as psychopathic that erst-while governor of New York, Lord Cornbury, who once a month dressed in women's clothes and paraded the Bat-tery. Although this custom caused him to be the topic of whispered conversation, he otherwise seems to have been quite manful. He was not the first, nor will he be the last, of British colonial governors who loved to strut. Even today a heavily gold-laced uniform and cocked hat seem to give some men of otherwise insignificant talents the momentary stature of greatness.

There were those merry Philadelphia wags, who, on the day after Christmas, 1702, exchanged sex in clothes. Dorothy Canterill, dressed as a man, was one, and Sarah Stimes an-other, accompanied by John Smith and Edward James, who

wore skirts. They walked the streets from house to house
and then danced in the home of John Stimes until the "unreasonable time of night," ten o'clock! when the constables
arrested them. All were haled before the court and their
crime condemned as "against ye Law of God, ye law of the
Province, and ye law of nature to ye staining of livly profession and Incoridging of wickedness in this place." [10]
Stimes was charged with keeping a disorderly house, which
it probably was.

But these are inconsequential masqueraders compared
with that monument of military pomp, Prince Grippy.


## Prince Grippy

It was not unusual, among Negro slaves, to find an outstanding man or woman who claimed, and with apparent
grounds to back it up, that in his or her veins flowed royal
African blood. We need not penetrate the mysteries of sable
aristocracy, since the African Almanach de Gotha still remains to be written. Nevertheless it is quite possible that
there fell into the hands of dealers in black ivory an occasional son or daughter of a tribal ruler. Brought to this
country, their own people here often respected their distinction, as was the case of Mr. Maverick's queen. The year
was 1639 and the place Massachusetts. Mr. Maverick had a
superior Negro wench whom he proposed to breed (this was
long before the rise of the New England conscience) and
supplied a likely young buck for the purpose. But the Negress
had been a queen in her own country. Other Negroes held
her in regard. One of them so respected her position that
she insisted on serving as her maid. Not only did the queen
refuse to yield to persuasion but, when forced to accept, her
fellow slaves set up such lamentations that the incident
found its niche in recorded Massachusetts history.[11]

With these observations before us, we will allow the claim of Agrippa Hull that he was the son of an African prince, and go on to show how he proved it.

The fortunes or misfortunes of war and slavery brought Agrippa to the enviable position of being body servant to General John Patterson. He stayed with that worthy patriot of the Revolution through many a campaign and finally went into rest camp with him at West Point. Here also was stationed Patterson's close friend and battle companion, General Kosciusko. "Grippy" was a great favorite with the officers at the Point, as he was intelligent and quick and witty in repartee. Kosciusko took a real fancy to him, and out of the generosity of his heart Patterson gave Grippy to the Polish patriot, who forthwith appointed him head and confidential servant, giving him, as a special charge, the care of his wardrobe.

Kosciusko had brought with him from Poland a costly and elaborate full dress uniform, including a coat heavy with gold trappings and medals and a chapeau crowned with a cluster of nodding ostrich plumes. Grippy devoted much of his time to the care of this finery. Moreover, the confidence Kosciusko placed in him and his own native wit made him the most popular of all the Negro servants at the Point, and their natural leader. Besides, had not Grippy carefully explained to all of them that he was the son of a prince?

On one occasion Kosciusko was required to go down the river and cross over, a duty that would take him away from camp for two or three days. Grippy was put in charge of headquarters. Scarcely had he packed off the general, than he improvised a dinner for all the other black servants. He put on the general's famous uniform and, as a substitute for boots and black stockings, blackened his legs and shined them.

For some reason Kosciusko was not able to cross the river

and he returned to camp the same day. Before he reached his quarters he was told of the dinner going on. He approached cautiously. The weather was warm and all windows were open. A screen had been placed before the opened door so that passers-by could not see the entertainment.

He crept closer. The party had been drinking his wine freely and were hilarious. At the moment he glanced round the screen, all were standing, glasses in hand, ceremoniously drinking Grippy's health, as they had seen their masters do. Kosciusko jumped among them. Some went out by the door, others through the windows. Grippy alone was left.

Sprawling himself at the general's feet, he cried, "Whip me, kill me, Massa, do anything with me, Mr. General." Kosciusko took his hand with great formality and replied, "Rise, Prince. It is beneath the dignity of an African nobleman to prostrate himself at the feet of any one." He made him put on the plumed chapeau and, thus attired, marched him across the grounds to General Patterson's headquarters. To all he met he introduced Grippy as an African prince and all received him with the ceremony befitting his station and royal blood. Finally the assembled officers made him sit down and smoked a pipe of peace with him.

After the war, when Kosciusko was about to return to Poland, he realized that Grippy had become indispensable to him. He must go along. They got as far as New York, but the night before sailing Grippy fled. He finally appeared at Patterson's headquarters and the general, in return for his faithfulness during the war, gave him his freedom.

When Kosciusko returned to the States for a visit, Grippy was taken to New York to see his old general, who received him with marked cordiality. Lafayette, too, on his second visit, remembered Grippy and shook his hand and talked over the battles long ago.

Finally Grippy bought a small farm at Stockbridge, Mass.,

where he rounded out his days well known, respected and beloved, as befitted a prince of royal African blood.[12]

## Sam Patch, the Jumper

The first quarter of the nineteenth century saw a mania for jumping spread over both the settled and frontier regions of the United States. Whether or not it was part of a national "keep fit" campaign is difficult to say. It was, however, part of a national tendency to demonstrate physical prowess which reached its high peak in the fabulous muscular accomplishments of Davy Crockett and Paul Bunyan. Young men dreamed of emulating and even outdoing them. One of these was a lad of Pawtucket, R. I., Samuel Patch by name.

Born about 1807, he first followed the sea, where he built up a rugged physique, and then settled down as a cotton spinner in a mill at Paterson, N. J. Here he developed a taste for the contemporary national custom of jumping.

At Paterson a bridge had just been built over the Passaic. So often and so loudly did Patch declare he would jump from it that the authorities arrested him. However, he managed to elude them and jumped from the rocks at the foot of the bridge. Later he jumped from the bridge itself, a successful drop of ninety feet—and thereby leaped into national fame.

Apparently there was good money in jumping, for he began traveling about the country demonstrating his prowess. He would drop from the yard arms and bowsprits of ships and dive from top masts and other high places that caught his eye. Niagara Falls next met his challenge, and he jumped more than half the height of the falls, dropping into the water from a rock on the highest point of Goat Island.

Each of these leaps was well advertised beforehand. A crowd always gathered and the shekels poured in. Sam made it a point to address the assembled populace before he jumped, telling them what a fine fellow he was.

Having put Niagara behind him, he next advised the world that he would jump from the banks of Genesee River at Genesee Falls, "into the abyss below, a distance of 125 feet." Usually he shot into space like an arrow. This time something went wrong. Either he lost his nerve or miscalculated the edge for, instead of going off head first, he tumbled awkwardly. The date was November 19. His body was not found until the 17th of March next, when it was picked up at the mouth of the river. It was buried close by.

Death made him an even more famous person than he had been in life. Plays were written around him, stories told, poems composed. He became a national symbol of quickness and power. And thus he remained for many years, until Steve Brodie, his linear athletic dscendent, by leaping from Brooklyn Bridge, snatched the laurels and won for himself a place in the song and story of those who delighted in muscular grandeur.[13]

## A Note on Grandfather's Architecture

In his bombastic perorations to jumping, Sam Patch used to liken himself to Napoleon and Wellington, two mighty heroes of his era. Wellington is no longer a simile for anything much and Napoleon is remembered today by most people because his name is attached to a complex. And, whether they called it so or not, many men down the years after Napoleon had terrified Europe developed his complex of overweening pride in personal accomplishments. It found many types of expression, not the least interesting of which was architecture.

Between the later '40's, when dignified Greek Revival lost
its hold on the imagination of those who would build
spacious mansions, and the end of the General Grant era,
this country saw the rise, prosperity and fall of the worst
domestic architecture in our history. Let a merchant creep
ahead of the ordinary run and he needs must build a house
that looked like a battlemented castle. Let a senator or a
rich lawyer or the heir to a comfortable heritage decide to
erect for himself "a stately pleasure dome," what did he
make of it? A lump of rocks and timber that sprouted un-
used and unlovely turrets like a potato grows warts.

Vaguely—very vaguely—reminiscent of Italian palazzo, of
Norman keeps, of castles on the Rhine, these hideous houses,
nevertheless, were attainments of dreams of architectural
grandeur. It was as though their owners had seen the clouds
of Wordsworth's vision:

> here, serene pavilions bright,
> In avenues disposed; their towers begirt
> With battlements that, on their restless fronts
> Bore stars,

had seen the vision, but lacking even the rudiments of taste,
snatched at the battlemented towers and missed the stars.

An earlier era of men who built homes in the grand manner produced some of our noblest architecture. Even though,
here and there, they disposed personal gewgaws about these
splendid façades, they could not entirely deface the apt
proportions and admirable lines.

With these few notes on the queer architecture of our
queer grandfathers, we can now stroll up High Street in
Newburyport, Mass., and halt before the square white
Georgian house which once was the home of Lord Timothy
Dexter.

## *"First in the East"*

The story of Timothy Dexter—"First in the East, First in the West and Greatest Philosopher of all the Known World," as he modestly claimed himself, is the tale of a man who had enough sense to stay sober in the morning. He went up on smart investments and shrewd Yankee trading—and slid down on a bottle.

Malden, Mass., which saw the nativity of many remarkable sons, records his birth as being on January 22, 1747. His schooling was meagre. At nine he was placed on a farm. At sixteen he went to Charlestown as an apprentice to learn the art and mystery of "dressing of skins for breeches and gloves." His apprenticeship over, he landed in the then bustling town of Newburyport in 1769 with a bundle and liquid assets to the total of $8.20 worth in British coin. He had sold his new "freedom suit," which apprentices received at the end of their service, for 5s. The following May he made his first long-headed investment—he married Elizabeth Frothingham, a widow (and consequently a woman hardened to housework) who, although she had four young children, was also in "good circumstances." She also owned a house down by the Merrimac River.

What disadvantage were four children compared with a house-owning, work-trained wife with a little money? He went to live in her house, hung out the sign of his trade, a wooden glove, and began working in earnest. There they labored and slaved, selling deer and moose skins and "a good quantity of Blubber" for twenty years. Two children were born to them, a son and a daughter. He seems to have been oblivious to a war going on. In 1776 he was elected the Town's Informer of Deer, a sort of primitive game warden, a position he held for many years.

Before the Revolution and with greater speed during it

LORD TIMOTHY DEXTER

and afterwards, the Continental currency gradually depreciated in value until it was considered wellnigh worthless.
Dexter took his savings—and probably some of his wife's
"good circumstances"—and bought up as much of this paper
money and as many state bonds as he could afford, at a fraction of their value. In 1791 Alexander Hamilton, after over-
coming bitter opposition, won his point on national credit
—the government was to assume debts incurred by the states
during the war. Dexter's hoard of depreciated paper soared
to par. He became wealthy overnight.

Others who once were rich were reduced to poverty. With
his newly-made wealth Timothy bought the home of Nathaniel Tracy, a gentleman of great wealth now in straitened
circumstances. As he had been made rich overnight, so overnight the humble glove maker announced himself a full-
fledged gentleman. He bought the house lock, stock and
barrel, which included the furniture, and shortly afterwards
added a coach and a pair of horses and a coachman to drive
them. He bought silver and stocked his cellar with wines.
The latter were both his downfall and making. But he always seemed to sober up by morning.

He next had a ship built, the *Mehitabel,* which he sent
on ventures to Europe and the West Indies. He bought odd
stocks that other people didn't seem to want or be able to
sell, and, if we are to believe his own boast, sold coal to
Newcastle—where there was a shortage because labor trouble
had closed the mines; sold cats to owners of rat-ridden ware-
houses in the tropics; cornered the market in whalebone,
which was used for women's stays, selling 342 tons of it at
a big profit; and in the West Indies sold 21,000 Bibles which
he had bought at 21 per cent under half price. He had
"Ready cash by holl sale. I was full of cash." Legend also
says that he managed to find a market in the Caribbean is-
lands for an enormous supply of warming pans, which he

sold as cooking vessels and skimmers for sugar boiling.
Mittens he sold in the Baltic. He was lucky in "spekkela-
tion." He also managed to get in on the ground floor when
the Deer Island Bridge was built over the Merrimac, becoming its largest stockholder. When the opening of the
bridge was celebrated on the 4th of July, 1793, he gave free
drinks to all at the near-by tavern and made a splendid,
though befuddled, speech.

Such a figure, even in Newburyport, was sure to gather a
following. Among his adherents and sharers in his bibulous
bounty was a local rhymster, Jonathan Plummer, a fish
pedlar who sold a sideline of broadside poems of his own
making. In impressive stanzas he exalted the virtues and
accomplishments of his patron, thereby becoming the earliest
of America's poets laureate.[14]

Dexter further managed to capture public admiration
when, on hearing in Boston of the execution of Louis XVI,
he rushed back to Newburyport, bribed the sextons of the
meeting houses to toll the bells, which brought the populace
out-of-doors—and to Timothy's front step. Encouraged by
this acclaim, he began writing to the local newspaper—letters
of muddle-headed philosophy on men and manners in the
most execrable spelling.

But for all the acclaim he was not received except by
hangers-on who ate his food and drank his punch. To force
the town to his doors, he kept a lion in his yard for a week
and advertised—at 9d. a head—for all to come and see. Still
he remained alone, except for a wife who took no delight in
his nonsense, and for which he avoided her, a son who turned
out a dissipated nuisance and a son-in-law who was a leech.
He tried to prove himself a good citizen by offering to build
a public market for the town—if they called it Dexter Hall—
but was turned down. Instead of respecting him, Newbury-
porters laughed at him openly. When his house was broken

into and robbed, he decided to shake the dust of the place off his feet. He sold his house—at the usual handsome profit —and moved to Chester, N. H.

Timothy had reached that age—he was 50—when some men, feeling the last bloom of youth, determine to do something to prevent its slipping from them. In Chester he not alone gathered about him a coterie of admiring cronies, but also began casting eyes at certain light village maidens. This we can understand. We can also understand why, when the Chesterites started referring to him as "Lord Timothy Dexter," he accepted the title. Now he'd show those Newburyport smirkers! "Ime the first Lord in the Younited States of Amercay," he wrote. "It is the voice of the peopel and I cant help it and so let it goe." Later he was to explain, "It is hard work to be a king. I say it is harder than tilling the ground—I know it is, for I find it is hard work to be A Lord —I don't desir the sound but to pleas the peopel at Large." He may have had his tongue in his cheek and he may not, but when he returned to Newburyport (having fought with one of Chester's swains over making overtures to his girl) he claimed for himself, ably assisted by his poet laureate, the lordship that Chester had dubbed him.[15]

His return to Newburyport was in the manner of a triumph. He rented and then bought the house of the Hon. Joseph Jackson, another first citizen of town, one of the finest examples of Georgian architecture in New England. And "Nater," so Lord Dexter declared, "has formed the grounds Eaquel to what you would wish for . . . the holl of the world cant exceed this." It was to be the background for Timothy's most lordly eccentricities. In March, 1797, Jonathan Plummer heralded this patron's return in bombastic verse, addressing it "to Sir Timothy Dexter." This princely welcome not only established Dexter's high rank in the minds of the people but also won for the laureate a

place in his master's household and a poet's livery—a long
black frock coat with silver stars on collar and front, shoes
with large buckles—a large cocked hat and a gold-headed
cane. Crowds of admirers gathered about the house and
wandered in the grounds, and Lord Timothy, taking advantage of his prerogatives, attempted improper liberties
with the less scrupulous of the lassies who came there.

Scarcely had he bought the house than he began "improving" it. "On the corners of the square roof and in many
other spots minarets began to arise surmounted by shining
gold balls that flaunted their lustre insolently upon the
broad street." In the grounds appeared new and exotic trees,
for Dexter was going horticultural. A huge gold eagle was
placed to cap the cupola—it is still there. He sent to France
for furniture, and good furniture, at that. He collected
books. Although it is doubtful if he ever read one of them,
they gave him the ambition for literary expression. The
library was his favorite drinking den. He acquired a coach
and had a coat of arms painted on its doors, and found a
pair of matched cream horses to draw it. Over this household, relieving Madam Dexter of worries, presided a huge
Negress, Lucy Lancaster, who claimed descent from an
African prince, since lords need be waited on by their own
kind.

Time and the excesses of living were beginning to tell on
Dexter. Gout brought him pain but did not reduce his drinking—although it sounded a warning to which he took heed.
In his garden he built a Temple of Reason intended for his
tomb, furnished it with an elaborate coffin—"panted with
whit Lead inside and outside, tucked with greane, with brass
trimmings eight handels and a good lock," that he could
open from inside. It was also equipped with "pipes and
tobaker and A speaking trumpet, and a bibel to read and
sum good songs." He wanted to be sure of having "fier works
in the toume."

He also wanted to be certain of a substantial funeral—and to enjoy it himself. So he staged a mock burial—named honorary pall bearers, hired a mock minister to pronounce a fitting eulogy and set out generous funeral meats and drinks. The procession passed through the garden to the Temple of Reason, with half of Newburyport on hand to watch the ceremonies. After it was over, rumor says, Lord Timothy beat his wife because she had not shed enough tears! To cap the affair, he gave a bell to the Second Presbyterian Church and further offered to pave the length of High Street if the town would change its name to his. This bid for fame was politely turned down.

The urge for being remembered as a philanthropist was on him. In 1801 he conceived the notion of making his own grounds into a museum to contain life-size figures of the great characters in history. "I wants," he explained, "to make my Enemys grin in time, Like a Cat over A hot pudding, and goe away and hang there heads Down Like a Dogg bin After sheep."

He called into service again the same ships' carpenter and figure-head sculptor, Joseph Wilson, who had carved the eagle for his cupola, and gave him a masterly assignment: "The 3 presidents, Doctor franklin John hen Cock and Mr. hamelton and Rouffous king and John Jea—2 grenadars on the top of the hous, 4 Lions below; 1 Eagel is on the Coupulow, one Lamb to lay down with one of the Lions— one younecorne, one Dogg, Addam and Eave in the Garden —one Horse. The Houll is not concluded as yet—Dexter's Mouseum." Then he added, "I will shoue the world one of the Grate Wonders of the world in 15 months, if No man murders me in Dors or out of Dors." And he did. Figures sprouted all over the place, figures out of the Scriptures, Noah, Abraham and Sarah, Joseph and Moses and David, Solomon and Hiram and St. Paul, St. Peter and St. John mingled with Washington, Adams, Franklin, Aaron Burr and other contemporary worthies.

In front of his door was erected a "Royal arch," seventeen feet high, surmounted by the three presidents. All of the figures, and there were forty of them, were carved life-size from wood and then painted in natural colors. On a pedestal near the front fence Lord Timothy erected a figure of himself inscribed, "I am the first in the East."

It was rumored that he spent $15,000 on this museum. As usual, Jonathan Plummer celebrated the event in a eulogistic poem. It began:

> Lord Dexter is a man of fame,
> Most celebrated is his name;
> More precious far than gold that's pure,
> Lord Dexter shines forevermore.

And so on for fifteen verses in which the contents of the house, the coach and horses that champed their silver bits and the images and the tomb are all given immortality.

But Dexter was uneasy. The public were not giving him the proper acclaim for his endeavors in art. In a pique, he offered to sell the house, its contents, its statuary and landscaped grounds. No one made an offer. Ah, well! So he settled down to his last great work—writing a book.

Before this period he had often broken into print, using a style all his own. Local newspaper editors tried to make it intelligible by adding punctuation and re-spelling the words. This time it would be printed as he wrote it. In May, 1802, it appeared, the sum total of the wisdom and experience of his long and colorful life. He called it, "A Pickle for the Knowing Ones, or Plain Truths in a Homespun Dress." In its pages he disregarded punctuation altogether and threw capital letters around willy-nilly. It comprised twenty-four pages in which he outlined his views on world politics, the nature of man and of religion and original sin, what he thought about the clergy and college learning, related his unhappy amorous episodes at Chester, described his plans for the museum and his ideas on bridges, and his own coffin and tomb, suggested an international peace congress and a scheme for lengthening the week by adding one more working day. Whatever had passed through his befuddled mind, whatever he had experienced, he set down in this *magnum opus*.

Newburyport, scornful of its local prophet, considered it a poor joke. Outside critics were more appreciative. Dexter gave the book away to anyone interested. It soon gained wide circulation. He lived to see it go into two editions— some say four—and in one of them Dexter added to his fame by answering those critics who had sneered at his lack of punctuation—he included a page of commas, periods, exclamation points and question marks and told them "thay may peper and solt it as they plese."

One of the editions was prefaced by an engraving of Dexter by James Akin (of whom more anon) showing him in his cocked hat with tassels on the corners and his gold-headed cane and his funny little dog. There are now ten editions of the "Pickle" in existence, no small monument to such a motley fool. "Whether intentional or not," says Marquand, his latest and most glorious biographer, "the 'Pickle' is like Dexter's life, a huge and ill-formed jest."

Time was pressing hard on His Lordship. His poor old head was growing more befuddled. Nevertheless he managed to stay a little sober in the morning. Crisp business notices of what he had to sell continued appearing in the paper. Meantime he and his museum attracted flocks of people from near-by towns, who came to gape, to admire, to laugh, to sneer. On one occasion, Dexter, angered at the actions of a visitor, fired at the ungrateful fellow from a second-story window. The shot went wild, and so did the visitor's wrath. He returned to Ipswich and swore out a warrant for Dexter's arrest. When His Lordship was sentenced to jail, he rode there in his coach with the true dignity of a nobleman.

After this sobering experience he turned to the written word again for consolation. From his pen there trickled a stream of observations—letters filled with combinations of words no one could understand, comprising comments on politics, on the cost of funerals and on whether or not angels had wings.

These problems were to remain unsolved. On October 23, 1806, Lord Timothy Dexter, First in the East, found use for his green and white coffin. Newburyport did not allow him the honors of his Temple of Reason, so he was laid away in the Old Hill burying ground, where a simple stone with modest inscription marks his resting place. His laureate, Jonathan Plummer, celebrated the sad event with a biographical eulogy. An extensive obituary appeared in the local paper, calling him "perhaps one of the most eccentric men of his time. . . . His singularities and peculiar notions were universally proverbial."

When his will was read, it must have come as a sobering shock to the Newburyport that had taken him so lightly. True, his estate was estimated to be worth a mere $35,000, yet, after caring for relatives and remembering friends, he left his native town of Malden $300 with which to purchase a bell for the meeting house and $2,000, the income of which was to be accumulated for a century and thereafter to be used "for the support of the gospel in the said town of Malden." To Newburyport he left an equal sum to be spent on the support of the poor outside the almshouse. It was the first charity bequest the town had ever received—and it is still active.

# II

## QUEER CONSCIENCE AND STRANGE VOCATIONS

*Conscience from New England to Virginia*

WHEN WILLIAM ELLERY, SIGNER OF THE DECLARATION OF Independence from Rhode Island, became collector of customs at Newport in 1790, he gave a demonstration of the sort of conscience which local publicists would have us believe to be peculiarly of New England. The incident was slight. His grandson, George G. Canning, destined to become a famous preacher, happened to drop into the old gentleman's office. He casually took a sheet of paper off the desk to write a letter. Ellery stopped him, saying, "My boy, if you want paper, I'll give you some, but that is Government paper." [1]

Today the memory of such rigid honesty in office would either send twinges of an affronted conscience through a politician or else cause him to smile indulgently.

Grandfather was queer as to conscience. Some New England grandfathers evidently started exercising theirs quite early. On his passage over from the old country, one Taylor of Lynn sold the milk of the cow he had aboard at 2*d*. a quart. After hearing a sermon upon extortion, he remembered this dairy matter and went distracted. [2]

Others considered their New England conscience elastic. Cotton Mather once preached a thundering sermon against the usurious habits of a Boston merchant. In 1639 this mer-

chant, Robert Keaine, was fined £200 for taking too large a
profit on some goods—6d. in the shilling and, in some small
things, above two for one. He held to the outrageous notion
that if a man lost in one commodity he had a right to make
it up in another and that he also might, in good conscience,
buy as low as he could and sell as high. Cotton Mather differed with him.[3]

Some New Englanders were ready to debate this matter of
conscience; hence the Yankee soon gained a nation-wide
reputation as a sharp trader. A truly conscientious Yankee
rarely ever missed his bargain. He claimed that if anybody
cheated him, his conscience would not let him rest until he
had made it right by cheating somebody else "about the same
amount." [4]

Natives of early Connecticut seemed able to whittle their
consciences down to a sharp edge. When Madam Knight
was passing through that colony in 1702, she picked up a
yarn about Fairfield. This particular hamlet had an abundance of sheep whose dung brought the town fathers considerable gain—with which they paid the parson's salary!
They rented the sheep out for a night. Before morning the
sheep would sufficiently dung a large meadow. One sharp
wag rented them, let them fertilize his field, and then, before
he drove them back, sheared off all the wool.[5]

Or the queer conscience might run to marriage. In a
near-by town, Derby, an old fellow by name of Parks married a woman whom both he and she thought to be a widow.
Several years later notice of her Enoch Arden's death was
published and Parks insisted that they should be married
again.[6]

By no means was conscience a virtue localized in New England. In time and in other colonies, it came to be classified
according to religions. During the famous Zenger case in
New York in 1734, the acquittal of Zenger establishing the

freedom of the press in this country, accusations flew thick and fast. The *New York Gazette,* commenting on the trial, insisted that there was a Quaker conscience and—quite different—a Presbyterian. It cited an ejectment case in the Jerseys. Fifty pistoles having been offered as fee to a Quaker, the client had forty returned to him. When the same fee was offered to a Presbyterian, that Scot's conscience directed him to keep forty and return ten! [7]

Pennsylvania history bristles with examples of Quaker conscience, especially in respect to holding slaves. In a trade the Quaker could be as sharp as any Yankee but, once he was convinced that his principles were wrong, he bent over backwards to correct the error and make reparation. For a long time the holding of slaves was debated in Friends' Meetings and many a preacher felt moved by the Spirit to assault the evil in their own ranks. In 1774-5, Walter Mifflin, slaveholding Quaker of Philadelphia, emancipated all his slaves, giving them wages for each year they had served beyond the age of twenty-one. [8]

An earlier and more extreme example was set by Joshua Francis Fisher. In 1743, after living for a time in Delaware, he sold his field hands and moved to Philadelphia, bringing along his house slaves. There he set up in shipping and prospered. One day he happened to hear John Woolman preach on the evils of slave-holding. His conscience began troubling him. He went back to Delaware and traced the field hands he had sold, even to the second generation, bought them up and set them all free, except a very old darkey, too old to work, whom he pensioned. [9]

Sometimes this Quaker conscience amounted to embarrassing obstinacy. Another of the Fishers—Samuel—a highly respected Philadelphia lawyer, was arrested for his Tory sympathies during the Revolution and promptly clamped into jail. He refused to plead one way or the other on the ground that he could not concede the legality of the patriots' regulation under which they had arrested him. He continued to sit in jail for several months, refusing the influence of friends and even the inducements of his captors, until finally he had literally to be pushed out of the place.

Not all Philadelphians were so strict. During the Revolution some of them went to no end of trouble to carry on an illicit trade with the enemy even though they were sympathizing with the patriots' cause. Lumber was in great demand in New York. In Philadelphia they'd load vessels to the gunwales with timber, sail ostensibly for foreign ports and then allow themselves to be captured by British cruisers lying off Delaware Bay. The officers were exchanged and the goods reached New York. With the proceeds from the New York sales, they then bought English goods that "found" their way to the American lines, where they were seized by American officers, transported in government wagons and finally brought to Philadelphia where their owners, now back home with their tales of capture on the high seas and final release, claimed the goods and turned another profit.[10]

Passing down the seaboard, we find an elastic conscience in Virginia. In 1732 land in the interior of that colony was being parceled out to heads of families. One wily German, Jacob Stauffer, managed to pile up more than his share of acreage by giving names to every horse, cow and pig he possessed and representing them as heads of families ready to settle on the land.[11] Well, maybe some of them were.

## A Rake Organist

But let us go back to Pennsylvania for just one more example of conscience. The place is Lancaster, center of the Pennsylvania Germans, the year 1744 and the episode concerns Col. Rigbie and Mr. Marshe of Virginia and a reformed rake organist.

The gentlemen from Virginia had come up for some sort of conference and, time hanging heavy on their hands, they went forth to see what attractions Lancaster might offer. One evening they visited a Dr. Adams, a German doctor, who was said to own an organ on which he played most sweetly. "It was with the greatest importunity he would favor us in playing a tune," reports Marshe, "telling us that unless he himself was possessed with a strong desire to play, he could oblige nobody." This prima donna reluctance having been overcome, "he at last complied, strumming over three or four High Dutch psalm tunes, to which he sang the words in most enthusiastic raptures."

To these Virginia gentlemen looking for a bit of excitement in rustic Lancaster the psalm tunes must have seemed tame. And yet every man has his story and, when Dr. Adam told his, the incident began to be sharpened with vivid highlights. He explained that "in his more youthful days he had been a consummate rake, but soon after he married turned himself to a sober and religious life and praised his Maker several hours in a day by playing on and singing to his organ." [12]

From these shreds of evidence picked up in other colonies, we may surmise that a lively conscience was not necessarily a product of New England. In fact, the finished and full-grown New England conscience, of which we hear so much today, probably did not begin to function until well into Abolitionist times. Before that it was said of the Yankee:

> His right hand fought from Britain to be loose,
> His left shipped slaves to Antigua for use

Let use consider conscience at work in the life of a picturesque and eccentric Virginia statesman.

## The Flute-Voiced Reformer

One of the strangest of gnawing consciences inhabited the tall, lean, liquor-washed body of John Randolph of Roanoke. A son of the Revolutionary War era, what he missed in education and peaceful home life was compensated for by a knightly sense of righting wrong and battling for lost causes. His stepfather furnished schooling of sorts, his mother supplied intelligence and the rare quality of his voice, and the family library, when the see-saw of battles did not prevent his being in it, furnished a wide range of reading. Later William and Mary, Princeton and Columbia were to add dabs of education and in Philadelphia, under his second cousin Edmund Randolph, he rested his spare frame long enough to read law. Randolph was then United States District Attorney. The young John also listened to political debates and dabbled in anatomy.

It is rumored that during this Philadelphia sojourn he also dabbled in gambling, acquired a thirst that was to stay with him through life and, being jilted by a famous beauty, Maria Ward, made an obscure and left-handed marriage. In matters of religion he appears to have been a pronounced skeptic and in politics a Jeffersonian of extremely rabid views. He inherited, however, the family estate of "Bizarre" in Prince Edwards County and settled down as a landed Virginia gentleman.

This is the background of one of the most brilliant and eccentric figures in the early administrations of the nineteenth century. By a single leap he mounted to the top. The country was arguing the Alien and Sedition acts and the Virginia legislature denounced them. Patrick Henry defended the President's right to expel foreigners without trial and John Randolph opposed him. In the next election he

JOHN RANDOLPH OF ROANOKE

attained Congress, where he quickly became Republican
leader of the House.

Six feet tall, emaciated—a mere skeleton of a man—nevertheless so poetically eloquent and forthright a speaker did
he prove that he soon had the nation at his feet. And he did
this in spite of his voice. For his voice was high-pitched and
flute-like, yet behind it was the power of a man of intense
loyalties and bitter hatreds. In this squeaky timbre he challenged and fought many a Congressional battle. It was once
silenced in 1830 when he accepted the post of minister to
Russia, a temptation to which he never should have yielded,
for the journey drew heavily on his small store of health
and arrested his political progress. Yet he was not entirely
broken when he picked up the Congressional reins again on
returning to the States. In a speech delivered a few days
before his death he stated that "his whole aim had been to
prevent, not to promote, legislation." Our Jeffersonian
Democrats in Congress today have overlooked his splendid
example.

Biographers have questioned his sanity. Some say it was
merely drink. Others the consumption that racked his
frame, for he rarely knew two consecutive days of robust
health. Still others claim that he was just plain mad. Eccentric and morose, his private life was marked by constant
shifts between queer decisions when drunk and outbursts
of generosity when sober. His affection for children, especially for a niece, was one of the tender facets of this many-
sided misanthrope. Although he drank much in public, he
drank even more in private. No one could tell whether the
intoxication came first or the madness, although on most
occasions they arrived together.

Evidences of eccentricity punctuated his private and public life and rolled up many a legend about him.

In 1810, for no special reason, he abandoned the comforts and broad acres of "Bizarre" and went to Roanoke on the Staunton in Charlotte County where he owned a large estate and hundreds of slaves. Here for years he lived in a log house in the midst of a dense forest. The yard was not enclosed "nor was there a flower or green shrub to relieve the wild aspect of the abode of this descendant of Pocahontas." [13]

When sober, his manners were gentle and kind but, had he been looking on the cup when it brimmed with potent Bourbon, no one could say what he would do. "He would drive a man as far as he could be driven; he had no mercy on him. In fact he took a pleasure in seeing how many humiliating things he could force a fellow creature to do. He would make sport of him in his own house and laugh him to scorn at his own table." Once, for instance, he invited the local minister to dine with him and some friends. It was customary, then as now, to ask the visiting clergyman to say grace, otherwise the host would pronounce it. Randolph placed the parson in the lowliest spot, neither said grace himself nor asked the minister to say it. As the chronicler of his vagaries observes, he purposely did this to make the minister "feel himself checked and handled."

On another occasion he invited the Rev. Mr. Clayton to pray for him. No sooner had he begun than lean John interrupted him: "Stop, sir, if that is the way you are going to pray, go into the garden or garret." On still a third visit of the clergy he halted the parson's prayer with "Stop, sir, if you pray after that manner God Almighty will damn us both." And then, in extenuation, his biographer falls back on the old excuse for this anti-clerical animosity, "it must have been something he ate": "his stomach was in such a delicate state at that period that he could not digest the fare he met with abroad and he brought snacks with him

from home, particularly when he went to a certain hotel."
There are times when all of us wish we had taken Mr.
Randolph's precautions.

On the whole he must have made a poor guest. He was a
frequent visitor at the home of Captain William M. Watkins, and so fond was he of horses, dogs and guns that
whenever he made a visit he brought some of his dogs with
him "and they were suffered to poke their noses into everything and to go where they pleased from kitchen to parlor." This sort of dog-bearing guests many of us today
know only too well and, like Captain Watkins, we submit
quietly to the breach of hospitality, knowing, as he knew,
that any unkind treatment of his dogs would have been regarded as an insult by his guest.

This long, lean champion of many causes finally succumbed to tuberculosis at Philadelphia while preparing for
a trip abroad. The legends that gathered about him in life
increased tenfold after his death. People said there never
was another like him. The public overlooked his excess of
drink: he had such fascination and charm that most people
really believed the drink had no effect on him. And yet for
all his weaknesses, he fought many bitter and losing battles
in Congress—the Yazoo fraud, the impeachment of Judge
Chase, the Embargo of 1811, States Rights, the Missouri
Compromise. The sword of his political conscience would
leap from the thin, drink-stained scabbard of his body and
flash clean and bright for a cause, although he might be
defending it single-handed and with the knowledge that it
would bring the alienation of many friends.

This bibulous orator with his eccentric figure and man-
nerisms, his wagging head, accusing bony fingers and strange
dress may have been the pattern for the colorfully crude dress
and habits of congressmen in many decades following John

Randolph's years in the national legislature. Some of them extend down to our own day and still capture popular fascination.

### Henry the Holy Shouter

Often the fixed idea which dominates the thinking and passionate pursuits of a "singular" character can be attributed to a queer conscience.

So tempting is the assortment of singular people offered in the first sixty years of the last century that the choice is difficult to make. Our arbitrary selection, then, falls on George W. Henry of Oneida, N. Y., who, in the Year of Grace 1859, himself wrote, printed and bound a volume called, "Shouting: Genuine and Spurious in all Ages of the Church. . . . Giving a History of the Outward Demonstrations of the Spirit, such as Laughing, Screaming, Shouting, Leaping, Jerking and Falling under the Power." This stout, well-printed and well-bound volume carries on its front cover a pious device of the Saviour standing between what appear to be two Gothic pew-ends and the slogan, "Stand Up For Jesus." Mr. Henry's other works were "Trials and Triumphs or Travels in Egypt, Twilight or Beulah," "Wedlock and Padlock, Temporal and Spiritual" and the "Camp Meeting Hymn Book." As is the custom of some authors who are proud of their craft, Mr. Henry used a portrait of himself and his son for frontispiece in his work on holy shouting.

Champion of good, hearty, abdominal Amens and Halleluiahs, Mr. Henry is quick to explain that there are false and true shouters: "Men may pass counterfeit money on ignorant men," he avers, "but it is not so easy to deceive a sanctified ear in regard to a genuine shout. . . . There is as much difference between the true and counterfeit shout and song as between the sounds of a maniac dancing to the music

GEORGE W. HENRY, THE HOLY SHOUTER

of his own chains and the sweet music that enraptures the saints in heaven."

As for the jerks, Mr. Henry explains that at camp meetings, "most usually, persons taken with the jerks, to obtain relief, as they said, would rise up and dance. Some would run, but could not get away. Some would resist; on such the jerks were generally very severe. . . . I have seen more than five hundred persons jerking at one time in my large congregations." But he had his doubts of the sincerity of those who wore fine clothes. "To see those proud young gentlemen and young ladies, dressed in their silks, jewelry and prunella, from top to toe, take the jerks, would often excite my risibilities. The first jerk or so you would see their fine bonnets, caps and combs fly; and so sudden would be the jerking of the head, that their long loose hair would crack almost as loud as a wagoner's whip."

Mr. Henry attests that he was converted and sanctified wholly at camp-meetings. Later he became a circuit preacher. In his after years, we suspect, he went blind. The night following his conversion, he woke suddenly and his mouth "was filled with loud laughter," so loud that the encampment was aroused and the "saints" gathered around the door of his tent. The word "Glory" rolled out of his mouth "like hot bomb-shells from a mortar." They exploded in the camp and set all on fire!

In the course of his study of these violent manifestations of the spirit, Mr. Henry considers John Wesley, with whom he disagrees on several points, Benjamin Abbott, Peter Cartwright and J. B. Finley, whose names were household words in the camp-meeting world prior to the Civil War. He also dips into Old Testament history and brings forth many a Father who danced and sang to express his joy at conversion. Altogether Henry makes out a fairly convincing case for the necessity for violence in religion.

It is amazing that a man so given to shouts, jerks and screaming could keep the steady hand that set the type in this book, kept the open eye that read its proofs without a flaw and bound it so stoutly and burnished its edge with fine gold.

## *James Johns, Penman*

If Mr. Henry pursued the typographical art with consuming ardor, what can we say of James Johns, to whom pen-printing, the noble daughter of calligraphy, was a passion for sixty-three years? Compared with the humble mediaeval monk illuminating books of hours through unending seasons, compared with Persian penmen writing their fantastic and exquisite script of romance in rose-bowered gardens, Mr. Johns of Vermont still stands mountain-high above them.

James Johns, son of a Revolutionary soldier, was born in Huntington, Vermont, on September 26, 1797. At his nativity both Orpheus and Gutenberg must have given him their blessings. That he was also destined to be a bachelor may or may not have influenced his choice of vocation and avocation.

At an early age—he began writing at thirteen—when he was not jotting down history and composing essays he burst into song—wrote lyrics which he sang on all occasions without urging (this must have tried the patience of the hardy Vermonters!), played the violin at country dances and invented a piano. It was the sort of piano that must have stirred the shades of Benjamin Franklin who, it will be remembered, invented a piano that gave forth tunes by rubbing the rims of tumblers. Mr. Johns' pianoforte consisted of pieces of glass of varying lengths suspended on wires which, being struck, sent forth harmonious tinkling notes.

But it is not for this blessing of Orpheus that the world

remembers James Johns. The Gutenberg touch was to be more pronounced.

First of all he lived his entire days either in his native town or in near-by Starksboro, leaving the Green Mountains only twice, so that the local scene was the complete and satisfying source of his inspiration. Being a congenital chronicler, for fifty years he kept records of the weather, births, deaths and accidents in his neighborhood.

At the age of thirty-one he published "Green Mountain Muse," his first book. Like many another author before him and since, he blamed the book's failure on the printer. We can surmise that he promised to pay for the job, for the printer sued him. This must have gotten Mr. Johns' back up. No mere printer should halt his flight into the higher realms of literature! And for the simple reason that he had a gift with which he could frustrate even the most agile setter of type: from the age of thirteen years onward he published a pen-printed newspaper, the *Vermont Autograph and Remarker*. In an amazingly beautiful and clear style of lettering he set down the public and private records of men and events in his locality, together with happenings in his own life. It took him only half a day to pen-print an entire copy. This custom he kept up until August, 1873, ceasing only eight months before his death. In all, this amounted to sixty-three years of composing and pen-printing a newspaper! Besides this monumental labor, he also composed and pen-printed a forty-four page booklet, "A brief sketch or outline of the History of the town of Huntington."

In 1857, evidently convinced that the only way for an author to get along in this world is to issue his own works, he bought a printing press and began sending out a spate of miniature broadside poems. He also printed a twenty-two-page book, with pages measuring only 3" x 4", which staggered under the lengthy title of "A brief record of the various fatal accidents which have happened from the first settlement of the town of Huntington to the present time." It may have been the tight-hearted little old bachelor in James Johns which made him produce miniature books.

In the same year, 1857, to keep the hungry maw of his new printing press satiated, he issued "Green Mountain Tradition" and in the next year, "Remarkable Circumstances." Seven years later "The Book of Funny Anecdotes" appeared. Also from time to time he printed on his press a small broadside paper, *The Huntington Remarker.*

In all, out of his seventy-six years, James Johns devoted sixty-three to the written and printed word. He was a sweet singer to one harp string—the Green Mountains people. Some 500 of his writings are preserved, which surely makes him one of the most prolific of our native writers.[14]

### Prosperous Communism in Missouri

America has always been a fertile ground for trying out economic and religious experiments. It has been estimated that between 1607, the time of the Jamestown Settlement, and 1894, these United States, to many citizens of which the word "communistic" connotes horrors untold, saw the rise and fall of no fewer than 200 communistic experiments. And, of course, this total does not include any of Father Divine's "Heavens." The Shaker communities, the successes of Noyes at Oneida, Jemima Wilkinson's at Penn Yan, Lorenzo Dow's attempts in the Ohio Valley and Robert Dale Owen at New Harmony, Ind., are only a colorful fraction of the share-and-share-alike living which have been attempted from time to time in this country.

Almost invariably the pattern was the same: the man who conceived and headed the movement was a dictator who

# Vermont Autograph and Remarker.

### Huntington Vt. October 10, 1834.

*It also will show you mine opinion -Elihu.*

## Introductory.

We have more than once since our paper was published under its present title been asked what was the meaning of the word 'Autograph'. Although we should think that any person might by consulting a dictionary easily satisfy his mind on that point still as we are willing to give information as to the meaning of words which we may use we will condescend to explain it for the edification of those of our readers who may wish to know its meaning. Know then that Autograph means a person's own hand writing; or any copy, or work executed with one's own hand. in distinction from that which struck off upon types at a printing office. We have adopted this word as part of the title of our little paper as being most characteristic of the manner in which it is executed: for there is no one who is at all experienc'd in reading but can readily percieve that this was done with a pen; and the reader may be assured that every paragraph is composed and written by the Editor himself. and that too without having first to draft it on another piece of paper which is more than can be said of the hundreds and thousands of super royal and imperial folios issued from the press. Writing with a pen was the only method of communicating ideas on paper till within four hundred years ago when the art of printing with types was invented, and even all the mighty works of learning that are issued from the press, are originally written with pen and ink under the author's own hand so that the world is still indebted to that simple instrument the pen for all the printed knowledge that ever filled a library from the first invention of letters down to the present day. A word respecting the course we have taken and intend to pursue with regard to the discussion of those subjects which are introduced into the columns of our paper. As it is composed wholly of original matter. it is of course the channel through which we occasionally express our sentiments on political and moral points which we intend to express boldly without fear or favor of any man or set of men. Against Executive usurpation, and against secret societies we feel it our duty to raise our voice and we hope the time will come when both will be put down by the influence of public opinion.

**JAMES JOHNS' PEN-PRINTED NEWSPAPER**

through force of strong character bent the people to his will and held them to his ideals. This capacity for command was usually forged on the anvil of uncommon circumstances: the novitiate was long and arduous, the struggle to leadership was up though a narrow path hedged on each side by stern convictions. It was driven forward by an unyielding conscience. Almost invariably it was bought at the price of renunciation. However much his or her followers believed him or her to be "led up" by God, the fact remains that this commanding personality did not spring full-fledged into leadership overnight. Consider the probation of Dr. William Keil.

A native of Prussia, Dr. William Keil came to America. A tall, commanding figure of a man, he was given to delving into mysticism, pursued the black arts and had his own way of curing human ailments. After his conversion in the German Methodist Church, he held a public meeting at which he burned his secret formula and renounced all necromantic practices. However, the teachings of his brethren in the church did not satisfy his questing spirit. He needs must go alone.

Already the fields in Pennsylvania and the Ohio Valley, to his thinking, were crowded. His people needed more elbow room and a wider horizon. In true Biblical fashion he sent men to spy out the land. In Shelby County, Missouri, so they reported, they found their Promised Land. On their recommendation Keil bought 2,500 acres and later 1,500 more, to which he gave the name of Canaan. Here he began building a town called Bethel. In 1845 he led 500 German pilgrims— some traveling by wagon train, others by boat—into this wilderness haven.

First they built a church and then a place to do business. Keil saw that all had bread, clothes and shelter and that the children were given an education. Along a single street they erected houses for themselves and buildings necessary for their well-being and progress—school, tannery, distillery, grist-mill, glove factory, drugstore, wagon shop. Soon the gloves and plows of Bethel became famous.

East of the town, on a plateau, Keil built himself a house of hand-made brick which he called "Elim." On the third floor was a spacious banquet hall capable of seating the entire community. Here he lived as a feudal king, governing the colony through his foremen and compounding his secret charms.

For ten years the colony thrived and grew. Though most of the people never saw a dollar for their labors, they never knew want nor lacked shelter nor clothes nor did their children miss an education or the community the benefits of a free living. Keil's idea was working. It was a pronounced success. His Church of the Living God, as he called his community, was rich and its people satisfied. If he could make the wilderness blossom like the rose in Shelby County, why not elsewhere? He dreamed of a chain of such colonies reaching to the Pacific.

In 1855 he was ready to undertake the work. He appointed Dr. Wolfe his successor at Bethel and began laying plans for another colony in the Northwest. Among Keil's children was a son, William, his namesake and favorite, on whose shoulders, he hoped, would fall the mantle of succession. To him Keil had promised that when they set forth to found the new Canaan, he should go along. As they were about to start, the boy died. Keil kept his promise: he laid the boy's body away in a lead coffin filled with alcohol, loaded it on a six-mule wagon, and with himself on the driver's seat, this grisly and pathetic relic led the way across plains and mountains for 2,000 miles until they reached Aurora. The poor boy's corpse and the father's grim determination to keep his promise gave courage to the followers who left their comfortable Bethel and took the long trek. It was the loadstone of their faith and, when they reached their appointed haven, it was the center of the new colony. Keil lived to see the new community established before he reached the end of his days in 1877.[15]

## Practitioners of the Black Arts

For one successful and prominent William Keil we could probably cite a dozen followers of necromancy and the black arts who filled only the tiny, miniature niches in local histories.

Romanies were in this country at an early date. It cannot be supposed that they laid aside "dukkerin" and other secret affairs of Egypt when they landed on these shores. Their presence is revealed in Virginia as early as 1695, by the refusal of a certain judge sitting in Henrico County court to accept the true bill found by his Grand Jury against one Joane Scot. He discharged Joane, "it being the opinion of this Court that ye Act Ag'st Fornication does not touch her [she] being an Egyptian and noe Xtian woman." [16] Besides being the first recorded evidence of Gypsies in this country, this little item also indicates that, contrary to the usual alleged chastity of Gypsy women, Joane was willing to practice more than black art.

The Colonial Entry Book, containing English laws applying to the colonies, provided that "all sturdy beggars or gypsies and other incorrigible rogues and wanderers may be taken up by constables and imprisoned at the next Assize or session they shall either be acquitted and assigned to some settled aboade and course of life here or be appointed to be sent to the plantations for five years under conditions of servants." [17]

In 1766 at Aimwell, Hunterdon County, N. J., was offered

an award of 40s. for the apprehension of a woman "who pretends to be a fortune teller." She wore a black and blue striped linsey short gown, a linsey petticoat and a leaden-colored stuffed bonnet. In the course of her pursuit of the black arts, this nimble-fingered Gypsy was suspected of purloining a quantity of goods—sheets, pillow cases, gowns, petticoats, women's caps, needlework and handkerchiefs.[18]

The most lusty of all these beggars was Bampfylde-Moore Carew, self-styled King of Gypsies, who first made his way from Maryland to the North in 1743. Near Darby, Pa., he overtook a crowd of people going to hear George Whitefield preach in an orchard. He joined them and, after the sermon, managed to get an interview with the famous exhorter, during which Carew told so pitiful a tale that Whitefield not only gave him much ghostly advice but also parted with several pounds in paper money of the province.[19] On his second sentence to the plantations, Carew was landed in Maryland and sold to Daniel Dulany, Sr., the famous lawyer. Carew claimed to be an expert gardener, a strange calling for a Gypsy if there ever was one. To his disgust, Dulany found that Carew didn't even know how to mow, and promptly turned him back.[20]

One suspects that "Old Shrunk" was a Gypsy who had gone sedentary when he found business good. In the early nineteenth century superstitious people of Philadelphia and lower Jersey used to consult this old fellow to have their fortunes told and to recover stolen goods. He would tell them where to dig and, for a special consideration, would surround the spot with magic incantations. He was particularly consulted on the whereabouts of pirate gold. There was one special cache, so legend said, where the pirate had murdered a prisoner and buried his body over the gold hoard so that his ghost would keep off thieves. Shrunk would not only attempt to locate the cache but also lay the ghost. In fact, he did all forms of plain and fancy hexing, used the diviner's rod where necessary and practiced the black arts in their various mysterious ways until he died at the ripe old age of eighty.[21]

The Pennsylvania Germans, if one were to believe newspaper reports today, might easily fall into this classification as practitioners of the black arts. Their barn decorations are said to be placed there for the purpose of keeping away witches. They are reported to be given to occult hexing. Facts reveal quite the opposite.

Doubtless some Pennsylvania Germans in the past did believe in witches, so did many people in the mid-eighteenth century. But witches did not seem to bother the Pennsylvania Germans half so much as they did the New Englanders of this period. The Salem trials and executions attest only too vividly to how real witches seemed to New Englanders.

The actual anti-witch sign of a Pennsylvania German barn was a triangle cut in the lintel or a small iron cow attached somewheres about the barn. The exterior decorative designs—stylized flowers and such—are found in other local forms of decoration—in quilts, cake molds and *fractur* or illuminating. "By association with Biblical motifs, their religious character is established." [22]

"Powwowing" was another Pennsylvania German custom that seems to deceive outsiders. It consisted in mumbling in a confused manner certain texts from Scriptures over a sick person. These healers, who had to be of the opposite sex, were believed to be invested with secret powers. So much for the legend. Powwowing is nothing else than faith healing or as a scholar of these customs has called it, "Christian Science without sophistication." [23]

On the other hand, Negro slaves in Early America often practiced voodoo and obeah, sometimes using obeah's extreme measure of poisoning. Like the Gypsies, they could

not be expected to give up their native customs and super-
stitions just because they were transported to these shores.
There were several serious slave uprisings of an obviously
planned character. New York had an outbreak in 1712 for
which twenty-one Negroes were executed; there was one near
Somerville, N. J., in 1734; and in New York again in 1741,
when eighteen were hanged, sixteen burned at the stake and
seventy transported. In addition to these there occurred a
number of mysterious poisonings of masters and other slaves
that indicate how active obeah was being practised.

In 1702 at Merion, Pa., Richard Harrison, on moving
his slaves from Maryland to Pennsylvania, had a grisly re-
minder of their discontent with this new home. He and his
family were at breakfast. Someone knocked on the door. In
getting up to answer the knock, Harrison tipped over the
table and spilt the breakfast chocolate. The household cat
lapped it up and promptly died. When the slaves were exam-
ined, conspirators among them confessed that they had intended poisoning the family.[24]

At another Pennsylvania farmhouse two Negroes were arrested after being overheard hatching a conspiracy to wipe
out their master's family with a "bush" drug. On them were
found both arsenic and some unknown roots.[25] Boston of
July, 1755, saw the executions of a Negro man and two
women, caught with poison which had killed their master,
Captain John Codman of Charlestown. Ten years before, at
Cambridge, a Negro woman was burned for the same offense.
When he was in Virginia in 1779, the English traveler, Anburey, found a case of herb poison administered to a rival
by a jealous Negro. It caused a lingering death that extended
over several weeks, and physicians were helpless to prevent
it.[26] In Charleston, S. C., ten years before this, a Negro man
and woman were burned alive for poisoning their master,
his wife and child.[27]

# III

## A BAGFUL OF ODD STICKS

IN THE INTRODUCTION, AS ONE OF THE EXCUSES FOR PRESENT-
ing these pages from obscure American history, we offered
the suggestion that the eccentrics and wags of old times were
ancestors of the preposterous and publicized eccentrics and
wags of our own days. Let us see then what we can trace, by
extracting from this bagful of odd sticks an assorted lot of
scientific hoaxers, medical quacks, petty rhymsters, crack-
brained inventors, lusty Amazons, macabre freaks, newspaper "personals" and merry fellows. Their kind is known
today. We can read accounts of their descendents in any
newspaper. Sunday magazine sections are especially good
hunting ground for them.

### Scientific Hoaxers

On May 13, 1784, there appeared in the *Journal de Paris,*
to be promptly copied by newspapers in England and provincial France, an article describing a balloon ascension alleged
to have been made in Philadelphia on December 28, 1783.
It stated that a man raised himself to the height of ninety-
seven English feet and came down again with ease. It also
explained that previous to this event Messrs. Rittenhouse
and Hopkins, eminent scientists and members of the Philosophical Academy, had been experimenting with inflated
bladders and then with somewhat larger machines. They

joined these bladders together and fastened them around a cage into which they placed several animals. The whole contraption having ascended, it was then drawn down by a rope.

Encouraged by this experiment, Messrs. Rittenhouse and Hopkins the next day induced a man to get into the cage and he rose fifteen feet, with the rope still holding him. James Wilcox, a carpenter, was then engaged—for a consideration—to try it, and rose twenty feet. He was then offered $50 if he would make an ascension with the rope cut. Dr. Jaune, the principal medical officer in the city, was in attendance in case of accident. Wilcox rose. The cage, lifted by seven balloons, climbed to ninety-seven feet and remained up there five minutes, when a sudden wind began blowing it towards the Schuylkill River. Following the instructions given him, Wilcox first cut loose three of the balloons, then the remainder gradually. As he glided down he fell on a fence and sprained his wrist. This, so the French report said, was his only injury.

Now the secret in creating a successful hoax is to approach, in some parts of it, the verisimilitude of truth. This account, which thrilled the newspaper-reading public of England and the Continent, was a hoax manufactured out of the whole cloth—but it was just realistic enough to gain credence. Though it had at the time and still has an American Philosophical Society, Philadelphia at this time did not have nor has it ever had a Philosophical Academy. Among the members of the former were David Rittenhouse, eminent mathematician and astronomer, but no Hopkins, although among its members was the famous Francis Hopkinson, signer of the Declaration, scientist and satirist. Also at this time no physician by name of Jaune resided in Philadelphia and the Philadelphia directory of the day reveals a John Wilcox but no James.

The first balloon ascension in America was made by Peter Carnes of Baltimore on July 17, 1784. Carnes, an amateur balloonist, rose to a great height in a basket held by a bag of hot air—and was thrown from the basket. The first fully successful ascension occurred, it is true, at Philadelphia—on the 9th of January, 1793, being accomplished by M. Blanchard, who before this had crossed the Channel in his balloon and made many ascensions in France. On his trip here, he carried with him a passport signed by Washington, directing whom it might concern and who had not seen a balloon before to treat the bearer with consideration. Blanchard's gas bag of green taffeta lifted him 5,812 feet and he was in the air from ten in the forenoon until he landed in Deptford Township, Gloucester County, N. J. He returned to Philadelphia at seven in the evening, where he went direct to the President and handed back his credentials.

The perpetrator of this Wilcox hoax is believed to have been Colonel Thomas Forrest of Philadelphia, who served valiantly in the Continental Artillery from 1776 to 1781, and who also enjoyed carrying his tongue in his cheek. In 1767 he wrote "The Disappointment," a comic opera announced for production at the Southwark Theatre but withdrawn. It satirized Philadelphia characters. A second edition appeared in 1796 under the authorship of "Andrew Barton." [1] As for his balloon hoax, the story was solemnly repeated, with improvements and embellishments, as late as the 9th edition of the Encyclopaedia Britannica.

That the Father of His Country should lend his approbation to such a scientific experiment as a balloon ascension was not unusual. It was an age when interest in scientific affairs indicated gentility and culture. Moreover this eminent person was as credulous as the most believing of his citizens. His household account books reveal, for instance, that at Mount Vernon he once "gave to a negro who calls him-

self Prince Achmet, $2.10." Later we shall see that he was
not above visiting human freaks.[2]

Another merry tale that set tongues a-wagging and the
credulous to speculating broke on the country in 1835 when
Richard Adam Locke first "proved" that the moon was inhabited. In doing so he also set the example, followed by
thousands of them since, of a newspaper building circulation
on scandal and pseudo-scientific stories. Locke was a New
Yorker by birth who had the advantages of an excellent education both at home and at Cambridge, England, from which
university he returned to the States in 1830 and embarked
on a journalistic career. The founder of the *New York Sun*
gave him his first chance and he made eminently good by
writing the Moon Hoax. It ran in the *Sun* from .August 25
to 31, 1835, and later appeared in pamphlet form in 1852,
1859 and 1871.

This series purported to be quotations from the *Edinburgh Journal of Science* on the result of astronomical observations of the moon made at the Cape of Good Hope by
Sir John Herschel the Younger. It proved that the moon was
inhabited by both men and animals. The human beings
were winged creatures and the animals not unfamiliar types.
Among them was a variety of superior biped beavers from
whose houses smoke could be seen issuing. The reports were
so convincingly spattered with astronomical terms and so
convincingly written that no one doubted them. The *Sun's*
circulation rose to 19,000, making it the most popular daily
of the time. Paris, London, Edinburgh and Glasgow papers
took the accounts seriously and reprinted them.

Locke's approach to truth was in attributing these reports
to the *Edinburgh Journal of Science*. There had been such
a publication, but it was defunct long before this smart
reporter began sharpening his quill. Scientists at Yale, realizing this, sent down a delegation to see the original copy

of the *Journal* from which Locke quoted. The hoax was exploded—but the *Sun* had its circulation by this time and the average readers much preferred to believe the *Sun* than the scientists, so the belief in lunar inhabitants still persists.[3]

## Quacks and Quackery

Among the pleasant memories we inherit of our great-great-grandmothers is the picture of that old lady working in her herb garden and concocting remedies from catmint and pennyroyal, sage, thoroughwort, tansy, wormwood and sassafras bark. Each had its own properties which these gentle old dames knew how to administer. Like as not she also had a copy of Nicholas Culpepper's "English Physician Enlarged"[4] in which that half-quack and half-botanist explained not only what herbs to use for what ailments, according to the Doctrine of Signatures or signs on the plants, but also how the herbs were to be gathered—the leaves at the beginning of Spring or towards the end of Summer, the flowers in their prime and the seeds when ripe. It was a poor family indeed which could not show, hanging from its garret rafters, bundles of herbs hung up to dry as Culpepper directed. Another handy volume each household might possess would be "Every Man His Own Doctor" by John Tennent, the Virginia physician. Tennent designed this little volume "for Those who can't afford to dye by the Hand of a Doctor." Naturally the profession criticized it, but the populace evidently bought it in great quantities, for in 1736 Franklin was printing a fourth edition of it.

That an abundance of herbs growing easily was an inducement to immigrants is indicated by one of the earliest descriptions of Pennsylvania, written by Thomas Makin, clerk of the Assembly and tutor in Latin at the Friends' Academy. It contained the welcome news that:

Here odiferous herbs and flowers grow
Useful to those who do their virtues know.[5]

In addition to these home remedies, local town apothe-
caries and pedlars' packs, as we have seen, supplied pills and
other specifics—Turlington's Balsam, Stoughton's & Daffy's
Elixir, Bateman's Drops, Hooper's, Anderson's and Lockyer's
pills, Hill's Balsam of Honey, Walker's Jesuit Drops, Golden
Spirit of Scurvy Grass and Swinsen's Electuary.

Even as today, quacks and quack medicines were plentiful.
The earliest of record was Tuscarora Rice, a preparation first
made from Indian corn by Mrs. Sybilla Masters of Philadelphia in 1711. She claimed it would relieve and cure tuberculosis and other ailments. An English patent, No. 401, the
first to any person in the American colonies, was granted to
her husband Thomas Masters for the new invention whereby
his wife was able to clean and cure Indian corn. She went to
England to make her fortune from this. The model of this
machine is still preserved in the Franklin Institute at Philadelphia.

Sybilla was evidently America's first woman inventor. In
1716 she was granted another patent, No. 403, for a process
of weaving palmetto chips and straws for covering hats and
bonnets and other improvements in that ware.[6]

Rattlesnake poisoning was a serious menace and many attempts were made to circumvent its effects. In 1745 Frederick Torres, a Frenchman resident at Philadelphia, advertised his "Chemical Stone," together with certain miraculous
powders that he claimed would cure snakebite immediately
if applied promptly to the spot. He also assured the believing
world that it would cure cancer, swellings, rheumatism,
toothache, labor pains and gout! [7] At the beginning of the
nineteenth century the North Carolina legislature granted
freedom and £200 to a local Negro named Caesar for his
"charm" against snakebite poison. It consisted of equal parts

of the juice of horehound and plantain taken internally and evidently was one of those Negro "bush" medicines mentioned in the previous chapter.[8]

It is a pity that Joseph Breintnall of Pennsylvania didn't know about Torres's "Chemical Stone" when the rattlesnake bit him in May, 1746. He would have been spared a long and heroic treatment. First he killed the snake. Then he took a chicken, ripped up its belly and put it on his hand to suck out the poison. Immediately it—the fowl—swelled, grew black and stunk. Breintnall kept his elbow bent and his fingers up. He bound his arm in a plaster made of turmeric roots. To let out the "bad" blood, he slit his fingers with a razor and cupped the back of his hand. Three days later he applied ashes of white ash and vinegar made into a poultice. He became delirious. His arm "swelled, gathered and burst"—and he recovered. This treatment had lasted from May until well into the Autumn.[9]

Four years before this, Richard Hockley of Philadelphia had sent to his friend, Thomas Hyam of London, a consignment of two dozen rattlesnakes, designed for William Penn, with the directions that they were to be pounded in a mortar and mixed with either wine or rum. The concoction was to be shaken two or three times a day for five days, when it would be ready for use.[10] This may have been the colonial forerunner of that specific so loudly hawked by circus barkers —snake oil.

It was the Dr. John Tennent of Virginia mentioned above who first extolled the virtues of Seneca Root, another of the barker's favorite cure-alls. He claimed it had virtues to solve many ailments, especially pleurisy and gout. The Virginia Assembly awarded him £100, but his creditors snatched it away before he could benefit from it.[11]

Quacks who claimed to be doctors abounded. Many of them, as we have observed, were smart Yankee pedlars;

others remained stationary. In his journey to Philadelphia
in 1723, at the tender age of twelve, Franklin stayed overnight at an inn near Burlington, N. J., kept by a Dr.
Brown, "an ambulatory quack doctor," who also amused
himself turning the Bible into doggerel verse.[12] Many years
later, in 1767, there moved from this same Burlington to
Philadelphia a "Dr." Thomas Wise, who advertised that "he
undertakes particularly to cure, with small expense and pain
to the Patient, cancers and wens without cutting them, the
King's Evil, venereal disorders without Sallivation, Rupture,
Strangury and Stone, etc." In fact, quite a range of bodily
troubles.[13]

The next year appeared the advertisement of another
Philadelphia quack—Daniel Goodman. He, being a seventh
son, claimed that, for a number of years in England, New
Jersey and Pennsylvania, he had cured divers persons afflicted with the King's Evil "by using no other means or
remedies than by stroking the parts affected with the hand."
He offered to help others and, generous soul, so unlike doctors today, assured them that "any person or persons will be
cured without fee or award." [14]

Fake oculists appeared too. Princeton, N. J., had its local
character who suddenly announced himself a specialist in
eyes. When one Benjamin Randolph lost his sight after
treatment by this quack, the newspapers warned the populace against him.[15]

## Petty Rhymsters

The colonial American was just as apt to break into doggerel as his descendants today. The broadside of the eighteenth century, with its confessions and accounts of extraordinary events celebrated in rhyme, finds some of its heritage
in those sheets "containin' woids av pop'lar song hits"
hawked on city streets today.

We have already seen how Samuel Temple set forth the wares in his general store at Dedham, Mass., and how Jonathan Plummer sang the virtues of Lord Timothy Dexter whilst peddling haddock, and eventually we shall encounter Rev. Mather Byles, the rhyming Boston parson.

So bright was the glow that surrounded Dexter in the previous chapter that Plummer, his poet laureate, may have been overshadowed. Let us do him honor now. His literary works—usually in rhyme—were "sold by him at his basket in Marketsquare, Newburyport." Nor were his poetic flights restricted to Dexter "Earl of Chester, Knight of the Four Open-Mouthed Lions in St. James's Park and Marquis de la Newburyport" as Plummer once dubbed him, signing himself,

> I am, my lord, in frost and summer
> Your Poet Laureat, Jonathan Plummer

No, occasionally Plummer wrote of other worthies and events and recorded local happenings, especially tragic accidents, in good broadside verse. He explained himself severally as a traveling preacher, physician, poet, trader, latter-day prophet and lay bishop; and in his "Looking Glass for lovers of strong drink" explained that he also was "no hermaphrodite." [16]

With this tribute to Plummer, let us turn to other Early American wags who spoke in poetic measures.

When, in 1767, Leonard Ware of Virginia found a stray steer wandering around his meadow, no mere prose would satisfy him. He needs must set forth the facts in verse and publish them in the *Virginia Gazette:*

> At Lily Valley a three year old steer,
> His mark is a ruff crop in every ear,
> His color is either brindle or brown
> And is posted and praised at two pounds and a crown.

His belly and thighs are part of them white,
And the owner may have him on proving his right.[17]

In various ways did John Watson of Pennsylvania claim his little niche among the locally famous: he was surveyor to the Penns, secretary to Governor Morris and in 1760 Surveyor-General of the Province. In Summer he generally went barefoot, but when surveying wore boots, as his father had died of a snake bite. He also—remarkable gift—both wrote and *spoke* in verse. Once he defended a thief in court. The evidence against his client was overwhelming, yet so passionately did Watson plead to the jury in impromptu verse that the thief was acquitted.[18]

A still smaller niche is occupied by Aquila Rose, one-time clerk of the Pennsylvania Assembly and otherwise occupied as keeper of a crude ferry crossing the Schuylkill. Between ferrying he wrote verse. So widespread grew his fame that when he was drowned near his ferry in 1823 the town mourned his death as a public calamity.

An earlier Pennsylvanian rhymster was Thomas Livezey. On June 29, 1764, to accompany thirty bushels of bran which he sold to a friend but of which he charged him for only fifteen, his generous heart welled up with these lines:

> Respected Friend, I've sent thee Bran
> As neat and clean as any Man,
> I've took great Pains, for fear of Loss
> To thee in foundering of thy Horse.
> Its ground with Bur and ground so nice
> It looks as 'twas bolted twice.
> But that's no matter, since its such
> Thy man can't ever feed too much,
> I mean can't founder if he would,
> I've took such pains to make it good.
> Nor will it ever dust his Cloaths
> Nor give thy horse a Mealy Nose,
> And further in its praise I'll say,

'Twill never make him run away.
But if on this alone he's fed,
A child may lead him with a thread.
Feed freely then, Nor be in Doubt,
I'll send thee more when this is out.[19]

The best laurels of all must go to George Sandys, treasurer of Virginia in 1623. Consider the circumstances under which he wrote. During the Winter following the massacre, when those who survived lived in constant terror and confusion, how did he employ his spare moments? In what did he find "escape," as modern psychologists would call it? He calmly went on translating into English the Metamorphoses of Ovid! It was the first poetry written in America.[20]

The great range of American broadside poetry offers many a quotable line and jingle—and some positively unquotable. It was a robust age. When, for example, the Maryland wit, George Alsop, felt moved to describe his critics, he used forthright language:

Arms all akimbo and with belly strut
As if they had Parnassus in their gut.

On the other hand, much of this broadside verse makes dreary reading. From the reams and reams of limping meters and non-rhyming rhymes, we can point to a rare one because it is devoted to an unusual topic. It shows that even as early as 1731 Yale was striving to set up some sort of *entente cordiale*—no matter how lowly the foundations—with proud Harvard. The authors must have been linear ancestors of the editors of the *Lampoon* and the *Record*.[21]

CAMBRIDGE, December 1731

Some Time since died here Mr. Mathew Abbey, in a very advanced Age: He had for a great Number of Years ferv'd the College in Quality of Bed-maker and Sweeper: Having no Child, his Wife inherits his whole Estate, which he bequeath'd to her by his last Will and Testament, as follows, viz:

To my dear Wife,
My Joy and Life,
I freely now do give her,
My whole Estate,
With all my Plate,
Being just about to leave her.

My Tub of Soap,
A long Cart Rope,
A Frying Pan and Kettle,
An Ashes Pail,
A threshing Frail,
An Iron Wedge and beetle.

Two painted Chairs,
Nine Warden Pears,
A large old dripping Platter,
This Bed of Hay
On which I lay,
An old Sauce-Pan for Butter.

A little Mug,
A Two Quart Jug,
A Bottle full of Brandy,
A Looking-Glass,
To see your Face,
You'll find it very handy.

A musket true,
As ever flew,
A Pound of Shot and Wallet,
A Leather Sash,
My Calabash,
My Powder Horn and Bullet.

An Old Sword blade,
A Garden Spade,
A Hoe, a Rake, a Ladder,
A wooden Can,
A Close Stool Pan,
A Clyster-Pipe and bladder.

A greasy Hat,
My Old Ram Cat,
A Yard and half of Linnen,
A Pot of Grease,
A Woolen Fleece,
In Order for your spinning.

A small Tooth Comb,
An ashen broom,
A Candlestick and Hatchet,
A Coverlid
Strip'd down with Red,
A bag of Rags to Patch it.

A ragged Mat,
A Tub of Fat,
A book put out by BUNYAN,
Another book
By ROBIN COOK,
A skain or two of spunyarn.

An old Black Muff,
Some Woolen Stuff,
A Quantity of Bardage,
Some Devil's Weed,
And Burdock feed,
To season well your Porridge,

A chafing Dish,
With one Salt Fish,
If I am not mistaken,
A Leg of Pork,
A broken Fork,
And half a Flitch of Bacon.

A Spinning Wheel
One Peck of Meal,
A Knife without a handle,
A rusty Lamp,
Two Quarts of Samp,
And half a Tallow Candle.

My Pouch and Pipes,
Two Oxen Tripes,
An Oaken Dish well carved,
My little Dog,
And spotted Hog,
With two young pigs just
starved.

This is my store,
I have no more,
I heartily do give it,
My Years are spun,
My Days are done,
And so I think to leave it.

NEW-HAVEN, January 1731-2

Our Sweeper having lately buried his spouse, and accidentally hearing of our CAMBRIDGE brother, has conceiv'd a violent passion for the relict, As Love Softens the Mind and disposes to Poetry, he had essay'd himself in the following strains, which he transmits to the charming Widow, as the first Essay of his Love and Courtship:

MISTRESS Abbey.
To you fly,
You only can relieve me,
To you I turn,
For you I burn,
If you will but believe me.

You may be sure
'Tis not your Dow'r
I make this flowing verse on,
In these smooth Lays
I only praise
The Glories of your perfon,

Then gentle Dame,
Admit my flame,
And grant me my petition,
If you deny
Alas! I die
In pitiful Condition.

For the whole that
Was left by Mat,
Fortune to me has granted;
In equal store,
I've one thing more
Which MATTHEW long had
wanted

Before the News
Of your dear Spouse
Had reach'd us at NEW HAVEN,
My dear wife dy'd,
Who was my bride,
In ANNO Eighty-Seven.

No Teeth, 'tis true,
You have to shew,
The young think teeth inviting,
But Silly Youths!
I love those Mouths
Where there's no fear of biting.

Thus being free,
Let's both agree
To join our Hands, for I do
Boldly aver
A Widower
Is fittest for a Widow.

A leaky Eye,
That's never dry,
These woful Times is fitting,
A wrinkled face
Adds solemn Grace
To Folks devout at Meeting.

Thus to go on
I would pen down
Your Charms from head to foot,
Set all your glory
In Verse before ye,
But I've no mind to do't.

Then haste away,
And make no stay;
For soon as you come hither,
We'll eat and sleep,

Make beds and sweep,
And talk and smoke together.

But if my Dear,
I must move there,
Tow'rds CAMBRIDGE strait I'll set me
To towze the Hay,
On which you lay,
If AGE and YOU will let me.

*Thus Father Abbey left his Spouse,*
*As rich as Church or College Mouse,*
*Which is sufficient Invitation,*
*To serve the College in his Station.*[22]

## *Cracked-Brain Inventors*

To the one Whitney who might invent a successful cotton-gin and to the Fitch who contrived a steamboat, there were dozens of mechanical visionaries in the opening years of the nineteenth century who gravely sought to lighten labor and increase production by complicated contraptions. Their kind is still with us.

Others were more picturesque. In Germantown, Pa., lived one Redheifer, a gambler and an otherwise worthless fellow. He enjoyed arousing his sleepy townsmen with bombastic claims and tall stories. At one time, after working on it with great secrecy, he announced that he had invented and built a machine which, once started, would run by perpetual motion. So loud and long did he proclaim the initial demonstration of this wonder of the ages that a large assembly gathered. He threw a switch, the machine began creaking into motion and, without further impulse, it carried on. The Germantowners might have accepted it as being all that Redheifer claimed, did they not know his

reputation. Sure enough, at last they discovered that the perpetual motion issued from a little decrepit old man concealed in an upper loft, who ground a crank.[23]

Of no such disreputable habits was Samuel Lamb, stone
mason of Kingston, Cumberland County, Pa. Up and down
the valley and far and wide thereabouts Sam Lamb's chim-
neys were famous. Well and truly laid, they rose to the sky
straight as an arrow. This was due to Sam's own method of
plumbing his work—he used to spit down the corners to see
that they were straight! [24]

The most thoroughly unnecessary inventions to which
Americans of the 1830's were subjected came to this country
under the aegis of John Nepomuk Maelzl. He had made a
continental reputation for his various contrivances and
brought them here as a traveling show. They included a
universal orchestra instrument called a "panharmonicon,"
an automaton trumpeter, speaking dolls, miniature birds that
sprang from the lids of little boxes, an act called the "Con-
flagration of Moscow" and an automaton chess-player. Edgar
Allan Poe, among others, proved conclusively that the chess-
player was controlled by human intelligence. Nevertheless,
Maelzl managed to attract crowds in the United States and
the West Indies for many years.[25]

### Lusty Amazons

In all wars and on every frontier of America, you could
find some lusty female who, hiding her sex under the garb
of a man, went forth to struggle and to fight. There was
Deborah Sampson, who joined the Continental Army and, so
her biographer assures us, "performed the duties of every
department into which she was called with punctual exact-
ness, fidelity and honor, and preserved her chastity intact by
the most artful concealment of her sex." [26] Stony Point,

Tappan Bay, raids on Tories, she went through them all safely and undisclosed under the name of Robert Surtlieff. She even filled the role of orderly to General Patterson, in which capacity she crossed the Alleghanies and fought with Indians in what is now Ohio. On a policing expedition to Philadelphia to quell riots among unpaid troops, she fell victim to fever. In the hospital her sex was revealed.

During the Civil War three women were known to have fought as men until their sex was disclosed—Louisa Wellman of Iowa and Sarah Stover and Maria Seelye. We shall let these three Amazons lie in peace, content that on each Memorial Day the Boy Scouts will wreathe their graves, and turn to pay honor to a frontier heroine, mad Anne Dennis Bailey Trotter and a female Marine—Louisa Baker.

From her beginning, life toughened Anne Dennis. Even in 1742 Liverpool was not a soft, cultural town to choose for birthplace. At 19 she was kidnaped—shanghaied is the more exact term—and carried off to Virginia where she was sold as an indentured servant. At 23 she married a man named Bailey (some say it was Trotter), a member of Col. Lewis's regiment, who was killed by the Indians in the Battle of Point Pleasant on October 10, 1774. Moved by revenge, she adopted male clothes, or as near to them as she could find— an old petticoat and a man's coat. She was prototype of all hill-billy women. The rifle rarely left her shoulder or the tomahawk and hunter's knife her belt. In this attire she followed the life of scout and spy and often carried information to the commandants of frontier forts.

In 1785 she married a soldier at Fort Clendenin on the Kanawha River, one John Bailey (or Trotter) and went to live in a hut built by herself on what is now called Mad Anne's Ridge in Alleghany County, Va.

Expert with the rifle and a superb horsewoman, "no mountain was too steep for her or her horse, no Winter too

severe, no Summer too hot, no enemy too cunning." Often
she made perilous journeys from the settlements on the
James and Potomac Rivers to Fort Clendenin and other distant outposts. One of her exploits was riding from Fort Lee
(now Charleston, W. Va.) to Fort Union (now Lewisburg),
to return with powder for the besieged garrison. For this
she was given a horse, which she named for her birthplace—
Liverpool. In one trip, going through the snow, she fell
asleep, tumbled off into a soft drift, and Liverpool came back
to give the alarm. At another time she appeared at Fort
Young with two Indian scalps dangling at her belt for
chatelaine. Besides being utterly unafraid, she used a mag-
nificently profane vocabulary, had a short temper and could
stand up to any man drink for drink.

The two authorities who are uncertain as to which swain
she married first also differ on the manner of her demise.
One finds her second husband killed in an Indian War,
whereupon she moves to Harrison township, Gallis County,
Ohio, with her son, William Trotter, and "in old age, she
taught school, displaying great mental and physical vigor"
until on November 23, 1825, she ascended to join the other
Amazons in Valhalla.[27] The second recorder is content to let
her die in the old rail shanty she had built herself.[28]

Our next heroine needs no such elaborate explanation nor
is there any dispute as to her matrimonial ventures, for her
whole career is set forth in a little pamphlet that, in the manner of long titles then fashionable, told everything. It reads:
"Louise Baker (a native of Massachusetts) who, in early life,
having been shamefully seduced, deserted by her parents and
become a distinguished associate of the vilest Bawds of
'Negro Hill' (so vulgarly termed), but becoming weary of
the sisterhood, she in 1813 (garbed as a male) entered as a
Marine on board a Frigate of the United States, where in
two or three engagements, she displayed the most heroic

fortitude and was honorably discharged therefrom a few months since with a discovery of her sex being made."

One wonders if it isn't about time the Marine Corps erects a statue to their sister-in-arms, this magnificent bawd, Louise Baker, who evidently always landed safely and "had things well in hand." It might even erect a companion statue to Emma Cole, the orphan who ran away to sea as a common sailor, was captured by pirates, in time restored safe and sound to her own people, and lived to a ripe old age without suffering so much as the loss of a sliver of her virtue.[29]

## Human Freaks

The story of human freaks in the salad days of this country is closely connected, of course, with the beginnings of the circus.

Both strange and malformed animals were shown at an early date, usually as solitary attractions. Then in August, 1771, the *Massachusetts Spy* advertised "a Maiden Dwarf, who is fifty-three years old and of but twenty-two inches in stature. It is by the counsel of some Gentlemen, that she is come to pay a visit to this place [Boston]; and she is willing to exhibit herself as a shew to such Gentlemen and Ladies as are desirous to gratify their curiosity, for one shilling lawful money for each person."

Calvin Phillips, native of Bridgewater, Me., appears as the first "Tom Thumb, Jr." Six years old, he was only twenty-six inches tall and weighed twelve pounds. Since his parents were in lowly circumstances, he managed to support them by being displayed, from 1797 to 1801.

In the town of Manchester, Passaic County, N. J., there once lived a monster in human form. At the time he was visited by Washington, he had attained the age of 27. The round part of his head measured 21". His eyes and nose were remarkably large and prominent, his chin long and pointed, making his features coarse, irregular and thoroughly repellent. The voice that issued from the slit between big nose and pointed chin was said to be sonorous. His further deformities included a body only 27″ long, limbs miniature and much deformed. He had the use of only one hand and he was never able to stand or sit up, as he could not support his enormous head. He was constantly in a large cradle with his head supported by a pillow.

Mankind made a beaten path to his door. Travelers would stop off to see him. He appeared to be especially fond of clergymen. When George Washington came to call, he asked this monstrosity if he were Whig or Tory, whereupon, so we are assured, the big head sententiously replied that he had never taken active part on either side.[30]

A companion piece to Calvin was Martha Ann Honeywell, the seven-year-old girl born with only one limb, having only the first joints of both arms and one foot with three toes. Nevertheless she could feed herself, write, do needlework and make cut-out paper portraits and scenes. By 1809, when she was seventeen, she had accumulated quite a gallery of her embroideries and portraits, which she exhibited along with herself.

Of the earliest Fat Ladies the records give the palm to Deborah and Susan Tripp. In 1829, aged respectively three years and five years and ten months, Deborah weighed 124 pounds and Susan 205.[31]

Many years later Texas produced Eli Bowen who is mentioned in a curious pamphlet by Felix O. C. Darley, published in 1847. Eli was born without legs. He lived with bears, snakes and wolves in the woods, to which he would escape on the approach of strangers. Evidently he lost his shyness or determined to make the sinister fate which gave him such a deformed body pay in good, spendable coin—he became a circus freak.[32]

Finally we come to that first of Barnum's ventures—Joice Heth. Her career is set forth in a pamphlet published at New York in 1837, in which it was claimed that Joice was the nurse who brought George Washington into the world. Though weighing only forty-six pounds, she still lived in 1837, aged 161 years. In Niblo's Garden at New York, 10,000 people came to see her. After her death an autopsy proved that her age was only half that which Barnum claimed, but by this time he had proved his belief in the unfailing gullibility of mankind.

### *"Personal"  Column*

Writers of letters to the newspapers we have always had with us and always will. Often the colonial editor depended on them to fill out his sheet. He also welcomed, within reason, "Personal" items, especially if they were of poetic or quixotic character. The editor of the *Connecticut Journal* in 1769 did not disdain this attack on a parson in Guilford, which must have caused no end of gossip: [33]

This may certify all whom it may concern that the art of barking is taught by Toby Ramshorn, bell-wether of the flock of Guilford. It is necessary to expatiate on the benefit arising from the noble art, lest it suffice that the flock in Guilford, under the instruction and direction of old Toby, have regained their liberty and are now barking at him after he is gone. Old Toby instructs at the lowest price, in all the various ways of barking—teaches to bark by note, both treble, tenor and bass, and is preparing a treatise upon the subject of barking. He proposes for ready money, to bark either for religion or liberty or against them; and will bark, gratis, monthly for public good. He at present bears the bell in the flock at Guilford, which is a fine flock, though he must confess very much hide-bound. . . . If any man, dog, wolf, sheep or any other kind of animal desires to be instructed in this noble art, let him repair to aforesaid Toby, who with all possible cheapness and diligence, will teach him the exercise of the windpipe.

Other editors were more careful to keep their columns "fit to print." Mr. Weyman, editor of the *New York Gazette,* in January 21, 1760, announced:

Mr. Z, if he pleases, may call for the piece he sent us last Week, when he shall have returned, one half of the Money he sent to have it inserted, whilst the other half we shall keep to pay for this Notice; as his Subject is unfit for a News-paper.

Three years later he was frequently known to state, without a flicker or a quibble:

Advertisements we must leave out this Week; our next will possibly make amends for it.

Today an advertiser at the mercy of a publisher would be news.

Mr. Weyman may have been unusually hard-hearted. Mr. Holt, who published *The New-York Journal;* or, *The General Advertiser,* had a softer heart—or perhaps, a harder head. On July 8, 1773, his paper ran the following advertisement:

WANTED, *incontinently,* "A handy, neat, well-proportioned, likely young woman, to wait upon a gentleman, keep his chamber, bed and furniture, in the neatest order and decorum, and take care that he be amply provided with every necessary accommodation according to the particular directions he shall from time to time occasionally give her—to take care of his clothes and linen, attend to dress and undress him, etc. She must be particularly skillful and assiduous in dressing hair, and giving the head all the fashionable decorations.

"If any young woman whose person and qualifications suits the above description, will leave with the printer hereof, a line directed to C. K. Q., Esq.; informing him of her terms, and where she may be found—he will let her know where to apply, and shall require no recommendation, as he proposes himself to be the judge of her qualifications.

"He is sensible that some of the services he requires, are usually performed by men, but being a person of delicacy, and having weak nerves, he cannot bear the coarse appearance, the strong effluvia, nor the rough touch of a male thing, to be so familiar with his person, and busy in handling and fidgeting about him.

"He hopes no one will be so unreasonable as to censure him for the singularity of his taste, as he is able to pay for its indulgence, and conceives his rights to it to be indisputable; since even the *Ladies,* who certainly are governed by the strictest rules of decorum and propriety, admit without scruple, of the like services from the other sex.

" *'Honi soit qui mal y pense.'* "

### Merry Fellows

From Mr. C. K. Q.'s obvious advertisement for a house-keeper-mistress it may seem a sheer drop into immodesty when we pass on to an incident that once happened aboard a ship heading for England. The *Boston News Letter* reports how this ship, outward bound from Boston, escaped from a devastating fate. The cabin next to the captain's was occupied by a British officer and what appeared to a New England Puritan on board to be the officer's mistress. Quarters were close in those early days and passengers more or less lived on each other's necks. This Puritan happened to be sitting by the fire in the common cabin when a curtain brushed into the coals and ignited. "Fire! Fire!" he shouted. Thereupon the officer's mistress rushed into the main cabin and extinguished the flames with the contents of her *pot de chambre.* Ship, crew, passengers and cargo were saved by the nimble wit of this loose lady.[34]

James Akin found other use for this convenience. A native of South Carolina, Mr. Akin eventually appeared in Newburyport, Mass., in 1804, where he entered the employment of Edmund M. Blunt as an engraver of maps. He also found time to do portraits—Lord Timothy Dexter's among them— and cartoons. His avocations were being a druggist and keeping a tavern. Once, during an altercation with his employer, Blunt threw a skillet at him. Akin made a cartoon of this incident. He also sought the utmost revenge on his employer—he made a portrait of Blunt and had it engraved on china—on chamber pots especially—and had the china sent to Newburyport where the natives snapped it up. To this day Akin's chamber pots are collector's items.[35]

Into quite a different mold was cast Andrew Jackson Allen. In the theatrical world and outside it as well, he was known as "Dummy Allen," for he had once been Edwin Forrest's costumer. After these years in the stage business, he retired to Albany and opened a restaurant. It was the sort of restaurant, offering an unusual cuisine in a pleasant environment, that naturally attracted the fashionable set and the legislators attendant at the capital.

Both at his restaurant and in the public press he announced once that on a certain day he would serve turtle soup and, to give the proper "build-up" to this famous dish, he had a large turtle paraded back and forth before his place. Then it disappeared—presumably into the soup pot. The restaurant was jammed. On several occasions he repeated this and his trade flourished. Finally one of the buyers, blessed with an observant eye, suspected that it was the same turtle and he marked it. Sure enough it disappeared just before turtle soup was announced. A week or so later, again the announcement, again the paraded turtle—and there it was, marks and all! Albany knew the story by sundown. Allen had made the turtle soup from calves' heads and he owned only this one old turtle, but the town enjoyed its laugh and continued to flock to his restaurant. And thus he built up a trade and lined his purse.

Space presses on us. We have room for only one more wag.
It is December 31, 1799.

> Ring out, wild bells, to the wild sky,
> The old year is dying, let it die.

That was precisely how Colonel Loammi Baldwin of Woburn, Mass., felt. But he wasn't going to allow the gorgeous
eighteenth century, with its memories of merry hours and
bitter moments, its recessions and advancements, its wars and
years of peace, its lovely women and gallant men, to pass
into the bourne of time without celebrating the occasion.
He gave a party. In fact he gave a magnificent ball at his
house and invited all the élite for miles around.

One of the attractions, placed at the end of the ballroom,
was the figure 1799 traced in colored wick lights. As the
hour of midnight approached, he ordered that all charge
their glasses. They gathered around the burning symbol of
the old year. The clocks and church bells announced the
end of one century and the beginning of another. Colonel
Baldwin began cranking a mechanism beside the lights. He
had invented this himself and lived for this hour to demonstrate it. Slowly the figures began to shift and reform until,
wonder of wonders, they spelled 1800! [36]

*Part III*

# CAVE DWELLERS AND SOLITARIES

# I

## CATACOMB ARISTOCRACY

### *Time and Place*

FOR MOST DESCENDANTS OF THOSE WHO CAME FIRST THERE stands an insurmountable barrier, a certain date, after which no one else can conceivably be a thorough-going, four-ply aristocrat. In this country two or three such dead lines are accepted. The War of Independence is still immovable. To older New Englanders, New Yorkers, Philadelphians, Marylanders, Virginians, and Charlestonians the belligerent era from 1776 to 1783, irrespective of which side their ancestors fought for or argued, continues to divide the sheep from the goats. The dates of first landings, of course, stamp the uttermost hallmark.

While one can sense this important matter of time in many centers along the Atlantic seaboard, it is particularly evident in Philadelphia where, above the effluvium from politics and the smoke of commerce, rises persistently the faint, nostalgic aroma of aristocracy.

In these restricted Philadelphia circles, even smaller inner rings expand their orbits as generation adds to generation. Here not alone time but also place creates a group destined to set themselves apart. And of those to whom time and place are imperishable barriers, the most amusing comprise the Catacomb Aristocrats.

## Delaware Bank Cave Dwellers

It is freely admitted by descendants of these Quaker troglodytes that their ancestors did not land complete with antiques. Nor did they move directly from shipboard into "brave brick houses" after the mode in London. They lived in caves. This gives their descendants a particular distinction.

The west bank of the Delaware, where Front Street runs today—then the first main street of the city—rose about twenty-five feet above the river level. In this high, dry bank many of the earliest arrivals found caves that the Swedes and Indians had dug long before Penn's first settlers came over. Like cowbirds, which raise their young in the nests other birds have abandoned, here they crawled in to live until houses could be built, or they were obliged to build them, or a new cargo of immigrants landed and took over the huts. Others dug more caves. Eventually, the length of that bank was fairly honeycombed with them.

They showed a commendable economy. Built half under the ground and half above it, they were cool in Summer and warm in Winter. Slabs obtained by clearing the near-by woods supported dirt walls, and planks formed the roof, over which was laid a thatch of swamp reeds to keep out the rain. Sods were piled along the projecting walls. A few more slabs for the east wall, a door, a tiny window, a chimney of stones, river pebbles and daub and the home was complete. In these snug burrows quite an appreciable number of Philadelphia's first families cooked, ate, slept, worked, bred and managed to carry on a fairly comfortable existence.

At the time, 1683, Philadelphia consisted of merely three or four cottages, the residue being woods, undergrowth, timber and trees, says Francis Daniel Pastorius, "among which I several times lost myself in traveling no farther

CAVES OF EARLY SETTLERS AT PHILADELPHIA

than from the waterside to the house. What my thoughts were of such a renowned city (I not long before having seen London, Paris, Amsterdam, Gandt, etc.) it is needless to rehearse unto ye here." [1]

Some of the caves were eventually turned into taverns, which greatly shocked the Plain Friends, who found the boisterous shouts issuing from these grubby little holes by night and day highly offensive. Besides, William Penn was laying out a pretentious city, his "green countrie towne which will never be burned and always be wholesome," where each house was to be placed in the middle of the lot so as to leave "ground on each side for gardens or orchards or fields." Since this was the lovely and ambitious program for his Holy Experiment, the shanty colony on the river front was scarcely calculated to be an ideal first view to impress visitors and newcomers. In 1685-86, when Philadelphia could count 600 houses, the Provincial Council saw no further good in tolerating these bank-side squatters. All dwellers in them were first summoned to appear before the Council for interrogation, and then the court ordered all empty hovels demolished, and the dwellers in the remainder to seek other and better homes. The edict threw some of the "firsts" into a panic. Patrick Robinson, clerk of the Privy Council, was so attached to his underground living that he begged for a whole month's time to pull it down and adjust himself to a house.

A cave couchant, whatever that might be, can well appear on the coats of arms of many a Philadelphia family today. They could point to it with pride, the way descendants of mediaeval pilgrims mention the palmer's shells on their arms, indicating the number of pious jaunts to the Holy Lands their forebears recorded.

Pastorius, the founder of Germantown and a man of outstanding qualities, arrived in Philadelphia on August 20,

1683, after eleven long perilous weeks at sea, and went directly to live in a Front Street cave. While he was plotting out the new village for his Crefelders or Mennonite weavers, he used it for an administrative office. In one of these dugout homes on the south side of town no fewer than thirteen families lived for a month, and there they cast lots for the choice of location upon the rich black soil that was to be Germanopolis or Germantown.

The Fisher dynasty, descended from window glazier John Fisher, would be granted a cave by any College of Heralds. John's widow Margaret, so the records show, found their hut a good real estate investment: in 1886 she was able to turn it over for sound cash.

Evidently these cave-dwellers followed the contemporary English custom of giving their homes, whether they be castle or cot, some picturesque name. One, which bore the pretty alliterative of "Pennypot," is remembered as being the place where John Key was born, his other distinction being the fact that he was the first child of English parentage to be brought forth within city limits.[2] So far, research has not revealed any especial aloofness among the Philadelphia Keys.

### Puritan Troglodytes

The wayward democracy of the Keys (pronounced Kay) might be attributed to their having heard the fact (which others of the Catacomb Aristocracy either never heard or promptly forgot) that long before the first Philadelphians began burrowing in the bowels of the earth, settlers of New Amsterdam and New England were confirmed troglodytes.

In 1652 (anticipating the Philadelphians by thirty years) Edward Johnson, town clerk of Woburn, reported that the first settlers there, "after they have thus found out a place of aboad, they burrow themselves in the earth for their first

shelter under some Hill-side, casting the Earth aloft up on
Timber: they make a smoky fire against the earth at the
highest side, and thus these poor servants of Christ provide
shelter for themselves, their Wives and little ones." [3]

At Lynn and Dorchester, Mass., and in the New Netherlands, the first settlers also dug into hillsides and river banks
for their homes; and at Concord, Mass., they dug cellars
which they spanned with spars and covered with turf, and
in these holes were as contented as moles. When the Secretary of the New Netherlands, Van Tierhoven, made his report in 1650, he gave a detailed description of the homes of
these troglodytes:

"Those in New Netherlands and especially in New England who have no means to build farmhouses at first, according to their wishes, dig a square pit in the ground cellar
fashion, 6 or 7 feet deep, as long and as broad as they think
proper, case the earth inside with wood all round the wall,
and line the wood with bark of trees or something else to
prevent the caving in of the earth, floor this cellar with
planks and wainscott it overhead with the bark or green
sods, so that they can live dry and warm in these houses with
their entire families for two, three or four years, it being
understood that partitions are run through those cellars,
which are adapted to the size of the family. The wealthy and
principal men of New England, in the beginning of the
Colonies, commenced their first dwelling houses in this
fashion." [4]

### Seekers of Solitude

So much for those who dwelt respectably in caves, or rose
in time from such humble dwellings to the loftier categories
of the social realm. We can leave them now, exuding the
aroma of their aristocracy down the generations, and pass
on to those who, for divers reasons, deliberately sought soli-

tude, to gather from it what William Penn felicitously called its "fruits."

On this point Dr. Johnson would dispute William Penn. "Solitude is dangerous to reason without being favorable to virtue," he said. "Remember that the solitary mortal is certainly luxurious, probably superstitious and possibly mad."

In our search for those who elected to live in caves, or alone, we shall find the luxurious, the superstitious and the mad. Some of our characters will hide for safety; some to shut out the association of their fellow men; some to gird them for battles to come. Some will be seeking wider horizons. Each of these in his or her own way finds a niche in our gallery of eccentrics. And, since we began this chapter at Philadelphia, we may continue from that point.

## A Fiery Gnome

If Philadelphians were characteristically slow in learning about their troglodyte competitors farther up the coast, they can take pride in having produced the first of odd sticks to live in a cave.

About six miles up York Road, in a district still called Branchtown, was a cave that gave shelter to as queer a character as even Philadelphia—a favorite haunt for eccentrics—ever saw. In the highfalutin terms of the times he was called "the singular Pythagorean, cynical philosopher." Benjamin Lay was his name. He was a native of Colchester, England, being born there of poor Quaker parents on November 26, 1681-2. Starting life with few educational advantages, he was apprenticed first to a glove-maker and then worked on a farm. When he reached twenty-one he took to the sea, and for the next seven years traveled as a common sailor on ships going to the Levant. In 1710 he left the sea, married

and settled down in London. There he attended Friends'
Meeting and promptly began making a nuisance of himself.
He was even so bold as to call on both King George I and
King George II, to present them with one of John Milton's
tracts that embodied his own particular enthusiasms at the
time. Finally, the London Meeting found "his Dark dis-
ordered Condition," his violent protests against the manner
of preaching, so intolerable that they disowned him. After
this rebuff, he returned to Colchester and opened a draper's
shop.

At Colchester, despite promises to hold his peace, he made
himself a nuisance to the Friends there and once more was
dismissed from meeting. Finally his wife Sarah, who had
clung to him faithfully through these two rejections and his
irresponsible ways, persuaded him to emigrate to Barbados.
They left England in 1729. At Barbados he obtained a piece
of land, built a cottage and apparently was settling down to
the calm existence of a merchant. However, the presence of
slaves on every hand disturbed him. On the Seventh Day
hundreds of them would gather about his cottage and he
would preach freedom to them. These violent denunciations
of the practice of slave-holding called down on his head the
anger of the planters. For a year he kept up this practice and
then, seeing that he was making no headway, resolved to go
north to Philadelphia where he surely would see no slaves.
Besides, the giddy pace the Barbadians lived shocked the
Quaker sensibilities of both the Lays. But in Philadelphia
he found the same evil rampant, so he promptly left the city
and went to live in the country, where, says his biographer,
he built a cottage resembling in its construction a cave and
around which he planted an orchard.

While in Barbados he had made a garden. One day a wild
pig ran in and rooted it up. In an outburst of justifiable
wrath, Benjamin slew the beast and hung its carcase on his

gate posts. His anger and its deadly consequences began prey-
ing on his mind so that he finally resolved thereafter to eat
no food and wear no article of clothing that involved the
death of any animal. This meant that henceforth he would
be a vegetarian and cease to wear boots or anything made of
leather. He also resolved never to use anything that involved
slave labor, and ever afterwards, to make his own clothes.

In Philadelphia, his strange habits and peculiar stature
soon made him a marked man. He stood not much over four
and one-half feet tall. His vegetarianism not only put him out
of step with the fleshy diet of the times, but his vociferous
anti-slavery agitation caused constant embarrassment to those
who tried to be his friends. He was the first public declaimer
against holding slaves, although the Germantown Mennonite
Friends, to which body he soon became attached while dwelling in his cave, had written against slavery as early as 1688.

Benjamin had no sooner moved into his grotto home than
he began traveling about on crusades. He would berate
officials and corner prominent citizens and speak rapturously
for his cause in Friends' Meetings. When he found his words
falling on deaf ears, he adopted methods that would do credit
to even our most highly publicized professional evangelists.

Once he stood in deep snow before the gate of Abington
Meeting with his right leg bare. To people who remon-
strated with him he replied, "You pretend compassion for
me, but you do not feel for the poor slaves in your fields who
go all winter half clad."

At another time he dropped in on the yearly meeting of
the Friends in Burlington, N. J. He wore a plain white
greatcoat with a single button. Under this was a soldier's
tunic with a sword that hung to his heels. In his arm he
carried a large book, from which he had cut out the leaves,
and between the covers he had concealed a bladder filled
with blood-red pokeberry juice. He found a conspicuous

place in the meeting, and when silence had completely enfolded all there, he rose abruptly and declaimed: "You might as well throw off the plain coat as I do," and, divesting himself of that garment, he stood revealed in his warlike uniform and sword. "Slavery," he continued, "would be as justifiable in the sight of the Almighty, Who beholdeth and respecteth all nations and colors of men with equal regard, as if you would thrust a sword through their hearts, as I do this book." Thereupon he plunged the sword into the bladder and spattered the bloody poke juice over those near him.

As in London and Colchester, so in Philadelphia, he made himself objectionable in Friends' Meetings. Once the Market Street Meeting found him so particularly odious that he was conducted from the building; and he promptly dropped into the gutter and stayed there until the meeting closed and the Friends came out. When passers-by asked if he needed help he nonchalantly answered, "Let those who cast me here raise me up. It is their business, not mine."

On another occasion he walked into an Anglican church dressed in sackcloth and insisted on standing all through the service. When it was over, he shouted, "I came to cry aloud against your practice of slave-holding," which must have made the ladies withdraw their skirts. He invariably refused to eat in a house where slaves were held. He would accept the invitation to the meal, sit down at table and then ask his hostess if he would be served by slaves. If she said, "Yes," he rose immediately, left the table and shook the dust of that house off his feet.

At another time, in emulation of the Saviour, he tried to fast forty days, meantime going about his labors. After three weeks, when he was at the point of collapse, lying on his bed tempting himself with a loaf of bread just out of his reach, his friends persuaded him to yield to the temptation and break his fast.

These dramatics were heightened by Benjamin's strange appearance. His head was large, his back hunched, his chest abnormally thrust forward, and his legs were mere match sticks. He allowed his beard to grow untrimmed and it soon turned snow white. He wore light-colored plain clothes, which, as we have seen, he wove himself. When speaking, he had the habit of standing in a twisted fashion, like a Palmer Cox brownie, with a hand resting on one hip.

Every now and then, as the Spirit called him, this minia-ture dragon would rush from his cave to protest against slavery or whatever other evil he thought to conquer.

> Fire in each eye and paper in each hand
> He raved, recited and maddened round the land.[5]

He was a prolific pamphleteer. In 1737 Franklin, after much persuasion and editorial bother, printed a book for him. Its title began, "All Slave Keepers," and then continued on for 157 words down the page, during which he dubbed slavery a "Filthy Leprosy and Apostacy" and claimed that he had written this "for a General Service" and the good of his own soul.

Once his publisher, Franklin, and the governor, Richard Penn, came to call. Setting his vegetarian dish before them, Benjamin Lay remarked: "This is not the kind of food you have at home, but it is good enough for you and me and, such as it is, you are welcome to it."

Not alone did he denounce slavery, but he made an equally violent protest against the importation of foreign spirits, rum especially, with which he claimed the populace was being debauched. He also made one of the first pleas in America against capital punishment, and advocated reform of the criminal code.

When he grew old and cave dwelling proved too much for his worn frame and the weakly condition of his wife, he went

BENJAMIN LAY, THE FIERY GNOME
*Courtesy of Historical Society of Pennsylvania*

to live with friends in Abington. There he built a grotto, in which he kept his library of 200 volumes and wrote incessantly. The following year, 1742, his wife died, whereupon Benjamin gathered together all her china into a big box that he dragged onto the Abington market place. When a sufficient crowd had assembled, he began haranguing them on the evils of drinking tea and, to prove his dislike of it, started smashing the cups and saucers with a hammer. The crowd intervened and carried off most of the china.

One gathers that, although her husband's "peculiar principles and conduct rendered him to many an object of admiration and to all a subject of conversation," Sarah Lay found living with him a little more than flesh could bear. Nevertheless, she was loyal to him through all those years. It is said that she resembled her husband, she having a crooked back. This deformity, however, did not prevent her from becoming an acceptable preacher at Friends' Meetings.

In his latter years Benjamin spent most of his time spinning, and his room was always festooned with skeins of thread that he displayed proudly to callers. He also took to making beehives and studying the complicated social commonwealth of bees. He died at the age of 80 on February 3, 1759. He had asked that his body be cremated and his ashes cast on the sea, but the idea was repugnant to the Friends of Abington, who laid him away in their burial ground. A few minutes before his fiery spirit took flight, he was brought the news that the Society of Friends had voted to put out of meeting those who did not dispose of their slaves. He shouted a thanksgiving and, falling back, murmured, "I can now die in peace." When his will was read it was discovered that not only had he left £40 for the education of poor Quaker children in Abington but that also he had left money to the meeting in his native Colchester. This legacy is still active.

So much a figure of Philadelphia did Benjamin Lay become that for fifty years after his death scarcely a Quaker household but contained his portrait. It was made by Henry Dawkins, local cartoon-engraver. The little old gnome with spindly shanks and white, fringed beard is issuing from his cave, book in hand and protesting fingers upraised. A basket of apples, presumably part of his vegetarian diet, rests by his feet. The caption reads, "Benjamin Lay, Lived to the Age of 80, in the Latter Part of Which he Observed extreme Temperance in his Eating and Drinking, his Fondness for a Particularity in Dress and Customs at times Subjected him to the Ridicule of the Ignorant, but his Friends who were Intimate with him Thought him an Honest Religious man." [6]

A creature of violent temper, eccentric to the extreme, obstinate to excess and invariably ungracious to his opponents, nevertheless Benjamin Lay served a noble purpose. He was, as Whittier called him, "the irrepressible prophet who troubled the Israel of slave-holding Quakerism, clinging like a rough chestnut-burr to the skirts of its respectability and settling like a pertinacious gad-fly on the sore places of its conscience."

### Penitence in Caves

Just what impelled Benjamin Lay to take up his abode in a cave has never been clearly established. In eighteenth century America cave-dwelling seems to have been a favorite custom among those whose consciences were burdened. Mount Holly, N. J., and Albany, N. Y., each provides an example of the penitent troglodyte.

When Hannah Callender, an impressionable Philadelphia miss of twenty-one, went on a journey in 1758, her diary traveled along with her. In New Jersey, she set down this item as being of especial interest: "Went to see the Hermit in a wood this side of Mount Holly. He is a person thought to travel along from Canada or the Mississippi about ten years ago, living in the woods ever since, partly on the charity of the neighborhood, partly on the fruits of the earth. He talks no English and will give no account of himself." [7]

Twenty years later, Surgeon Albigence Waldo of the Connecticut Line was passing that way, and dropped in to see the hermit and evidently was able to make him talk, for his diary furnishes quite an extensive description.[8] By that time the old man had lived for twenty years on bread and water, wild berries and such other food as the neighbors gave him. His cave was under a large oak that had been blown down by a storm, in a spot two miles from Mount Holly and four from Burlington. It was dug about 1½ feet below the surface and covered with boards and bark, and was just large enough to sit up in. The hermit would crawl into this hole and pull the boards over him for blanket and roof. The inside of the cell was lined with cast-off clothes and rags given him by neighbors. He never lighted a fire and even in the coldest weather never approached one.

This peculiar cell he called his grave. He explained that God had warned him in a dream to live that way. A deeply religious man, he knelt before a particular tree each day to say his prayers. In his cell were Latin and other books, and to while away his time he used to read these and to write. When anyone called, he kissed his visitor's hand and then the crucifix that hung round his neck. He thankfully received all gifts excepting money, which he spurned. When his food supply ran low, and not till then, he would shoulder his sack and go from door to door begging. Whatever was handed him he received gratefully, giving the donor his blessing with the crucifix.

Like Benjamin Lay, he was small of stature and had a delicate frame. He wore a beard which, at the time Surgeon

Waldo called on him, he "did" up in a club under his chin.
Some time after this, rude boys attacked the old fellow and
lopped it off—after which he always trimmed it meticulously.
He spoke very fast, using German and Latin and sometimes
Italian and Spanish, although his English seems to have been
limited to a few words. He appeared to be a man of violent
passions.

In his latter days he explained that if he continued in this
penitential state until he was 80, he expected to come out
purified and thereafter would live as other folks did, or like
Elijah, to whom God first said, "Go hide thyself," and then,
"Go show thyself." It was rumored that he had been an
officer in both the French and German armies and, while
in the former, he had killed a fellow officer in a duel. This
so sobered his fiery temper that he fled to America, wandering through the wilderness seeking peace for his gnawing
conscience, and finally settling down in the Mount Holly
cave for his long penitence.

Fate, however, did not allow him the time necessary to
attain perfection. On January 19, 1778, a kindly neighbor,
bringing him food, found the old man very ill, but he refused the neighbor's offer to take him to his home. The
next morning he was found dead in his cell. In his hand was
the crucifix and by his side—one wonders why—lay a brass
fish. There were also found the scissors with which he
trimmed his beard after the boys lopped it off, and a blank
book in which he scribbled and drew religious pictures. And
so he came to his end, after he had lived in his cave almost
a quarter of a century. Although he was believed to have
been a Roman Catholic, his worn body was laid to rest in
the Friends' burial ground at Mount Holly.

Rumor has a way of playing tricks and pranks and it toyed
with the name of this hermit and legends about him until,
today, anyone digging through the jungle of these legends

has to penetrate quite a distance before he comes to the facts. Through several accounts we find him named Francis Furgler, whereas his name actually was Francis Adam Joseph Phyle. This and his history he had related in 1756, through an interpreter, to Col. Charles Read, member of the Supreme Court, when he had been living beneath his fallen tree only a few weeks. At first he had found shelter in a haystack, but when the hay was hauled off to the barn he was forced to make the cell under the fallen oak. Once the Moravians offered him a home with them at Bethlehem, which he politely refused. In 1777, when an engagement was fought near his cave, he merely remained underground and let the bullets whistle over him. Nor did he show the slightest excitement over the affair, which, considering his previous life, might seem odd.[9]

He was a Swiss, a native of Lucerne, from which he had gone to France and joined the army there. He came with the French troops to Canada and, growing disgusted with a soldier's life, had deserted and wandered down to New York and thence into the Jerseys. He was under great stress of mind when Col. Read spoke to him, hinting at the weight of his sin, occasioned by having killed an adversary in a duel. When first interviewed, he wore the uniform of a French soldier and was completely ignorant of English.

One more word and we shall leave him under the anonymous sod of the Friends' burial ground. So long as he lived, Joseph Burr, the owner of the woods in which his cave was located, would never allow the land to be cleared, or the hermit disturbed in any way.

Francis Phyle's New York counterpart and contemporary (who knows but it was Francis himself en route to New Jersey!) is reported to us by Mrs. Anne Grant, that chatty chronicler of Albany in the days of the fascinating Madam Schuyler. Her time there, before she finally retired to Scot-

land to marry and eventually pursue the literary career that
was to bring her a modicum of fame and the acquaintance
of the great, was from 1762 to 1768. In her "Memoirs of an
American Lady," writing of one of "those sequestered vales"
around Albany, she says that in her time it was "inhabited
by a hermit. He was a Frenchman and did not seem to in-
spire much veneration among the Albanians. They imag-
ined or heard that he had retired to that solitude in remorse
for some fatal duel in which he had been engaged, and they
considered him an idolator, because he had an image of the
Virgin in his hut. I think he retired to Canada at last." [10]

Alas, that Mrs. Grant's information was so indefinite. A
subsequent historian of Albany merely quoted the passage
without attempting to verify the rumor of this Ishmaelite
and his aloofness. At this late date it is practically impossible to identify the second of our penitent troglodytes. Who
knows but that he retired to Albany's sequestered vale to
spend his time, like Descartes, trying to prove his own existence!

Let us now cut across country until we reach the environs
of New Haven, where we will find something more tangible
than a worried conscience pursuing cave-dwellers into the
crannies of the rocks.

### Regicides Among the Rocks

Among the first man-hunts in recorded American history
was the pursuit of the judges who condemned Charles I to
the scaffold. Edward Whalley and his son-in-law William
Goffe appeared in New England and for a time lived quietly
in or around Boston. Meanwhile, Cromwell's regime having
ended and Charles II come to the throne, these three soon
found a price had been put upon their heads. They quietly
moved southward. When the authorities in Boston discov-

ered that their birds had flown, they commissioned two mes-
sengers, Thomas Kellond and Thomas Kirk, to follow hot-
foot and capture them.

On their way through the Connecticut wilderness the
regicides had discovered many old friends among the leading
citizens, who gladly gave them shelter and blandly denied
to the commissioners any knowledge of the culprits. Whalley
and Goffe lived under aliases in New Haven and were soon
joined by the third culprit, John Dixwell. Their presence in
such a small town was a matter of common report and it
must have aroused some whispering, for they were well received by the minister and the magistrates. Governor Leete
had no intention of turning them over to the commissioners.
Since the commissioners could find no trace of them there,
they went chasing a false scent to New York. Meantime
Whalley and Goffe had successively hidden in closets, in an
old mill, and under a bridge, and now sought a more secluded hide-out.

The day after the commissioners had left, they retired
to a cave on West Rock. They called it Providence Hill, but
to this day New Haven natives call it the Judges' Cave. A
group of huge broad stone pillars fifteen to twenty feet high,
it was well surrounded by trees which concealed them from
observation. Being on the top of the mountain, it is a spot
that commands a wide panorama and from it could be seen
any approaching stranger. Here they lived three months.
Only in stormy weather did they leave it to seek shelter at a
neighbor's house, the home of Richard Sperry, who also
supplied them with food which he brought himself.

Meantime the New Haven magistrates solemnly called a
meeting of the General Court and ordered each marshal in
each plantation to search for the regicides. Evidently the
hounds were on good terms with the foxes, for they never so
much as poked a nose into the Judges' Cave. After this, when-

ever things in New Haven grew warm for them, they disappeared and the friendly rocks swallowed them up again. Their final cause for abandoning the cave came not from pursuers. The country thereabouts was a haunt of wild beasts. One night a catamount, his eyes blazing, put his head in between the rocks. The apparition so thoroughly frightened the refugees that they fled to Sperry's house.[11]

This compounding of a felony with the accused by those in high places—among the earliest examples of our judges tipping the scales—made life in New Haven a little merrier in that Spring of 1661. Today West Rock stands in the neighborhood of Baldwin Drive, that skirts the top of the ridge and from which a splendid view of New Haven and the Long Island Sound can be gained. The Judges' Cave is protected by a fence and, as it is now included in a State Park, picnickers and visitors to the city haunt the historic spot.

### An Atrocity Hermitess

In rumors that terrify the public, all wars have a sameness. The solitary atrocity is elaborated into mass action as the report spreads through homes and taverns. Scarcely a horrible deed attributed to the armies on either side during the Great War, or any other, but finds its counterpart in rumors that terrified the countryside during the Revolutionary War. At this distance of time it is difficult to find convincing proof of any one isolated atrocity that may have set rumor a-rolling. So, then, what actually happened to Sarah Bishop to cause her to take up a solitary existence can only be conjectured.

Through most of the Revolution, homes on Long Island were subjected by loyalists and rebels alike to forays, night reprisals and raids that left behind them trails of destruction and the fabric of many a legend that is now firmly imbedded in the Island's history. Others found no permanent report. Among the latter was the attack on the Bishop home. Her father's house, as Sarah related, was burned by the British and she, cruelly treated by a British officer. The experience set her wandering, as though she feared to associate with friends and come in contact with strangers. Sarah was heard to say that she had no dread of any animal on earth but man. She finally appeared in the neighborhood of Ridgefield, Conn., choosing for her abode a cave at the foot of a rocky precipice just the other side of the New York State line.

It was wild country at the time, as parts of it still are. The woods were thick and the terrain rocky. In this shelter, bear, deer and foxes and a multitude of other wild animals found a safe home. These were Sarah Bishop's companions—she was unafraid of them, they unafraid of her—until her death in 1810. Now and then she came down the mountain and appeared in Ridgefield of a Sunday to go to church. These visits were the only glimpses the natives had of her. Otherwise she was content with her solitary life.

She kept no animals—neither cat nor dog, nor even chickens. A clearing in the woods, a rich half-acre of soil, she cultivated for her provisions. It was a pretty spot, walled with the tangled growth of wild grape that made an impenetrable hedge to protect her few hills of corn, cucumbers, beans and potatoes. Peach trees supplied her with fruit. Close by her cave was a fine spring that gave her water.

For clothes she wore a mass of rags patched together without any order. Her hair she left falling in uncombed, slatternly gray strands around her face and shoulders. The profane curiosity of her fellow men bewildered and puzzled the old woman. When visitors approached, she would retreat into the cave and barricade it with shells of tree stumps. Those who did manage to win her confidence and penetrate beyond

her barrier found a single room without furniture. Her only
utensils were an old pewter basin and a gourd shell. A few
rags heaped on a rock ledge served for bed. Occasionally she
indulged in the luxury of a fire. When stormy weather descended—spells of rain and snow—she stayed indoors.

In addition to her vegetables she lived on roots, berries
and nuts gathered from the woods. Her only amusement

THE JUDGES' CAVE, NEW HAVEN, CONN.

seems to have been reading the Bible, for she was of a religious turn of mind. To those who talked with her, despite
the unkempt clothes and dire poverty of her chosen life, she
appeared of sound mind.[12]

It would be easy enough for us of a swift and ruthless
world to dismiss Sarah Bishop as "touched" and defective in
temperament, an obvious case of anthophobia. And yet
this Connecticut anchorite was only one of a long line of
women, stretching back to the days of the Egyptian eremites,
who found their ultimate satisfaction in solitude. Today
pious people account them as holy. A philosopher of our
time, Alfred North Whitehead, has said that "Religion is

what the individual does with his own solitariness." And
two centuries before, the old solitary of Ephrata, Pa., was
praising it in his beautiful hymn, "O blessed life of loneliness, where all creation silence keeps. . . ." From all reports, they cared no more for their personal appearance or
creature comforts than did Sarah Bishop.

## The Hag of Plymouth

Not so solitary was Aunt Rachel, who once lived alone
in a tumble-down fish house hanging over the waterfront
near Duxbury, Mass. An ancient, decrepit hag, bundled in
whatever tatters she could pick up, her external appearance
hid a woman with a keen eye for the sea and a canny knowledge of the seasons.

Her favorite diversion was wandering alone in the night
—and the darker the night, the better. She would stumble
along the rocky foreshore and "watch the flux of the sea"
or penetrate far inland, wherever her feet led her—searching, searching. Searching for what? Who knows?

Most of the respectable natives avoided her, since she had
a rough side to her tongue and made no bones about using
it; but now and then a minister, a schoolmaster, or a physician would consult her before starting on a journey. It was
among the fishermen, though, that she found her sworn
allies. From her knowledge of the sea, the wind and the
sky, she told them what the weather would be. They would
ask her advice before launching their boats. Coming back,
they left a choice fish before her hut, and let her help herself from the fish flakes where the salted catch was drying.

This hearty trust and friendship of the fishermen afforded
the one bright spot in her drab and lonely existence. It was
the anchor that gave stability to her living. No man who
went down to the sea in ships from Plymouth ever failed

her. . . . Then one day the *Betsy,* a sugar boat from Boston, put into the harbor. Strange sailors landed. They thought to make sport of her and pretended to ask her advice. She sensed their insincerity and accused them of being "Moon Cursers"—men who set false beacons and wreck ships for plunder—such as had made her childless and a widow. She laid the poor man's curse on their boat and warned them not to sail on her. "May he who rides upon the pale horse be your guide," she concluded her prophecy. They further teased and harassed the old tatterdemalion, saying they'd "put a stopper in her gab," till her violent temper flared up, and she cursed the lot of them "from Hell to high water."

The next morning, in retaliation, one of the brutes set fire to her hut and the others rushed back to the boat shouting imprecations. At sight of the flames the whole town tumbled down to the waterfront—"every inhabitant but the infants and decrepit." They found Aunt Rachel mounted on a rock. She was wrapped in the remains of an old sail cloth. Her matted hair floated out like streamers upon the wind, her long, bony arms were extended in threatening gestures. She foamed at the mouth and "howled in the most distressing accents." Her eyes seemed starting out of their sockets. She leaned forward in an ecstasy of expectation as she watched the crew climb aboard, watched the anchor creep up the side, watched the sails ripple up the masts and belly in the breeze as the boat headed out to sea. When the brig passed Beach Point the old harridan's ravings increased. She lifted up her voice and laid a curse on them.

Surely enough, the boat struck a reef and sank. The cargo was lost and one man—the one who had fired her hut—was drowned. So enthralled was the populace by the sinking of the vessel that no one noticed Aunt Rachel pitch forward. When someone finally approached the bundle of rags on the rock, he discovered that the old woman was dead.

The town buried her on the spot where her hut had stood. For many years after that, the reef was known as Rachel's Curse.[13]

## Beachcomber and Wanton

Of quite a different breed was the beachcomber whom William Byrd of Westover encountered living in solitary, though not single, bliss when he went to survey the dividing line between Virginia and North Carolina in 1728. "A Marooner that modestly calls Himself a Hermit," Byrd describes him, "tho he be forfeited that Name by Suffering a wanton Female to cohabit with Him." This treasure Byrd found on the seacoast. He was not afflicted with either conscience or ambition and let a woman wait on him.

"His Habitation was a Bower, cover'd with Bark after the Indian Fashion which in this mild Situation protected him pretty well from the Weather. Like the Ravens, he neither plow'd nor sow'd, but Subsisted chiefly upon Oysters which his Handmaid made a Shift to gather from the adjacent Rocks. Sometimes, too, for a change of diet, he sent her to drive up the Neighbor's cows, to moisten their mouths with a little Milk."

This hermit must have been a forebear of our present cartoon hill-billies. His beard grew prodigiously long, and he depended on it mostly for raiment. His wanton bawdy-basket did the same, using the length of her hair brought decently forward "and the rest dangled behind quite down to her rump, like one of Herodotus' East Indian Pygmies." William Byrd, who together with other commendable qualities had an observant eye and a merry pen, concludes his report of this pair with the observation, "Thus did these wretches live in a dirty State of Nature and were mere Adamites, innocence only excepted." [14]

# II

## SOLITARIES ABOVE AND BELOW GROUND

### A Virginian Mr. Parr

AMONG THE ENGLISH WORTHIES DESERVING OF REMEMBRANCE
through all time was "The Old, Old, Very Old Man"
Thomas Parr, a native of Alberbury, near Shrewsbury, whose
length of days was celebrated by John Taylor, the water
poet.[1] He is said to have lived 152 years, marrying a second
wife at the age of 120, and having a child by her. His death
was caused by a visit to London in 1635, where he went on
an invitation of the King, who was curious to meet an Englishman who could so successfully survive to that great age.
The excitement of the presentation, the change of climate
and the rich food with which he gorged himself brought the
old man to his end. It is related of this visit that the King
asked Mr. Parr which of his experiences in these long years
he considered unique. Mr. Parr (stout fellow!) replied, "Sire,
I believe I am your Majesty's only subject who has done
public penance for fornication when past the age of 100
years!"

Mr. Parr and his ribald answer find a place in these seemly
pages only as a peg on which to hang an explanation for our
next hermit. His existence, so far as search has revealed, is
not given a place in recorded Virginian history. We encounter him on a broadside printed in the first quarter of
the nineteenth century. Now broadsides comprised one of
our earliest and most popular types of fiction for the masses.

The writers of them often drew on their imaginations. Some may have drawn on their reading. The writer of this particular broadside may have heard of the very old Mr. Parr and determined to match him on this side of the Atlantic. He even went so far as to make his account appear authentic by giving names and dates. The story runs this way:

Captain James Buckland and Mr. John Fielding of Virginia left their homes on the 16th of June, 1816, to explore the West. For seventy-three days they penetrated the wilderness, forded streams, climbed mountains, crossed prairies and battled with wild beasts until, on a certain unnamed mountainside, they reached a cave. After they had done a little shouting, as one naturally does in the mouth of caves, a hermit appeared. The ceremony of mutual introductions finished, they got down to asking personal questions. The hermit was only too happy to explain himself.

First, he assured them he was no less than 227 years old, which would figure to about 1589 as the date of his birth. London was his birthplace. Although his father was only a mechanic, he sent the boy to a gentleman to be educated. While in this improved environment he fell in love with a noble's daughter, which met with a stern rebuke from the parent. In fact, the girl was snatched from his very arms. The separation was too much for her: she fell sick and died. Deeply grieving, he wandered over the Continent, finally reaching Italy, where he shipped as a sailor. The boat was wrecked on the shores of America. Then began a long vagrancy through the wilderness until he found this cave, where he had dwelt ever since. Nature was kind to him. It furnished food and drink. Even the animals were gracious to him in his loneliness, he said; as for Orpheus, the beasts of the forests came and danced before his cave.[2]

Captain Buckland tried to persuade the hermit to come along with them back to the comfort and civilization of

Virginia, but he refused. After all, who would not refuse
who could have wild beasts dance for him?

### The Love-lorn Hermit of Wolf Rocks

It is inevitable, as we go through these stories of Early
American troglodytes, that unrequited love should emerge
as the impelling force to drive men and women into the
solitary habitation of caves. The previous hermit of the
broadside was one, and here is another.

A certain craggy hilltop in Bucks County, Pa., was known
for a long time as Wolf Rocks, evidently gaining this name
from the wolves that found a safe harbor there for their lit-
ters. It also gave shelter to Albert Large, hermit and mystery man of the Buckingham Mountains.

He was born about 1805. Schooling, even the informal
teaching of the little red schoolhouse, made every fiber inside the boy stiffen with rebellion. He was a child of Nature,
born outside society and unable to tolerate even its easiest
complications and simplest refinements. Instead of dutifully
attending school, he would wander off into the woods by
himself. His mother died, and a stepmother soon succeeded
her. Home life grew uncongenial. Besides, he had other interests: he suffered a heart-stirring over a girl in the valley.
She thought him queer (which, doubtless, he was) and firmly
refused his advances. This rejection even further warped
his twisted mind. He disappeared into the wilderness and,
after family and neighbors had searched for him without
avail, was given up for lost. They apparently hadn't searched
a certain cave in the Wolf Rocks.

As caves go, he made it quite comfortable. He arranged
a kitchen with a chimney, and a boarded-in bedroom. His
front door was a huge stone which he rolled away, Biblical
fashion, whenever he wanted to go out. By day, he wandered

through the thick woods; at night he descended to near-by farms where he stole provisions and investigated hen roosts. He even ventured into a town now and then and managed to filch a jug of liquor. In fact, Albert Large was the most sybaritic of our hermits; he denied himself nothing of food and drink. When the weather turned bad, he merely stayed indoors, cooking his stolen food and enjoying sips from the pilfered jugs. Once, in a hard Winter, he remained at the cave for six weeks on end, indicating that he had provided well for himself.

In this comfortable solitude he lived twenty years, during which time he refrained from cutting his hair or beard, so that the former fell well down upon his shoulders, and the latter covered his breast.

He had long been considered lost by the neighbors. So it was quite a shock to the valley folk when, on April 9, 1858, some hunters discovered the cave and, encountering Albert behind his stone door, drew from him the story you have just read.[3]

## Bathsheba Bowers

A tidy little study might be made (and life would prove richer for having read it) of what men and women do when crossed in love. It is generally conceded that women grow tight-lipped and acidulous and men become unconscionable rakes or dour penny-pinching grouches. Some fly to solitude, as did our previous recluse, Albert Large. Others take to religion, that broad and comfortable bosom on which the broken in heart can lay their troubled heads. Into the latter category would fall the next of our solitaries, Bathsheba Bowers.

Her grandmother was the niece of Henry Dunster, first president of Harvard, who had sent to England for her to come and live with him. Her father, Benanuel Bowers, being turned out of England for persisting in his Quaker beliefs, emigrated to New England. In those days, it was scarcely the ideal spot for Quakers: the vigorous minions of the Lord, who held to the zealous faith of the Presbyterian Party, displayed scant patience towards those who waited for the "light within" to move them. Benanuel was constantly being fined for some infraction of the Puritan code, once for the simple decent human act of giving a cup of milk to a Quakeress who had been whipped and imprisoned two days without food and water. However, Bathsheba's father managed to brave this harsh intolerance and succeeded in buying a farm of 20 acres outside of Boston. Here he cultivated the soil diligently and saw to it that there were arrows aplenty in his quiver, for he had no fewer than twelve children. He also displayed a literary bent: he wrote his biography in doggerel verses, which are still preserved.

As Philadelphia was a more congenial atmosphere for the simple faith of Friends, he sent four of his daughters down there, one of them Bathsheba. As you have already anticipated, Bathsheba (what else could happen to a girl with that name?) attracted her quota of admirers. But men in those times, as men today, were undependable lovers. At eighteen, Bathsheba found herself nursing a broken heart. Then it was that she laid her tormented head on the calming bosom of religion. No longer was she

> like a milk-white lamb that bleats
> For man's protection.[4]

A girl of middle stature, and quite beautiful when young, she grew stern and morose. Mrs. Ann Bolton, her niece who lived with her when a child and who wrote the account we quote, found her very cruel.

Although she had no regard for riches, she made a beautiful home and garden on what is now South Second Street.

Half a mile away, under Society Hill and close by a spring—the best spring in the city—she built a small cottage and furnished it with books, a table and a cup. It came to be known as Bathsheba's Bower. In both her home and her bower, "she retired herself as free from Society as if she had lived in a cave underground, or on the top of a high mountain." Here she wrote, read her Bible, argufied on religion to all who called and offered them her excellent spring water by way of refreshment. For twenty years she lived an ascetic life, eating no fish nor flesh. From the balcony of her Bower George Whitefield, the celebrated revivalist, once preached to a large assembly.

During this retirement she penned a pamphlet on her religious experiences to which she gave a characteristically long title: "An Alarm Sounded to prepare the Inhabitants of the World to meet the Lord in the way of His Judgement." This was printed in 1709. In the pages of this pamphlet she recounts how, when she was no more than six or seven years old she had "strange and numerous apprehensions of the future state and a fear to dye," and that at fourteen, pride became her enemy; and that she found release from these religious problems in gardening. She also wrote a history of her life which she distributed gratis. Her niece remarked of this public distribution, "Like Absalom, I suppose, she was willing to have something to bear up her name and, being too strict a virtuoso, could not expect fame and favor here by any method than such of her own raising and spreading." No copy of this pamphlet-biography has ever been discovered.

Another of the means she found to while away her time was keeping a diary, which she wrote in the form of letters addressed to her physician, Dr. Anderson of Maryland. She also filled several manuscript books with dreams and visions "and a thousand romantic notions of her seeing various beasts and bulls in the heavens."

What induced her to give up this retirement may never be known, but leave it she certainly did, and we find her first living alone in the country near Philadelphia, then in South Carolina. She chose a wild district where life was far from certain or secure. Indians swooped down unheralded on the settlement and fever took off those who could not resist it. She fell sick. In the midst of her most desperate illness, Indians attacked the colony early one morning. At the house close to hers several persons were killed. She refused to move from her bed, saying that Providence would protect her. Two men, taking pity on her condition, lifted her and her bed to a boat and carried her away to safety through a rain of Indian bullets and arrows. And so she, who had sought the security of peace and retirement, finished in excitement and danger. She died in 1718, in her 46th year.[5]

## The Human Mole

It is quite common, as many a wife knows, to find among grown men some boyish trait or hobby or superstition that continues with them to the end of their days. There is nothing peculiarly offensive about this retarded development; rarely does it interfere with the maturing and improving of other traits. Small boys who hate washing behind the ears may grow into old gentlemen who are not ashamed of spots on their waistcoats. The shanty-building urge which possesses all normal boys at a certain period in their extreme youth often reaches its sublime accomplishment when, as grown men, they build homes. Small lads who follow the thrill of "digging down to China" may become miners—or gardeners. Often the persistence of such a trait indicates the authenticity of a vocation that smoulders throughout life because circumstances do not permit it to be followed.

Remembering these, it is possible to understand the particular life habit of Mr. Sutliff, long a resident of Plymouth, Conn., at the beginning of the last century. His public vocation was that of a miller—a respectable and, we hope, a successful miller. His private vocation was that of a miner.

When a young man, he became obsessed with the notion that the mountain in the rear of his house held a rich store of gold, silver and other precious metals. He also caught from somewhere the idea that if he dug into the mountain he would find these metals in a liquid state and all he had to do when he reached them was to ladle them out. Doubtless he dreamed of the day when, these gold and silver pools at his command, he could give up the dust and noise of his grist mill. No more wrangling with farmers over the price of grinding this corn. No more bother with sluice-ways that rotted and water-wheels that wore out and heavy millstones that had to be constantly adjusted and bolting boxes that had to be repaired! So he started digging, started behind his house and each day devoted his spare moments to heading underground towards that mountain and freedom.

Dynamite and the science of using it were apparently unknown to him. Nor was he acquainted with methods of surveying that would have plotted a direct course for him to follow through the bowels of the earth. As the old song goes:

> He wore his compass under his hat
> And he always knew where he was at!

When he came to a rock, he merely dug around it and went on. His course became very circuitous; in fact, without realizing it, he was heading for the turnpike instead of the mountain. One day, a townsman who was passing by heard a noise under the road. He concluded it must be John Sutliff. Himself digging down at the spot, he uncovered the human mole. John's anger at being interrupted became Plymouth's standing joke.

Although perfectly sane on all other subjects—so the local chronicler assures us—John Sutliff continued digging a little every day for the greater part of his life—a labor that extended between thirty and forty years—until the infirmities of old age compelled him to desist. Who knows but that in the silence of the cool earth and in burrowing through it he found exercise and peace and the satisfaction that only solitude can bring to men frustrated by circumstance in the pursuit of their dreams! [6]

And yet there may have been more to that dream than we suspect. Even up to our own generation, robust and romantic natives in the Hudson Valley behind Hudson, N. Y., and inland to the Massachusetts line have been spurred on to digging by a legend that Hendrik Hudson salted away great quantities of gold somewhere in that region.

### A Solitary Farmer and His Ilk

While Mr. Sutliff's passion for the "earth beneath" is unique in these annals, the desire to be alone, which drove men deeper and deeper into the wilderness, was a commonplace in our frontier history. They were men who loathed the nearness of others. They demanded elbow room. Born to wide horizons, they must ever be seeking them. The farther frontier always held for them a fresh glamor. This social claustrophobia might be illustrated by many cases. Cape Cod, for instance, produces the remembrance of retired sailors who, on leaving the unbroken skyline of the sea and its solitary paths, retreated to little farms far inland and distant from villages, where they lived out their remaining days without benefit of wife or friend, contented and at peace.

One old retired seaman settled down in the neighborhood of Bourne, raised chickens and cultivated a small patch. His favorite diet was crackers and cheese. He rarely ate his own fowls, but exchanged them and their eggs for cheese whenever he ventured into town.

For others, swamps held a peculiar fascination. The marshy stretches in southern New Jersey around Bridgeton hid many a recluse a century or more ago. One of them, Mike Link, found a cave in which he lived for years. On the death of his wife he retired from the association of his fellow men and was satisfied to live alone with the memory of her. But, like Theseus, who unwound the cord the fair damsel Ariadne had given him before he descended into the Cretan labyrinth, Mike kept one contact with his former life. He didn't mind living as he did, but he wanted to be buried like Christian folks, so he deposited a largish sum with a neighboring farmer with which to pay for a "good" funeral.

In the dense Morris River swamp of the same district various hermits have found their homes from time to time and even today an island in the marshes gives shelter to a recluse who lives there, and has lived there for ten years, alone with a dog. He cultivates a patch of provisions and comes out of the swamp only once a year. Natives of this same region also used to find the huts of itinerant umbrella menders—the only homes to which the poor old tinkers could return when the road proved too long and the going too hard.

Another example of men who seek release from social claustrophobia might be cited in David McQuain, the hermit farmer of Waterford, Mass. In the year 1777, Mr. McQuain, having bought a parcel of land far out in the wilderness for $40, left his family and acquaintances and departed for it alone. There he built a hut. He had no household furniture beyond a pail, a dish and a spoon. He had no domestic animals except a dog and he completely eschewed women. For many years he worked single-handed on his tract, clearing woods and sowing crops. He prospered by this hermit farming until he owned 800 acres and kept 40 head of cattle. As the work increased he brought in laborers—men only, for he appears to have been wary of spinster and widow alike. Lacking a dairymaid, for instance, he was content to feed the milk to his hogs, and the hogs waxed enormous and fetched correspondingly big prices. A large truck patch and a flourishing orchard fed him and his laborers.[7]

### Robert, the Slave Hermit

It is not too far from John Quain's wilderness farm beyond Waterford to the old border line between Massachusetts and Rhode Island. In those days the boundary came close to Providence, and it is from Providence we hear of Robert, the Slave Hermit.

In a thirty-six page pamphlet, bound in blue paper and published there in 1829, his story is revealed. Its frontispiece is a crude woodblock portrait, and the title page reads:

Life and Adventures
of
Robert
the
Hermit of Massachusetts
Who has lived 14 years in a cave, secluded
from human society
comprising
An account of his Birth, Parentage, Sufferings and providential escape from unjust and cruel Bondage
in early life—and his reasons for
becoming a Recluse
Taken from his own mouth, and published for his benefit

Since the price for this pamphlet was 12½ cents, Robert may not have been embarrassed by overwhelming royalties.

Were he living today, he would find himself fabulously rich, for his life story now fetches $3.50. Evidently all Rhode Island knew of him. He must have been as public a figure there as was the celebrated Stephen Duck of England, who presided as resident hermit in the cave at Richmond Park which the architect Kent designed for Queen Caroline in the lush days of England's rustic sentimentality.

"It is a fact well known to almost every inhabitant of Rhode Island," begins the pamphlet, "that on the summit of a hill, a few rods east of Seekonk River (within the state of Massachusetts) and about two miles from Providence Bridge, has dwelt for many years a solitary hermit, bearing the name of Robert—and, although familiarly known to many of the inhabitants of Providence and its vicinity for his peaceable and agreeable disposition, yet his history as regards his birth, the cause of his seclusion, et cetera, has until recently remained a profound secret, having carefully avoided answering any questions relative thereto of hundreds who, prompted by curiosity, have been from time to time induced to visit his cave."

Robert's life story would furnish as good a ready-made plot as any period novelist could wish for. It has suspense and adventure. Its hero stumbles from Grace and regains his footing. He follows his Grail to a tragic awakening. Then, in the end, his burial aligns him with the rest of us.

He was born at Princeton, N. J., in 1769-70, and, as was his mother (who was of African descent), in bondage. His father he understood to have been "a pure white, blooded Englishman," a gentleman of considerable eminence. The only other child was a sister who was included in the patrimonial portion of his master's older daughter when she married. When four years old Robert moved with his master's family to Georgetown, D. C., after which he had no recollection of his mother.

At 14 his master apprenticed him to a shoemaker, but, showing little proficiency as a follower of St. Crispin, he was taken back to the estate, where he served as gardener until his twentieth year. It was at this age he first met the one woman in his life—Miss Alley Pennington of Cecil County, Md. Her sole requirement of him before marriage was that he obtain his freedom. Since his master had no intention of manumitting him, Robert borrowed £50 from a supposed good friend—one James Bevens—with which to buy his freedom; Bevens accepted his promise to pay eventually both principal and interest by the fruits of his industry. Mr. Bevens bought his bond, Robert married Alley, and all seemed rosy.

For three years they were blissfully happy. The union was blessed with two children. By industry and economy he managed to pay back part of the loan, neglecting, however, to ask for receipts. Late one evening Bevens and another descended upon this happy family, seized Robert and carried him off. He was put aboard a schooner and, to prevent escape, heavily shackled. Eventually the schooner made Charleston, where Robert was disposed of to the highest bidder. After serving some time he managed to escape on a sloop bound for Philadelphia, a journey made without food or water while hidden in the hold. He left the sloop undiscovered, picked up a Quaker to whom he told his story and who presented him with half a crown and extracted his promise to return the next day. Meanwhile, however, people in his lodgings suspected him of being a runaway slave and reported him to the authorities, who clamped him into jail. After nine days in the prison he was put on a boat, again heavily shackled, bound once more for Charleston and his former master. Apparently this Charlestonian had sickened of his purchase, for he put Robert up at public auction.

His next master was Dr. Peter Fersue, a man of consider-

ROBERT THE HERMIT

able wealth, for whom he worked eighteen months, at the end of which he managed to escape again and secrete himself in an empty cask on a boat bound direct for Boston. After five days at sea, emaciated with hunger and tormented with thirst, he revealed himself to the crew. The captain, who happened to be a Quaker, saw that he was given food and drink, and finally set him free on Boston docks.

From Boston he walked to Salem, where he lodged in a sailors' boarding-house. In the course of the next day he met a ship owner who was in quest of hands for a voyage to India. Robert signed up, traveled the long way there and back, returning to Salem after an absence of fourteen months. He remained on shore only a short time when he shipped for a second voyage to India. For a period of nine years he continued to sail as a common hand from the ports of Boston and Salem to different ports of Europe and India.

Such time as he was on shore he lodged with a mother and family consisting of three daughters aged respectively eighteen, twenty, and twenty-five. As he had by now given up hope of ever seeing his wife and children again, he married one of the daughters. The family's kindness further induced him to rent a small house and provide for them. He was about to sail for India once more and he arranged that part of his wages be sent his wife. When he returned he discovered that he had become a father. After three months ashore, spent blissfully with his wife, Robert assures us, he shipped on board the *Herald*, Capt. Derby, bound from Boston to Canton.

On this voyage he was away eighteen months. Apparently his spouse found such solitude not to her liking or changed the course of her affections, for when Robert returned, loaded down with gifts from China, he was bluntly informed that, had he never returned, she would be the last to lament it. After a few months' vain attempt at reconciliation, he started southward—walked to Providence and found a berth in a shipping line that plied to New York, work that kept him busy for the next nine years and, incidentally, won him over to Providence.

Twenty years had elapsed since that night Bevens tore him away from his beloved Alley and their children. He was now well-nigh sixty. The remembrance of them began haunting him. Finally, he shipped to Baltimore and thence made his way to Georgetown, in search of his wife and children. His old master was long since dead. Bevens had gone west. He heard rumors that shortly after he was kidnaped, his wife had died of despair, and that her helpless children did not long survive her. There was no further trace.

"I then felt but little desire to live," Robert says; "there was nothing then remaining to attach me to this world—and it was at that moment I formed a determination to retire from it, to become a recluse, and mingle thereafter as little as possible with human society."

He returned direct to Rhode Island and built a hut at the uninhabited tip of Fox Point, where he lived for several years "until annoyed and discommoded by the youth of the town." He then applied to the Hon. Tristram Burgess, who gave him land on which to build another hut. Here he dwelt for nine years. Once or twice a week he left his hiding place, crossed the bridge into Providence, talked with old friends, bought a few necessities and returned again well satisfied to his peaceable dwelling.

Robert died a natural death on April 1, 1832. His obituary in the *Providence Journal,* printed the next day, reads:

In Seekonk yesterday morning, at his Hermitage, near Washington Bridge, Robert, generally known as Robert the Hermit, aged three score years and ten. He lived a solitary life, rejecting the society of man and communing alone with his God. Funeral this afternoon at one o'clock, from his late residence.[8]

So Robert the Hermit communed alone with his God. So in their own ways did Sarah Bishop and Bathsheba Bower and Francis Phyle and that shadowy hermit who dwelt in the sequestered vale near Albany. Being driven underground, they lifted up their eyes.

Their seeking contact with Deity may have been a logical outcome of the solitary lives they led. It compensated for their eccentricity. It gave their "singularity" a *raison d'être*. They were God-searchers, and down through time God-searchers who held themselves aloof from the world have been set down as a "peculiar" people. Vicarious anchorites, they gathered in their loneliness the fruits of solitude.

After this solitary way the next step is to follow the monastic life—the communal life of discipline in the wilderness.

### John Kelpius and the Schuylkill Brethren

One of the earliest manifestations of the monastic life in America is dated at 1694, when hermits newly come to America retired from the world to live according to a religious rule on the Ridge above the Schuylkill near Wissahickon beyond Philadelphia—then a wilderness. They were John Kelpius, John Seelig, Bernard Kuster, Daniel Falckner, Daniel Lutkins, Lewis Alderman and several others to the number of about forty, most of them learned men and all single. In 1704, they were joined by Conrad Matthews, Christopher Witt, Daniel Geissler and some others.

John Kelpius, their leader, was a German from Transylvania, member of an eminent family who had studied under the famous Dr. John Fabricius at Helmstadt. An inclination toward Pietism, which was then being hunted down by the church, caused his dismissal from the University. Kelpius kept a journal of the long journey to America in Latin. Be-

sides this tongue, he wrote in Hebrew, Greek, German and
English.

The group these brethren formed was called The Society
of the Woman in the Wilderness. They believed that the
woman of the wilderness in Revelations symbolized the great
deliverance of the Church by Christ. She was "to come up
from this wilderness leaning on her beloved," so the beloved
in the wilderness, which their chosen home at this time certainly was, laid aside all other concerns to await her coming.
They strictly observed the signs of the times—meteors, stars,
color of the sky, and wind and rain. According to their beliefs there were three wildernesses or progressive states of
holiness—the barren, the fruitful and the wilderness state of
the elect of God. In the last, the high stage of holiness could
be attained only by those who dwelt in solitude, even as
Moses had dwelt for forty years in the wilderness, and John
the Baptist and Christ forty days. Thus trained, men would
be qualified to go forth and convert whole cities and work
signs and wonders. The habit of this Pietist society was a
coarse gown. Truly the Old Testament saying had come
about: in the wilderness was found a lodging place for these
wayfaring men.

In 1708, their brilliant leader Kelpius died. He was only
thirty-five. He passed away in the garden he had planted—
the first botanical garden in America—surrounded by children he had taught. Perhaps they sang to him some of the
lovely hymns he had written. After his death the others gradually returned to the world. Some married. But before their
order disbanded they were joined by Conrad Matthews and
Christopher Witt, the latter a physician and diviner. For
many years after this John Seelig and Conrad Matthews continued to live alone as hermits and, like their former brethren, sought immediate and strange revelations and lived in
daily expectation of the second advent.[9]

When Dr. Witt left the order he went to live in Germantown, where he proved himself a devoted physician and an all-round versatile man. He was a skilled botanist—he planted America's second botanical garden—a famous clockmaker, an expert organist and an artist, among his portraits being one of Kelpius which is still preserved. But his reputation was even more deeply engraved as a follower of Rosicrucian philosophy. He cast nativities and, from his mathematical and astronomical learning, wrote horoscopes. He had a disciple, one Fraily, who proved adept at curing the diseases of horses and cattle that baffled the local veterinarians. He also prescribed for sick people without seeing them,[10] which, at best, must have been under precarious diagnoses!

### Conrad Weisser's Vernal Urge

Another of the picturesque sects in early Pennsylvania were the Sieben-Taegers, or German Seventh-Day Baptists, commonly called Tunkers. At Ephrata, 56 miles northwest of Philadelphia, John Conrad Beissel formed a monastic community. The sect grew to such an extent that other colonies were established near York, Bedford, and Snow Hill. Beissel, a native of Eberbach in the Palatinate, and a persecuted Pietist there, arrived in this country in 1720 and settled at Mill Creek, Pa., where he was baptised by the German Tunker minister five years later. He soon became an ardent advocate, not only gathering about him many followers, but also growing vociferous in his protests against changing the Sabbath from the seventh to the first day of the week. He claimed that celibacy was the highest order of the Christian life and determined to set about proving it.

About 1728, after he had dwelt in the wilderness meditating on the subject, he formed the Ephrata Society. It was a monastic group of men vowed to celibacy and the advance-

ment of learning. They wore a robe similar to that of the
Capuchins and, on entering the order, took monastic names.[11]
Soon pious women clamored to be set apart for a conventual
life, and Beissel formed the Order of Spiritual Virgins, or
Roses of Sharon, who also bound themselves by a pledge.
These two communities for a time lived together in the same
house, a structure called Kedar, and many a man left his
wife to join it and many a wife her husband.[12]

Such was the background of Conrad Weisser's vernal urge.

Weisser was a born frontiersman. He held the office of
ranger, justice of the peace, provincial interpreter and Indian agent under James Logan, positions that brought him
a wide reputation and the friendship of the leading men of
Pennsylvania, including Benjamin Franklin. He always wore
the fur jerkin of the trapper and carried a large silver watch,
his prized possession. By the fairness of his dealings he soon
commanded both the respect of the community and the confidence of the Indians. Like others of the Pennsylvania Germans, he had a marked religious inclination; he served as
an elder in the Lutheran Church.

Now it happened that once John Conrad Beissel, the
"Superintendent" of the Ephrata order, went on a journey
into the wilderness; and on his return Weisser guided him
through the dense mountain trails. The man's piety so impressed Weisser that, forgetful of his responsibilities and his
wife and family, right there in the zenith of his career he
decided to leave all and follow. He retired to Ephrata, under-
took the monastic way and settled down to solitary existence
in a cell. His fur jerkin and silver watch he laid aside for
penitential garb.

But a man so used to power and the free life of the wilderness could not easily bend his will to discipline. He envied
the Superintendent's place in the community and was not
above listening to whispers against him. Indeed, the "heav-

enly intercourse" to which the male and female sides at
Kedar devoted themselves threatened to take realistic shape
for Conrad Weisser. Of all this the saintly Superintendent
was evidently well apprised.

One day, in the course of a ceremonial foot-washing, the
Superintendent "noticed from the feeling of the feet to what
temptations he was most exposed," so the chronicle runs,[13]
and he said to Weisser, "The Brother must take heed against
the female sex." Conrad was so moved that he later confessed
all to the Superintendent, who thereupon "took his burden
upon himself so that the good Brother was freed from temptation." Nevertheless, because "he did not take sufficient
heed to himself," Weisser was assailed anew by the tempter
and would probably have been overcome "had not God put
it into the heart of the Sister to seek out the covenant and
have herself re-baptised. Then the cords of the tempter were
torn and they again became as strangers to each other."

We can only imagine how embarrassing the situation
thereafter must have been. What efforts to avoid each other!
What struggles to overcome! Fortunately quite a different
temptation relieved the impasse.

The governor, to whom Weisser's frontier services were
invaluable, had little patience with this monastic nonsense.
Also, he had been hearing rumors and gossip about the community at Ephrata. He, being wise in his ways, did not express his thoughts; instead, he sent to Weisser an offer to
make him the local judge. As the community was vowed
never to take recourse to the law, the idea of one of their
members accepting such a post horrified them. But the
Superintendent, who evidently was only too glad to snatch
at a way of escape for this lusty Brother, ruled that it should
be decided by Weisser's conscience. To the assembled chapter
of brothers Weisser stated, after the proper heart-searching,
that his conscience did not feel the slightest twinge.

And so ended his monastic fling and its romantic succumbing to the Tempter—and temptress. He forthwith returned to his wife and settled down once more to being a substantial citizen and the father of thirteen children. When troops were called for the Braddock campaign, he enrolled immediately and rose to be a colonel. After peace was declared he conducted a general store in Reading, a town he had helped to lay out in the beginning, and prospered to such an extent that he was able to loan money. An enthusiastic musician, he played the organ and assembled quite a collection of printed music, which he kept in a special room at his house. His daughter married the famous Henry Melchior Muhlenberg and that young man later testified that "he gave me his daughter as my wife and helpmeet, because at my first visit I played and sang the edifying Halle songs on his house organ or seraphin." [14]

It is pleasant to end the story of this intrepid frontiersman, Indian interpreter, judge, store-keeper, money-lender, musician, and ex-monk with the information that at his funeral in 1762 there were consumed nine gallons of wine, 5½ of rum and "an incredible amount of punch."

# III

## GUILTY MEN AND INNOCENT WANDERERS

### Broadsiding Crime

THUS FAR IN OUR PROCESSION OF THOSE WHO LIVED IN CAVES or pursued the solitary life above ground there have filed past, with one exception, fairly innocent men and women. The regicides at New Haven provided the exception; and their misfortune, brought about through no fault of their own, was that they belonged to the wrong party. Now come into sight four characters who, through their *own* fault, were confined in quarters as close as any cave.

Modern penologists and psychiatrists doubtless could run through the calendar of Early American criminals and deftly pigeon-hole each where he belonged. Their work would be lightened by the confessions and "warnings" of these criminals which appeared in broadsides or pamphlets, prose or verse, and provided racy and salutary reading to our great-great-grandfathers. The authors and those who "ghosted" these confessions saw to it that the path down from innocence to Avernus was well marked.

Let Levi Ames approach his execution in Boston on October 21, 1773, and the whole of his dissolute career from childhood to sentence for burglary serves as a warning to sinners. Indeed, Levi seems to have attained the stature of a complete criminal before he danced on air: two broadsides were devoted to him. One, grisly illustrated, is headed "The Dying Groans of Levi Ames" and starts:

217

> Ye Youth. Who throng this fatal plain
> And crowd th' accursed Tree;
> O Shun the path that leads to shame,
> Nor fall like wretched me.

The other, likewise decorated with the scene of an execution, bears the title:

> An Address to the Inhabitants of Boston
> (Particularly to the Thoughtless Youth)
> Occasioned by the Execution of
> Levi Ames
> Who so early in Life, as not 22 years of age, must quit
> the Stage of action in this awful Manner

Levi's second author not alone ran on for thirty verses but really spread himself in the grand poetic style. He began:

> The Day's far spent, the Night comes on apace,
> Rebellious Man has almost run his race;
> This Day brings forth the Fruits of Sin and Shame,
> Which shews the Frailty of the human Frame.

On April 6, 1754, William Wieer swung as a moral object lesson on the gallows for the murder of William Chisin of Boston. His "Warning to Young and Old" was calculated to deter any youth who might think to tread the primrose path.[1]

Some of these confessions and warnings may have been written by parsons—old Cotton Mather was not above doing some of these "dying speeches"—but one suspects that journalists and printers, their tongues snugly in their cheeks and one eye on the main chance, set to work on them with as much ghoulish enthusiasm as any sob-sister employed by a tabloid today. And it is evident that the former drew as much on their imaginations as do the latter.

Out of a great collection of broadsides and pamphlets of this character we can select four curious items which describe criminals who were a little different from the average run—

## A *Warning* to Young & Old:

In the Execution of *William Wieer*, at *Bofton*, the 21ᵗʰ of *November*, 1754, for the Murder of *William Chifin*, on the 6ᵗʰ of *April* laſt.

**I.**

BEHOLD good People now I pray,
  And give you Heed to what I fay;
Your due Attention I do crave,
That you the Benefit may have.

**II.**

The Subject of my prefent Rhime,
Is *Will'm Wieer*'s wicked Crime:
A Crime for which he now muſt die,
By his own Act of Cruelty.

**III.**

Poor *Chifin* he in Anger flew,
Without a Provocation too;
This poor Man's Life he took away,
Not having Time, one Word to fay.

**IV.**

And now his Paffion he witholds,
And to his great Surprize beholds,
The Wound was Mortal which he gave,
But hopes for Mercy yet to have.

**V.**

But where fhall he for Mercy Cry?
But to the Sov'reign GOD moſt high:
Who has in facred Writ declar'd,
That fuch Men's Lives fhall not be fpar'd.

**VI.**

Ah! Paffion now, that ran fo high,
As to afcend the Clouds and Sky;
Where there is neither End nor Bound:—
But *Murder!* 'Tis a dreadful Sound.

**VII.**

Now *Wieer* for this horrid Crime,
Is doom'd to die before his Time;
He did'nt intend, (as he doth fay,)
To take poor *Chifin*'s Life away.

**VIII.**

But whether he did or no, 'tis true,
By GOD's juſt Laws, he has but due;
For *Murder* is a dreadful Fact,
Which none I hope will dare Tranfact.

**IX.**

Here's an Example for you all,
Both for the Great, as well as Small;
The Old as well as Young may be
Accuftom'd to this fatal Tree.

**X.**

That GOD whofe Ways are juſt and true,
Doth ev'ry wicked Way purfue;
Therefore be always on your Guard,
In all your Doings pleafe the LORD:

**XI.**

Correct your Paffions in due Time,
Left you commit this horrid Crime;
The Crime of Murder, few's fo great,
And you repent when it's too late.

**XII.**

Keep free from Slander and from Pelf,
And love your Neighbour as yourfelf,
Be thus to them both kind and true,
As you'd have them be fo to you.

**XIII.**

Let GOD's Commands be your Delight,
In all your Dealings be upright:
Be always careful to fulfil
The Sixth Command, (*Thou fhalt not Kill.*)

**XIV.**

'Tis GOD's free, rich and fov'reign Grace,
That we're not in this poor Man's Place;
Then let us fhun all wicked Ways,
Before the *Gallows* end our Days.

**XV.**

Happy they'll be, and happy thrice,
Who will take Counfel and Advice,
From this poor Man's unhappy Fate,
To view their own moſt fad Eſtate.

**XVI.**

If GOD's Commands you do obey,
Depend on Him, and often pray,
He will in his abundant Grace,
Preferve you in your righteous Ways.

**XVII.**

His glorious Grace will then come down,
And all your wicked Paffions drown:
Then take the Wing, to JESUS fly,
And fee thy GOD above the Sky.

**FINIS.**

CRIMINAL CONFESSION BROADSIDE, 1754

a counterfeiter in a cave, a lady horse thief, a prison puppeteer, and a mighty impregnator.

### John Richardson, Seducer

The family name of Richardson can cover a multitude of
sinners but, in his time, John Richardson committed enough
offenses along one particular line to allow the rest of the
family to live comparatively innocent lives.

Born in New York late in the seventeenth century, he
soon entered on a long career of seduction. It began with
the daughter of a carpenter with whom he found work. Then
he went to sea, landing up at Amsterdam, where he overcame
the scruples of a Dutch seaman's wife, whom he also robbed
of a considerable quantity of goods. With these ill-gotten
gains burning a hole in his pocket, he made Boston and,
retiring to a country hamlet on the outskirts of town, so in-
gratiated himself into the favor of several rural girls with
his gifts of the stolen Indian handkerchiefs that in a short
time all of them were pregnant. Meantime the daughter of
the farmer with whom he stayed had taken his attentions
seriously, but insisted that bans be read before they married.
When these were published the rest of the maidens, declar-
ing him responsible for their condition, insisted that he
marry them, but since his intended bride found herself in
the same state, he thought to dissolve his dilemma by marrying her. This he did on the agreement that her father hand
over £300 local currency for dowry. The decision so angered
the others that they promptly had him arrested, and he was
obliged to give surety for the maintenance of his future
children.

With what remained of the dowry in his hands, John departed for New York, to find work by which to meet all
these obligations. There a Quaker ship-builder gave him

employment, and the Quaker's wife found other occupation for him. On being caught *flagrante delicto*, he shipped to Philadelphia and went to lodgings kept by a widow. After the proverbial manner of some widows, if we may believe the account, she welcomed the attentions of this swaggering ruffian. She had two daughters, and each in turn shared their mother's predilection until they discovered that their sin was surely going to find them out. The lusty John married one, inducing the mother to part with £100 and half her plate as dowry.

Again he had the problem for support of unborn infants on his hands, so he shipped to South Carolina and thence to Jamaica and back, proving a good navigator. Christmas found him in the home of the ship-owner and there also, was the inevitable daughter. On the way home from a dance, "he received convincing proofs of her kindness"; indeed, so attracted was she by him that she arranged for his easy entrance to her bedroom. The consequences were soon apparent, so John gallantly offered to marry her. The father, thankful to find this way out of his troubles, presented his new son-in-law with a vessel. En route to Barbados, through no fault of his own, he lost his boat, and was rescued only in the nick of time.

The Barbadians he found to be a gullible lot. By claiming to be the son of prominent men, he managed to collect enough to live on. Once he even was awarded an inheritance. Eventually Barbados got too hot for him and he left the island as a common sailor.

After making the other side, the boat headed for Turkey. On board was another sailor, Richard Coyle. Evidently by this time Richardson had wearied of sexual redundancies, for Coyle and he conspired to slay the captain, which they managed successfully. It was the irony of fate that one who had pursued an uninterrupted course of seduction for so many years should spend his last moments on a very small platform at the end of a rope for so unimaginative a crime as murder. He and Coyle were hanged on Execution Dock, London, on January 25, 1738. Of the two, John Richardson is remembered by occupying a place in the famous Newgate Calendar.[2] To this day, Richardson is also a fairly common family name up and down the Atlantic seacoast.

## Miss Perkins, Horse Thief

On a May day in 1839, from a miserable cell in the Madison County Prison, Ky., a certain penitent young lady sighed her confession. The same year a New York publisher brought it forth to the delectation and horror of all and sundry under the alluring title of—

The
Female Prisoner
Once respected and beloved, but late the most wretched
of womankind
Narrative
of the Life and Singular Adventures of
Josephine Amelia Perkins
A young woman, who, in early life was deservedly esteemed for her exemplary behavior, yet for three years last past (friendless and unprotected) has been unhappily addicted to a criminal propensity, more singular and surprising in its nature (for one of her sex) than can be found on record; in the commission of which, she has been four times detected, twice pardoned on account of her sex, once for reasons of supposed insanity, and the fourth and last time, convicted and sentenced to two years imprisonment in Madison county jail, Kentucky. Annexed is a well-written Address to Parents and Children.

In a word, Josephine was a horse thief. She "got that way" through love and skill in handling horses learned in childhood. She claimed to have been born of "peaceable and

JOSEPHINE PERKINS, LADY HORSE THIEF

well-disposed inhabitants" of Devonshire, England, in 1818. When little more than thirteen she learned to manage even the most high-spirited horses and could ride them at great speed. At the age of seventeen, she fell in love with a naval officer eight years her senior. Her father objected so strenuously to the match that they determined to elope. They arranged a rendezvous at Portsmouth, 117 miles away, where

his ship was loading for a cruise to America. She intended to
join him and ship as a common sailor. Taking her father's
fastest horse, she started early in the morning, managed to
outride her parent who chased her, covered the distance in
a day and a night, sold the horse on reaching Portsmouth—
and discovered that her lover's vessel had sailed. No other
course was left the poor girl but to take the next ship, which
was bound for St. John's, New Brunswick. Like many an
English person then and since, her knowledge of the geog-
raphy of the United States left much to be desired.

A storm drove the ship far off its course and so wrecked
its rigging that the boat had to be abandoned. The survivors
were picked up by an American pilot boat and landed at
Wilmington, N. C. There Amelia stood *sans* lover, *sans*
money and possessing only the clothes on her back. In this
desperate state she wandered out to the country and her eye
fell upon an especially fine horse grazing in a pasture. Having been successful in stealing a horse from her father and
cashing in on it, she yielded to the temptation. But the
horse, after she had ridden him twelve miles, turned home-
ward and brought her to the doorstep of the astonished
owner. He gave the famished girl a meal and then took her
over to the justice of the peace. With proverbial southern
gallantry, this authoritative person dismissed the charge on
the ground that "an instance of the prosecution of a female
for the crime of horse stealing was both novel and without
precedent."

Thereafter her course in crime came easily. She stole
horses and sold them until, at the tender age of twenty-one,
she was convicted. While in prison, she was visited by some
religiously minded women who convinced her that confession was good for the soul, whereupon she wrote her life
story. She rounded it out with a warning to children to obey
their parents and with a good sound bit of advice to parents

not to be so hardhearted when their daughters were in love. Her portrait, with wrists bound, shows her to be profoundly repentant.

### Counterfeiter in a Cave

Scarcely had the various colonies begun issuing money than counterfeit currency and bills popped up to bother the authorities. Some of it was crude, some in admirable imitations. It added to the criminal class who would get rich quick. That many otherwise respectable young men were lured into this dangerous business is attested by court records and confessions. New Jersey in the middle of the eighteenth century developed a serious counterfeit case involving some of the best known scions of the day.

After the turn of the nineteenth century, Connecticut produced William Stuart, who crammed his days so full of crimes and escapades as to bring him eventually to the "horrible pit in Simsbury." It also furnished a vivid "Life" which is one of the choice items prized by collectors of American curios. Printed first in 1854, and probably "ghosted" by a parson with a literary turn, it has been re-printed as lately as 1932 in New Milford, Conn., where Stuart finally ended his days.[3]

So much has been written about him (for Connecticut boasts even its best criminals), that we shall pass him by with this casual mention and proceed to a counterfeiter who chose a cave for his nefarious operations.

In 1765 Gilbert Belcher migrated from Hebron, Conn., with a family of nine small children and an aged mother, to Great Barrington, Mass., and set up there as a silversmith. He bought, for what was evidently a song, a property known as Bung Hill, a wild, rattlesnake-infested section which offered only two desirable features, a little house at the foot of the hill and a cave half-way up it. He settled his numerous family in the house and proceeded to work at his trade.

On October 30, 1772, he and three others—Ethan Lewis, J. Adams and Wane Case—were captured by a posse of militia who surrounded the cave and committed them to jail for "manufacturing counterfeits in imitation of 'York' money,

WILLIAM STEWART, COUNTERFEITER

that is, coins and currency bearing the official imprint and accepted as standard in the Province of New York and in the provinces of New England also." ⁴ At the same time there were rounded up, in various parts of New England and New York, a dozen other accomplices. All were marched to Albany and clapped into jail.

During the trial it was brought out that Belcher had engraved the plates and printed them with Ethan Lewis's help while the others passed the counterfeits. Supposed to be working at his silversmithing in the little house at the foot of the hill and keeping food in the mouths of his nine children and aged mother, Belcher was actually making spurious notes and coins in the cave. Retorts which he borrowed from a physician, on the lame excuse that he wanted to try experiments in alchemy, Belcher used for melting down silver. Evidently charcoal, which makes but little smoke, provided the fire. To this day the cave shows evidences of being heavily smoked and a corner of it marked with the effects of a fire.

One of the accomplices, John Smith, made a confession, which later found its way into print. Belcher and John Law Lovey, another accomplice, remained defiant throughout the trial and up to the very day of their execution. One of the gang, son of a prominent citizen, turned King's evidence and was pardoned. He had merely passed some of the bills. Before trial some of the gang made an effort to break jail, but were apprehended. Smith went to the gallows on February 5, 1773, and Lovey, "Dr." Bill and Belcher on April 2. A few days before their execution they were caught trying to fire and blow up the jail. What was claimed to be Belcher's last speech, confession and dying words appeared in a Hartford newspaper, but the effort was of so literary a character that one suspects an enterprising journalist.

The cave on Bung Hill was not only the factory for the counterfeit notes and coins but also the cache and rendezvous for the gang. From that time on Belcher and his accomplices found quite a number of imitators and it became almost axiomatic among the authorities that if you started searching for counterfeiters you would eventually find them in a cave somewhere. Police in the eighteenth and early nineteenth century were not given to romancing over troglodytes. They suspected all caves of being dens of flagrant iniquity.

On the whole, compared with William Stuart's, Gilbert Belcher's career was humdrum and sordid. Behind it stood the economic necessity produced by a numerous family. It lacked the dark streak of vagrancy that· gave Stuart's life its charm and impelled him to wander on his counterfeit-passing trade up and down from Canada to the South. It lacked the boozing and belly-cheer and rowdy rabblements in taverns and the random assignations with obliging wantons. In short, Belcher's career lacked romance, for even at best nine children could not conceivably creep under that heading. As in the case of beggars, no comets were seen the night Gil Belcher dangled on the twisted hemp.

## Henry Frederic Moon, Puppeteer

It is pleasant to turn to a more engaging character. Although we last find him doing time in the same abandoned copper mine, at the grim underground prison in Simsbury, Conn., that held William Stuart for so long, Henry Frederic Moon, alias Henry Frederic More Smith, alias William Newman, proved to be by far the most cunning criminal in the annals of early nineteenth century American crime. So unparalleled were his artifices, impostures and mechanical ingenuities that Walter Bates, High Sheriff in King's County, New Brunswick, N. S., felt moved to write an extensive narrative of his conduct and adventures.[5]

Moon, a likely-appearing young fellow, well spoken and educated and equipped with a trunkful of good clothes, appeared in Windsor, Nova Scotia, in 1812, where he found employment on a farm, proving steady, careful and industrious and thereby gaining the confidence of his employer, a Mr. Bond. Soon the attachment between Moon and Bond's daughter Elizabeth became too close to be unobserved. Moon asked for her hand, but the parent would not give his consent. She then left her father's house and married Moon in March, 1813. After this he claimed to be a tailor, although he pursued no regular business, and seemed somehow to come by enough money to live on. An exemplary person,

he was never known to be intoxicated, never used bad language and seemed to be addicted to no bad habits. In 1814
he was arrested at New Brunswick for stealing a valuable
horse. When asked his occupation, he replied, "No one in
particular." He claimed to be a graduate of Cambridge and
acquainted with four languages, including Latin.

After being a short time in the jail at Kingston, he apparently fell sick and as the days passed grew seriously ill. Doctors visited him and could not diagnose his case except to
agree that he was past recovery. To let him die in peace, his
irons were removed. As he lingered day after day, the sympathy of the entire community increased. Kind-hearted
women sent him dainties. Ministers came to offer spiritual
consolation. Finally one sympathetic citizen, determined that
the poor fellow should not die on the wretched straw of his
cell, sent a boy to the prison with a feather bed. When he
arrived there, the jailer discovered Moon's cell was empty.

Enraged at this "unparalleled and abominable deception,"
a posse started on his trail. It was easily picked up and followed a long distance through the forests and over water by
a succession of bold thefts. Eventually he was cornered,
young, alert and hearty, and hauled back to jail.

From that time on he presented a constant problem to
the authorities. Again and again, without any outside help,
he managed to free himself from his irons. Sometimes he
broke them into pieces. On several occasions he wrecked the
walls of his cell. Extra guards and the heaviest chains had
no effect on him—he invariably eluded the one and slipped
out of the other. Brought to trial, he laughed at his judges,
kicked up a rumpus in the court and, though sentenced to
death, played amusing antics. He was building up for himself a convincing alibi of insanity.

Back in his cell again, he ceased being violent and started
displaying his mechanical ingenuities. One day his jailer

found that he had made a convincing semblance of a woman
out of braided straw and kneaded bread. But let Sheriff
Bates tell it:

"He now produced an effigy of a man in perfect shape
with his features painted and joints to all his limbs, and
dressed him in the clothes that he had made, in good shape
and fashion out of the clothes that he had torn off himself
(being now naked) which was admired for its ingenuity.
This he would put sometimes in one position and sometimes
in another, and seemed to amuse himself with it, without
taking the least notice of anything else; continuing in his old
way, hallooing. . . .

"The most wonderful and mysterious of all is that in seven
days, he had prepared undiscovered and at once exhibited
the most striking pictures of art, taste, genius and invention
that ever was, and I presume, ever will be produced by any
human being placed in his situation, in a dark room, chained
and handcuffed, under sentence of death, without so much
as a nail or any kind of a thing to work with, but his hands,
and naked. . . .

"It consists of ten characters, men, women and children—
all made and painted in the most expressive manner, with
all the limbs and joints of the human frame—each perform-
ing different parts; the features, shape and form all express
their different fashions and suitable to the stations in which
they act. They appear as perfect as though alive, with all the
air and gaiety of actors on the stage. . . .

"He sits in his bed by the side of the jail—his exhibition
begins about a foot from the floor and compasses the whole
space of the ceiling. The uppermost is a man whom he calls
the tambourine-player, or sometimes Dr. Blount, standing
with all the pride and appearance of a master musician, his
left hand akimbo, his right hand on his tambourine. Next
him, below, is a lady, genteelly dressed, gracefully sitting in

a handsome swing; at her left hand stands a man neatly dressed, in the character of a servant, holding the side of the swing, with his right hand, his left hand on his hip, in an easy posture, waiting the lady's motion. On her right hand stands a man genteelly dressed in the character of a gallant, in a graceful posture of dancing. . . .

"Beneath these three figures sits a young man and a young girl (apparently about 14) in a posture for tilting, at each end of a board. Directly under these stands one he calls Buonaparte, or sometimes the father of his family; he stands erect, his features are prominent, his cheeks red, his teeth white, set in order, his gums and lips red, his nose shaded black representing the nostrils, his dress is that of a harlequin; in one hand he holds an infant, with the other he plays or beats music. Before him stand two children apparently three or four years old, holding each other by one hand, in the act of playing or dancing with a man, dressed in fashion, who appears in the character of a steward. This makes up the show.

"Then commences the performance. The first operation is from the tambourine-player or master, who gives three single strokes on his tambourine, that may be heard in any part of the house, without moving his body. He then dances gracefully a few steps; the lady is then swung two or three times by the steward; then the gallant takes a few steps; then the two below tilt a few times in the most easy, pleasant manner; then the two children dance a little, holding each other by the hand." [6]

Moon's puppets soon became one of the town's attractions. Visitors were taken to the jail to see them. He gave performances for children. Money trickled into his hands. He was offered a fife and a fiddle with which to furnish music. He could play both, and on the fife was ambidextrous—"would play any tune either right or left-handed." Whereas, before, he had used charred sticks and his own blood for coloring, the jailer now gave him pen and paints and articles of cloth-

HENRY FREDERIC MOON, CRIMINAL PUPPETEER

ing. He continued repairing and improving his family until it included twenty-four characters; "six beat music in concert with the fiddle, while six dance to the tune."

When he had completed these, he began practising a new mystery—telling fortunes from tea leaves. He even prophesied he would be pardoned. Sure enough, the court met to reconsider the charges against him and, although he celebrated the occasion by trying to burn down the jail, he was finally ushered out of the province and headed towards the United States.

Mad? Not a bit of it. He passed through Portland, thence to Boston and New London to New Haven. From a hotel in the last named city he decamped with a quantity of silver spoons and a number of other articles.

He was now traveling under the name of William Newman. Apprehended in New York for this theft, he was brought back to New Haven for trial. Although Sheriff Bates positively identified him as Moon, he denied ever being in New Brunswick and said he was a Frenchman educated in England. Connecticut judges were not to be bamboozled by any such whimwhams as feigned sickness or puppets. He was hustled off to Simsbury, where he spent his nights in "that horrid pit" and each day was brought forth to the light to labor in chains and fetters. Among the wretched victims in this jail at the time, Sheriff Bates attests, "William Newman appears like a distinguished character."

Little wonder! For was he not a versatile person? He could play on almost any instrument of music. He was equally skilled as a blacksmith, shipwright, tailor and farmer. He had the "strength of a lion and the subtlety of the Devil." And so astonishingly quick and active was he in his motions that he could catch mice even when wearing handcuffs!

## Deluded Solitaries

We can now pass from those on whom the solitary life was forced through their own fault, to those strange, sad, happy and mad fellows who talked to themselves and lived alone.

Scarcely a community but has remembrance of at least one of them. What addled their brains, what brought the cloud to settle on them, need not concern us here. At least they were harmless, and the village saw that no harm was done to them. Their only claim to fame was that they were extreme eccentrics without any other redeeming features. So that they may find representation in this collection of odd sticks and, presumably, be thereby honored, we cite two examples.

### Yodeling Sam and the Pumpkin Scratcher

In the middle years of the last century, what was then the rustic village of New Canaan, Conn., harbored a fantastic creature known as "Crazy Sam." He lived alone in a hut and, being very much afraid of people, never showed himself by daylight. At dead of night he would wander into the village and there, in the small hours of the morning, awaken the inhabitants by the exercise of his one talent—beautiful Swiss yodeling. He always wore home-made leather clothes and a sombrero. One of his eccentricities was a passion for coins, which he strung around the brim of his hat. He was believed to have been a German.[7]

Cross the Connecticut state line in the northeast corner, and you are soon in Westerly, R. I. There, without house or home, lived in the forest an extreme eccentric, David Wilbur. Uneducated yet seemingly gifted, he was afraid of all humankind. On their approach he would flee. Even the sight of children sent him to cover. And yet in this solitary existence he studied the stars and clouds and winds so that he became weatherwise. Local folks knew him as the "Astronomer." In Summer he lived chiefly on berries and fruit and slept in a swamp under the shelter of a large oak. In Winter he fed on nuts and grains that he had stored, squirrel-like, and such game as he could trap. He was constantly on the move, traversing great distances, yet very few people actually saw him close to. His particular eccentricity was a penchant, when passing through cornfields, to scratch numbers, signs and figures on pumpkins.[8]

It is conceivable that David Wilbur might have been more worthily employed, but he apparently was satisfied with his solitary wanderings, his life close to Nature, and his cabalistic scratchings. "There is a joy in being mad that only madmen know."

## Johnnie Appleseed

In a recent book on Connecticut, the authors claim for that state, among other remarkable accomplishments, the impelling force which drove Johnnie Appleseed to retire from the ordinary paths of his fellow men and to follow the trails and waterways of the Middle West to plant seeds of apple trees. This impelling force was a maiden in Clinton, Conn., who told Jonathan Chapman in no uncertain terms that she would not marry him.[9] In the light of what he accomplished thereafter, this incident may have been merely a spiritual catharsis, leaving him free to pursue his greater purpose. Jonathan lost a wife, but the American people gained an imperishable legend.

Born near Springfield, Mass., in 1775, his youth was passed among people whose eyes were turned westward. On all sides men wearied of farming in rock-strewn fields were talking about the fat soil and sunny slopes of the Ohio Valley. For two decades the wagon trains had been pushing westward from Massachusetts and Connecticut—a constant migration of families with all their worldly goods, eager to start life afresh in this new Eden. Perhaps migration did not appeal to the anonymous miss of Clinton. So Jonathan went alone.

He first appeared at Licking County, O., with a sack of

apple seeds he had collected en route at cider mills in New
York and Pennsylvania. The year was 1801. Wherever he
found a favorable spot he planted his seeds. Five years later
he drifted down the Ohio with two canoe-loads of apple
seeds lashed together, making for what was then the western
frontier. A harmless enough fellow, the Indians treated him
with respect. Even during the War of 1812, while other
white settlers were being slaughtered by these native allies
of the British, Johnnie Appleseed passed unmolested.

There was a reason for their reluctance to harm him. He
was a religious man after the Swedenborgian persuasion, a
type of faith that seems to impart serenity and happiness to
its followers. In addition to his apple seeds he carried Bibles,
and he preached to Indians and settlers alike whenever he
could gather a handful of them to listen to him. To those
who lacked them, he gave Bibles. When he reached the end
of a journey he would turn back and retrace his old trail,
so that he could cultivate the seedling apple trees.

At first glance he might have been put down as "touched."
He was not a prepossessing person. Of medium height, with
light blue eyes and long, light brown hair, he wore scarcely
any clothes. Sometimes he was content with wearing merely
an old coffee sack with holes cut out for legs and arms. Often
he traded apple seedling trees for old clothes. Winter and
Summer he went barefoot. In lieu of a cap or hat, he wore
a tin pan in which, when it was not otherwise in use, he
cooked his food.

It has been estimated that by 1838 the seed he planted had
grown into trees bearing fruit over an area of 100,000 square
miles. How many miles he traveled on his peculiar solitary
journeying as sower of the Word and the seed it would be
impossible to calculate. Forty-six long years, traveling afoot,
by boat and a-horseback, he pursued his mission. He lived
to see the seed he planted and the scions of the new Jona-

than or "Rickey" apples he set out grow into fruitful trees and produce their own generation of orchards.

As he had lived kindly, so Death was kindly to him. One dusk in 1847, having tramped twenty miles that day, he finally reached the home of friends near Fort Wayne, Ind. His seventy-two years were telling on him. He sat down wearily on the doorstep, and the kind people brought him bread and milk. In return for their courtesies he read the Beatitudes to them. . . . "Blessed are the poor in spirit, for theirs is the kingdom of heaven. . . . Blessed are the meek, for they shall inherit the earth. . . . Blessed are the peacemakers, for they shall be called the children of God. . . ." Then he stretched on the floor to sleep. In the morning, when they looked at him lying there, they saw that he had entered into even a fuller life.[10]

To most of his contemporaries Johnnie Appleseed was just a queer old fellow, a failure, harmless, whimsical, pious. As the years pass, his shadow grows longer. He has become not alone one of our most romantic figures, but the symbol of the sort of idealism our world sorely needs. His trees grew and fruited abundantly and their offspring gave increase. Today Johnnie Appleseed is the saint for Arbor Day, the patron and ghostly guiding spirit of those who would make trees grow where none grew before. As the fruit reddens on the bough they think kindly of him and thank Heaven that he lived.

### The Leather Man

If Johnnie Appleseed has become the patron saint of arborists, perhaps in time Jules Bourlay will attain a faint halo as a sacrifice to business failure. It would not be beyond the realm of possibility that a world which has suffered through a decade or more of economic depression and business uncertainty might choose him as a romantic figure. The leather trade in particular could point to him with a sardonic sort of pride.

In 1857 there first appeared in Connecticut a strange figure who attracted much countryside attention because he wore leather clothes—leather coat, leather breeches, leather hat, leather boots. It was soon realized by country folks that he was following a well-defined circuit. Twice a year thereafter and for thirty-two years, this small, swarthy, bearded old fellow could be depended upon to appear at regular intervals. People began wondering who he was and why he wandered, and why he wore leather clothes. The usual tales were woven around him that are fastened on all strange wanderers—that he had been disappointed in love, that he was doing penance for a crime, that he had failed in the leather business.

"Avoiding cities and main highways, the Leather Man followed a course of nearly 365 miles, year in and year out. Although not always traveling over the same ground, his roundabout course, two-thirds of which lay in Connecticut, was made on schedule time. He rarely stayed more than a few hours in one spot unless his clothes were in need of repair, and then but a few days.

"No one remembers seeing him traveling in the rain. He is believed to have slept in caves which he had discovered, staying in them most of the Winter and reappearing with Spring. Once or twice he was known to construct huts from railroad ties or to sleep in sheltered spots of the underbrush. Any cave on his route came to be known locally as 'Leather Man's Cave.' New Canaan, Conn., claims two of them. Here he slept without bedding or blanket, here he repaired his clothes and cached the scraps of food and leather he did not need at the moment." [11]

Since he could speak only a phrase or two of English, and

these with a French accent, the natives said he was a Frenchman. And they were right.

Jules Bourlay came to this country from his home in Lyons. The son of a prosperous wool merchant, he was given a good education. In due time he inevitably fell in love and, like Amelia Jenkins, the lady horse thief, found parents could be hard-hearted. The girl's father was a leather merchant who held to strict business ideas, up to which Jules, apparently did not measure. However, Jules persuaded him to make a trial. Jules was to serve a year's probation in the leather firm. If in that time he proved his worth, the girl was his.

During that year the bottom dropped out of the leather market. Unexperienced and young, Jules tried to stem the tide of a 40 per cent drop in prices. Bankruptcy descended on the firm his prospective father-in-law had entrusted to him, and with bankruptcy inevitably came the loss of the girl. He fled to this country and started his vagrancy.

The leather clothes may have been his choice of penance. They may have been a bitter mockery. However, at no time did he seem violent nor display any signs of anger, nor was he ever known to harm a soul. His big blue eyes were always remarkably bright and intelligent. "He never begged for food, but, as the years went by, he picked one or two homes in each village where he could go unmolested for food and tobacco. He never entered a house, never returned if he was questioned, never took any money or worked for what he got." Perhaps that year of probation shattered any illusions he may have had in the nobility of work. He was never known to steal fruit or vegetables from the gardens he passed. He would pick up only stray bits of leather and string to patch his clothes.

His usual custom was to knock on the kitchen door, and when it opened, would put his fingers to his mouth and

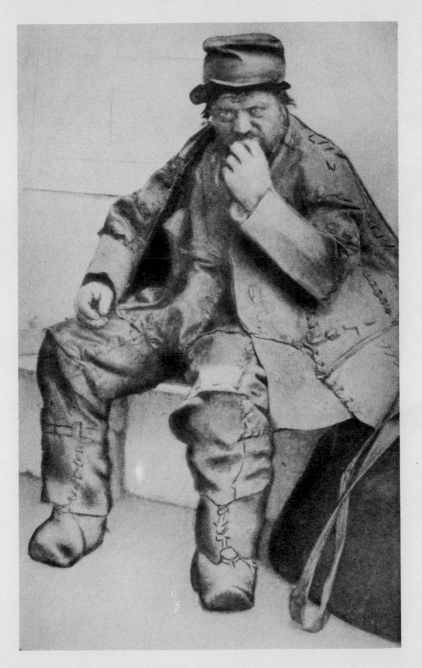

JULES BOURLAY, THE OLD LEATHER MAN

mutter, "Piece to eat." Then he would sit on the wash bench
by the door until food was set down by him. What he
couldn't eat he would stuff into his pockets. His coat, which
was loose and hung almost to his knees, had huge inside
pockets.

The rest of his queer garb consisted of a leather cap and
badly fitting leather trousers that he stuffed into high leather
boots with wooden soles. He wore a blue woolen under-
shirt. This was his one concession. Even though they were
offered him, he refused to wear any clothes but leather. He
carried a stout walking stick and on his back was a leather
bag containing a few personal belongings, an iron hatchet,
a tin plate and pail, an axe, an awl, a jack-knife, scraps of
leather and a French Catholic prayer-book. He wore a small
crucifix around his neck. Thus clad, he creaked his way
from town to town and from cave to cave.

When the blizzard of March, 1888, isolated the Connecticut countryside, the old Leather Man suffered griev-
ously. He was then sixty-five. Thirty-two years of wandering
had taken its toll of him. Caught in the snow near Hartford,
both his hands and feet were frozen. Rescuers took him to
the Hartford Hospital, where it was found that he also was
suffering from cancer. A few hours later, he escaped from
the hospital and feebly started off on his circuit again—to
North Haven, through New Canaan and other towns en
route and across the New York State line. A farmer, seeing
his pathetic appearance, vainly tried to persuade him to sleep
in the farm barn but the old fellow pressed on. In a cave
not far from Ossining he was found dead on March 24, 1889.
Cold and cancer had caught up with him. The town authorities laid his body away in the Potter's Field at near-by
Sparta, and the coroner deposited his leather costume in the
local museum.

*Part IV*

# THE GOSPEL-GLUTTED

# I

## ECCENTRICS IN PARSONAGE AND PULPIT

### *The Parson a Superior Person*

F OR MANY YEARS AFTER THE COLONIES WERE FOUNDED, whether in Puritan New England, Dutch Reformed New Netherlands, Quaker Pennsylvania, Catholic Maryland or Anglican Virginia, no one would dream of laughing at the parson. Not even in the privacy of the home would a parent tolerate so much as a fleeting smile at any eccentricity the minister might display. He was above criticism.

In both New England and the South, the clergyman was part and parcel of the government. In small towns he served many other capacities—judge, lawyer, teacher, physician, mechanic. He not alone claimed this omniscience, but "he had his claim allowed." To smile at him, then, would have constituted *lèse majesté*. To criticize him was little short of criminal. In the Pilgrim Society at Plymouth is preserved a document unique for its character: the testimony of James Cole, innkeeper, before Deputy Governor Bradford, dated 1691, that he *did* hear John Gray call the minister a "dirty fellow"!

Because of his superior education, the parson was generally several intellectual notches above the mental average of his congregation. Consequently he led and directed such thinking as its several members might indulge in. For those who disagreed with him the punishment was swift and efficacious. Barring grave illness, he accepted no apology for absence from public worship. An oracle on theology and Scriptural interpretation, he often also could be consulted on other learned subjects—mathematics, physics, astronomy. He could be depended on to teach Latin and sometimes Greek and Hebrew. He was the person *par excellence* in his little domain. Save in rare instances, he proved a faithful, though stern, shepherd of his sheep. He and his church were the natural centers of good thought and good works.

## Versatile Clergy

Many ministers were also physicians to their flocks. "Ever since the days of Luke the Evangelist, skill in physic has been frequently professed and practiced by persons whose most declared business was the study of divinity," declared Cotton Mather in the funeral sermon on his friend, Thomas Thatcher, pastor for a long time at Milton, Mass., and the town's only physician. It was not unusual, then, that when the parishioners of Rev. Michael Wigglesworth of Malden, Mass., came to lay away their faithful old minister, they should carve on his tombstone the lines:

Here lies in silent grave below
Maulden's physician in soul and body too.[1]

Sometimes the clergyman served humbler purposes, as did Rev. John Cuthbertson, first Reformed Presbyterian minister to arrive in America. He came here in 1751. His charges lay scattered through the back regions of Pennsylvania and he rode on horseback from one community to another, preaching, marrying, baptising, administering the Lord's Supper, counseling and comforting his people—and he was also available for any little jobs of butchering cattle at the various places where he called.[2]

Middletown, Conn., had a minister, Mr. Fuller, who was

also schoolmaster, constable, ran a store and conducted a tavern.[3] The most versatile seems to have been Rev. John Harriman of Elizabeth Town, N. J., who served there as pastor of the Presbyterian Church from 1687 to 1705, and was equally good as a surveyor, farmer, miller and presser of cider. For a number of years he was a member of the Legislature and still, with all these activities, found time to keep a boarding school and to buy and sell real estate.[4]

The parson, wherever found, possessed at least the nucleus of a library and so became the leader of culture. Most of his books were theological. His normal interest in the "Queen of Sciences" accounts for the presence of such works in the homes of the laity, as he would naturally direct the reading of his people along the lines in which he was most concerned. John Dunston, early New England bookseller, writing in his journal of 1686, attests that "parsons are the greatest benefactor to the bookseller." [5]

When a new town was to be settled in the New England wilderness, it was usually the parson who led his people thither, sharing with them exposure to the attacks of wild beasts and savages and the perils and weariness of the way, and when they reached their appointed place he helped direct the layout and building of the new village. Under his leadership, especially in New England, the building of the meeting house was among the first concerns and it was given a position of importance on the village green. Here it would serve not only for church but for schoolhouse and place of town meeting as well.

For the parson, ministerial lands, or a glebe, were set aside. Often this was an extensive area, so large, in fact, that the parson could not be expected to farm it himself nor could he afford to hire help to cultivate it. From its natural resources came some part of his salary, in kind or supplies, as in one New England village where the records of 1663 show that "22 cords of wood were cut and sold to pay for clothes of minister." [6] After the church and provision for sustaining the minister came education. So we see the New England township as essentially a congregation with the pastor at its head. Through his influence it was formed and extended. Many generations later, when the Ohio Valley and Illinois were being opened up, we find the ecclesiastical descendants of these early New England parsons leading their people forth into the wilderness and beginning their new settlements in much the same order as they were first started back home.

The early parson in Virginia, on the other hand, had no such compact parish, nor did he sway such a sphere of influence. His congregation was scattered over a wide area and rarely could he minister to the spiritual wants of all save when they came in to church. Whereas in New England most of the official business was conducted by the town, in Virginia and farther south it was under the jurisdiction of the vestry of the parish. The vestry made contracts for building churches, opening roads, levied fines, etc. The minister either counseled or led this board or meekly acceded to its dictates. Nevertheless, as we shall see, his position was upheld and respect for his cloth maintained.

## Competitive Preaching

There were times when the minister himself was the cause of a migration. Such was Roger Williams' leading his band of rebellious believers away from the orthodoxy of Massachusetts into the free wilderness of Rhode Island and, in turn, the moving southward of the pious and valiant Hooker who opened up Connecticut. Sometimes those who followed the parson into new fields were supporters he had weaned away from a competing preacher. The settlement of Woodbury, Conn., is directly traceable to a dispute over preachers.

In 1665 the congregation at Stratford chose for its pastor a fledgling minister, Rev. Charles Chauncey. Some of the congregation, being opposed to his ordination, called in his stead Rev. Zechariah Walker. As Stratford could boast only one meeting house at the time, and a primitive affair it must have been, both ministers conducted public services in the same house, "spelling each other," as the Yankee saying goes. Chauncey preached first in the morning and Walker was allowed two hours at noon, with Chauncey coming in again, directly he had finished, to start the afternoon service. The town was soon divided between the Chaunceyites and the Walkerites, a sorry state of affairs.

As the weeks passed, Walker developed into a prodigious preacher. Often he was just nearing his seventh point, with two more and a "finally" to go, when Mr. Chauncey and his followers were gathered outside waiting to enter. In retaliation, Mr. Chauncey began preaching the hour glass twice over and more besides in the morning, while the Walkerites cooled their heels outdoors.

This oratorical contest—for in those days pulpit verbosity was the hallmark of a good parson—went on until the Walkerites tired of the impasse, and determined to go off by themselves where they could listen to their preacher without interruption as long as his breath held out. Led by Walker, they penetrated deeper into the colony—a pious migration of families and their belongings and their cattle—until they reached their chosen Eden and set up the beginnings of what is now Woodbury. The year of this hegira was 1672.[7]

Competitive preachers could occasionally afford a village as much excitement as local baseball teams or rival boxers do today. Sandwich, Mass., supplies an early example of this ecclesiastical sport. Revs. Richard Bourne and Thomas Tucker (the latter adjudged by some a little "touched") each had his own followers. So bitter became the controversy over

them that the town fathers finally decided that he who attracted the most adherents at a meeting should be the
preacher for the day.[8] That, of course, was one way of getting
people to go to church. "All out for Parson Tucker! All out
for Parson Bourne!" Nor did it appear unseemly to the
pious folk of Sandwich that they were acting as referees to
preaching bouts.

### Ups and Downs of Piety

Although the New England theocracy lasted and spread,
it was inevitable that cracks should eventually appear in the
temple the clergy had so carefully and solidly built for themselves. In matters of both Church and State they held the
leading place in Massachusetts Bay Colony. They advocated
all improvements that did not infringe on their prerogative
or dignity. They led the movement for education, were the
literary men of their day, as we have seen, and "labored to
exalt the dignity of spirit over matter."

Their influence, however, was not always extended in favor
of justice and liberty. Those who disagreed with their theology were given short shrift or, as the saying went, "God
do no where in His word tolerate Christian states to give
Toleration."

By 1690 it was evident that the reign of the saints was passing. The number and importance of the Boston merchants
had increased with the trade of that port, so that "they had
attained the dignity of an economic and social class which
challenged the supremacy of the Puritan priesthood." [9] By
this time, too, a considerable degree of freedom was allowed
to most Christian sects to conduct their worship as they
pleased, a liberty that was definitely granted them by the
charter of 1691. A wide crack appeared in their temple walls
in 1703, when Governor Dudley quarreled with the Mathers.

From that day the ministers' prestige and power as politicians gradually waned.

The same was true of other colonies with other 'faiths. Maryland's original ecclesiastical set-up gave the Jesuits control over the religious interests of the Maryland palatinate.[10] No marriages were to be considered valid except those performed in chapel by a priest, and all children must be baptized in the conventional manner. The lord of the manor and the priest were to receive the accustomed fees and tithes. All Protestants were considered fit subjects for proselytizing. Such was the plan. But it soon broke down and the priest had to take his place alongside the dissenting parson.

In the beginnings of Virginia the Established Church was equally well seated in the saddle. An edict passed May 10, 1618, declared that "Every person to go to church Sundays and Holy Days or lye neck and heel on the Corps du Guard the night following." [11] Baptism was a public order. "Every person that refuseth to have his children Baptized," says the ancient Virginia law, "when he hath opportunity by a lawful Minister in ye country, shal be fin'd 2000 lbs Toba., ½ to ye parish, ½ to ye informer." [12] Departure from the straight and narrow path of orthodoxy met with swift reaction. When in 1648 Rev. Thomas Harrison, originally of the Church of England, changed his faith to Puritanism and headed a congregation of dissenters, he was promptly banished from Virginia by Governor William Berkeley.

For an indication of how strongly the clergy of Virginia were entrenched in the early days, consider the experience of the rebellious and terrible-tempered Henry Charlton. The aforesaid Henry acquired a dislike for the Rev. William Cotton, rector of Hunger's Parish. He even went so far as to boast in church that "if he had Mr. Cotton without the churchyard, he would kick him over the Palysodes and calling of him black coated raskall." For this offensive remark he was sentenced to build a pair of stocks and sit in them "three several Sabbath days at the Church door during the time of Divine Service and there ask Mr. Cotton's forgiveness publically." [13]

Eventually inertia became the prevailing clerical trait in Virginia. The laity were moderately pious in a placid, undogmatic fashion, attending service quite regularly either from religious impulse or because it was good form or because church services afforded occasions for social comminglings.

Another cause of the cracks appearing in the solid front of the clergy both in New England and the South were the schisms in their own ranks and the multitude of sects that increased with the landing of new settlers from both England and the Continent. "As people increased," said John Winthrop, "sin abounded."

It was not to be expected that the piety and fervor of the average man and woman could be maintained at the white heat which characterized it in the very early days of apostolic simplicity. Life became easier and safer. Frontiers were being pushed back. Comforts, luxuries and conveniences began to soften the fiber of the people in towns. Many were backsliders; indeed, many never darkened the door of a church except on particular occasions.

In both Boston and Philadelphia the populations were many times larger than the total capacity of all of the churches in each of these cities, indicating that many stayed at home on the Sabbath. "In 1690 Boston churches could accommodate only about one-fourth of the town's inhabitants and in 1720, one-fifth. In Philadelphia they seated 1700 out of a population of 10,000." [14] In New Amsterdam, at the time of the surrender to the British, there were only six Dutch ministers for thirteen churches, in 1740, nineteen for sixty-five churches and in 1771, thirty-four for over a hundred.[15]

Even as early as 1704 Madam Knight, in her famous journey alone from Boston to New York, saw signs of relaxed religious and social conventions. Men and women began thinking for themselves and disputing clerical dictums and wrangling over the established theologies. Nor were the clergy of the various sects above stealing each other's sheep.

This condition grew to such an extent that by the first quarter of the eighteenth century both New Englanders and Southerners might be said to have touched their lowest point intellectually and spiritually. The revolt against Calvinism spread in the North and in New York, the Jerseys, Pennsylvania, Maryland and Virginia comfortable contentment blanketed congregations.

Upon religious practice fell a lethargy from which it was not aroused until Jonathan Edwards of Connecticut and the Presbyterians of New Jersey began a stirring in 1726. These were followed by a nation-wide frenzy thirteen years later, when George Whitefield and his revival preachers began dragging their Gospel nets up and down the Atlantic seaboard and "shaking the dry bones" until they showed signs of life. Fire and brimstone sermons were the happy medium of these ghoulish evangelists. They believed the only way to bring hardened sinners into the Kingdom was to scare them out of their seven senses by dangling them over the pit. Their tireless and awesome exhortations in time caused a grave schism in the ministerial ranks between the New Lights, who held to this blood and thunder perambulating revivalism, and the Old Lights, who clung to the more dignified and stationary way of saving souls.

People surely began laughing at preachers of the opposing camp when they read either the saccharine adulation poured upon them in prose and verse by their doting followers, or

the vitriolic condemnations uttered by those who did not
share their views. Words such as those written by Dr. William
Douglas, the Boston wit, who declared that Whitefield and
his disciples, "seemed to be great promoters of impulses,
ecstacies and wantoness between the sexes. Hypocritical professions, vociferations and itineracies are devotional quack-
ery." In return, Gilbert Tennent called the Old Lights,
"hirelings, caterpillars, letter-learned Pharisees, Hypocrites,
varlets, Seed of the Serpent, foolish Builders whom the Devil
drives into the ministry, dead dogs that cannot bark, blind
men, dead men, men possessed of the Devil, rebels and enemies of God."

This sort of ecclesiastical back-chat finally died down, for
by 1744 the frenzied revival had spent its force. The people's
attention was distracted by their own internal troubles.
Churches entered into another somnolent era.

Up to the early years of the eighteenth century, congregations might be scandalized, as we shall see, when some un-
sacerdotal action of their pastor could not be overlooked,
but less than scandal would not permit them to give way to
smiles. When the parson was forced down to the human level
of those to whom he preached, his eccentricities and weaknesses began to be a matter of public comment and record.
To some of these human failings we can now turn our attention.

## Parson's Nose Grows Red

According to the way you look at it, tippling was one of
the curses or one of the commendable amenities of eighteenth
century America, and the minister enjoyed it or suffered
evil from the custom.

The country parson had laid down his supply of hard cider
in the cellar by the time snow began to fly. Cider was the
common, three-times-a-day drink with meals in New Eng-

land and the middle colonies. Rev. Edward Holyoke, president of Harvard, used to lay in thirty or more barrels of cider each Autumn for entertainment. Later in the Winter he drew off part of it and into each barrel poured a bottle of spirits. A month later this blend was ready for bottling.[16] Inventories of the estates of several of the clergy list barrels of cider along with their Sabbath clothes and theological works.

The town minister, following the custom of his contemporaries, had his Claret and Madeira and, if in New England, he further fought chills and impending epidemics with rum. Down South his brothers of the cloth found emergency sustenance in potent peach brandy. In New Jersey he would have recourse to applejack or the equally stimulating brandies distilled from cherries, plums, persimmons or pears. Or he might partake of flip, or, being in a penitential mood, content his thirst with negus. In the country his parishioners would offer the homely fare of "health beer," a Spring tonic concocted from pine chips, pine bark, hemlock needles, roasted corn, dried apple skins, sassafras roots and bran mixed with hops and a little malt. Or, again, it might be currant wine, made lovingly by the hands of one of his pious followers. It is doubtful if the parson, unless he was utterly depraved, ever sank to the level of "Strip and Go Naked," as gin was popularly called.

Since parsons were no less subject to human failings than the male members of their congregations, it was only to be expected that some of them should fall from grace through private tippling or tavern-haunting. One doctor in eighteenth century New Jersey remarked that he knew no fewer than forty immoderate drinkers among his parsonage acquaintances.

The early pastor of a church in Elizabeth Town was obliged to resign his pulpit owing to intemperance.[17] Rev.

Stephen S. Buckingham, pastor of the church at Norwalk, Conn., in 1725-6, had his salary stopped and was dismissed because, "though an excellent preacher, it was said that he drank too much." [18] At Sharon, Conn., Rev. Peter Pratt, the town's first minister, was ordained in 1740 and dismissed five years later for intemperance.[19] In May, 1742, the Virginia Council met at Williamsburg to hear complaints against Rev. James Pedie of Mattaway Parish, for being "guilty of many Immoralities as Drunkeness, Profane Swearing and Lewd and Debauched Actions." He was ordered to be turned out of his parish.[20] Indeed, some of the clergy in the Anglican Church of Virginia led most Bacchic lives, and yet they continued a dignified influence for many generations and exercised commendable tolerance towards dissenters.

Often the congregation connived in the minister's downfall. At Deerfield, Mass., the church was supplied with an oblong flask with a round hole in the top just large enough to admit the small end of a goblet. In this, on Winter mornings, was kept warm the parson's toddy, so that he could have it at just the right temperature after he had finished preaching.

Or the parson might connive with the congregation, as happened once in New Jersey, and no one thought it out of the ordinary.

At Bedminster one Sunday morning the congregation enjoyed an excellent sermon from a supply preacher. On descending the pulpit stairs, the elders gathered around him and, as was the custom, paid his fee on the spot in crisp, half-pound notes. "Gentlemen," said he, "will you walk out with me?" Crossing the road, they entered a tavern and the visiting minister ordered mine host to "set 'em up for the boys." When he and they had had their fill, he handed the tavern-keeper a half-pound note, remarking, "Take it out of this.

I just received it for preaching the sermon." Then they all trooped back to the church and soon began the afternoon service. Doubtless the preacher was even more eloquent then than he had been in the morning.[21]

In New Haven the elders were more considerate: at the installation of a new minister they would arrange with an

TAVERN CLOSE TO CHURCHES AT NEW MILFORD, CONN.

adjacent ordinary to serve drinks to the congregation, for which the church paid the bill. When in 1729 Rev. Edwin Jackson was ordained at Woburn, Mass., among the items of expense were four that aggregated £23—"6 Barrels and a one-half of Cyder, 28 gallons of Wine, 2 Gallons of Brandy and four of Rum, Loaf Sugar, Lime Juice and Pipes."

Often an especially good beer was brewed called Ordination Beer, and in Connecticut it was customary to give an Ordination Ball at the tavern when a new young minister was introduced. Here is the tavern bill for an Ordination Ball in Hartford:

To keeping Ministers

|  | | £ | s. | d. |
|---|---|---|---|---|
| 2 | Mugs toddy | | 2 | 4 |
| 5 | Segars | | 5 | 10 |
| 1 | pint wine | | 3 | 9 |
| 3 | Lodgings | | 9 | |
| 3 | Bitters | | | 9 |
| 3 | Breakfasts | | 3 | 6 |
| 15 | Boles Punch | 1 | | 10 |
| 24 | Dinners | 1 | | 16 |
| 11 | bottles wine | | 3 | 6 |
| 5 | Mugs flip | | 5 | 10 |
| 5 | Boles Punch | | 6 | |
| 3 | Boles Toddy | | 3 | 6 |

Endorsed on the bill was "This is all paid except the Ministers rum."

At Beverly, Mass., when Rev. Joseph McKean was ordained in 1785 we can note from the bill that the congregation was well fortified before the service:

    30 Boles of Punch before the People went to meeting
    10 bottles of wine before they went to meeting
    44 bowles of Punch while at dinner
    18 bottles of wine
     8 Bowles of Brandy
       Cherry wine

The bill also indicates that out of the entire congregation only "6 people drank tea."

House raisings, which the parson often attended to give his blessing, were occasions for long and manful drinking. Judge Sewall of Boston reports taking a ten-quart jug of Madeira to one house raising. When the meeting house was raised, the whole congregation had to celebrate. In July, 1731, the meeting house at Braintree, Mass., being raised, the town provided "Bred cheap, Sugar, Rum, Sider and Bear" for purposes of celebration.[22] Funerals, too, were occasions on which the parson might be tempted to drink more than he could conveniently carry.

Here and there we encounter a minister who had more than passing interest in rum. New Jersey had a parson-distiller, Rev. Jacob G. Green of Morris County, a versatile fellow who served also as lawyer and doctor. His still produced applejack, for which New Jersey has ever been famous. Hartford, Conn., also had its pastor in the trade— Rev. Nathaniel Strong, Jr., pastor of the First Congregational Church from 1744 to 1815. Together with his brother-in-law, Reuben Smith, he operated a distillery. The business failed. Writs of attachment were issued against the property and persons of both of them. Smith fled to New York, but Strong stayed to face the music. Fearing arrest, he never dared stir out of his house except on Sundays. Nevertheless Princeton thought so highly of him that in 1801 it gave him a D.D.[23]

Just what the Anglicans and clergy of other persuasions consumed at their meetings has escaped this historian. The Presbyterians of New Jersey appear to have been a hardy set of topers. In 1792 the Trenton Presbytery met and ran up a bill of 40s. 10d. for beer alone; at another, eight gallons of Lisbon wine and five of spirits were consumed.[24] As most of these Presbyterian ministers were of Scotch or Scotch-Irish birth or descent, we can safely assume that they carried their liquor like gentlemen.

## Mr. Belchoir's Regrettable Lewdness

It has been calculated that in mediaeval times the Church could figure on one out of every seven of the clergy so yielding to the temptations of the flesh as to warrant his being unfrocked. It is not surprising, then, if in this newly settled

country a parson here and there should supply cause for
scandal to his congregation and neighborhood.

In 1686, so Judge Sewall reports in his diary, Thomas
Chiever, pastor of Malden, was accused of "scandalous
breaches of the Third Commandment" and "shameful and
abominable violation of the Seventh Commandment" and
he also used light and obscene expressions in an ordinary at
Salem. He had been ordained only the previous July, so that
it was just as well that the congregation halted him in the
beginning of his career. He failed to show proper repentance
when faced with his sins, and was promptly suspended.[25]

Philadelphia also had its early ecclesiastical scandal. Person Francis Phillips of the Anglican Church, in August,
1715, was arrested for talking too freely of his amorous con-
quests among some of the town's most respectable ladies,
several of whom were married. His arrest and prosecution
produced riots, much violence and numerous broken windows, which caused him to be released. James Logan, secretary of Pennsylvania, says that he "appeared a most vile
man, not only in practice but in conversation and [yet] he
still holds the church and a number of hearers." Later, however, he was dismissed from his pastoral care. This incident
won its niche in Philadelphia history not alone because Mr.
Phillips' boasting of "undue intimacy with some women of
reputation" caused the ructions that followed, but because
he was also challenged to a duel by one Peter Evans, who
resented Phillips' "basely scandalizing a gentlewoman." It
was the first challenge to a duel in Philadelphia history. The
authorities stepped in before the amorous clergyman could
answer it.[26]

Virginia suffered from just such a bad boy and, as things
turned out, he should never have been in the ministry anyhow.

In 1755 there appeared in Virginia, off one of the British

men of war that came to Maryland, a naval chaplain, by name Belchoir. He was accepted socially and entertained with that open-handedness which always characterizes Virginian hospitality. Indeed, he was so moved by the reception that he proposed writing a history of America in which he would set forth the politeness of the people. Slick of tongue and smooth, he impressed his acquaintances to a degree with which he found no difficulty borrowing money from them for his proposed literary venture. Picturing himself as heart-loose and fancy-free, he paid his addresses to several of the young ladies. Eventually he married one of them. She was well born and had a little fortune of her own.

He induced her to hand over most of the money and with this he paid his debts. Then he found it necessary to return to England to arrange his affairs. For his passage she also provided the money, he leaving her enough, of course, to be comfortable while he was away. Shortly after his return he was advertised for stealing a horse, but he managed to talk his young wife out of her suspicions and then convinced her that they should really go on to Philadelphia and sail for England, where all would be well.

Various gentlemen of the neighborhood, among them Col. Harrison, were not so easily taken in. They had received confidential reports on the Rev. Mr. Belchoir. It seems he had been dismissed as naval chaplain for gross wickedness— and also that he had a wife and family living in England! Col. Harrison rode full speed to Philadelphia, rescued the young wife and managed to capture Belchoir for the authorities, who by this time had a warrant out for his arrest. On the return journey Belchoir escaped and, with two ruffians, tried to break into the inn where Harrison and the young wife were staying. Harrison managed to save himself from assassination and the girl from capture. The disillusioned miss was finally brought home in safety. As for Belchoir, he doubtless soon afterwards went the way of evil flesh.[27]

### "The Amorous Mr. Batchiler"

It was customary among early New England chroniclers, when setting down any scandalous falls from grace, to recount every fact and rumor in order that they might draw their moral, which invariably was to show God's vengeance on sinners. Consequently, before we recount what led to the downfall of one naughty old parson, let us find how this sinner felt the avenging hand of Providence. "In his time," runs the account, "his house and nearly all his substance was consumed by fire." Now we are ready for the story.

"This year (1641) Mr. Stephen Batchelour, pastor of the church at Hampton (having suffered much from the hands of the bishops about the ceremonies) when he was eighty years of age was complained of for soliciting the chastity of his neighbor's wife. Being dealt withal for this offense, he denied it (as he told the woman he would) and complained to the authorities of the man and woman for slandering him, yet was forced soon after, by the terror of his conscience, to confess it openly in church and for the scandal of the same, he was cast out of the church and two years after, upon his repentance, he was released of his sentence." [28]

Either Mr. Batchiler was emulating the career of the "Olde, Olde Very Olde Mr. Parr" of a previous chapter or, having had a way with him, he was caught in the meshes of his own senile folly. He was not the first clergyman to fall victim to the adoring women of his parish nor will he be the last. His kind has suffered—and enjoyed—pious and ardent ladies ever since Teckla pursued St. Paul.

There is much that is appealing about Mr. Batchiler. His story, as it unfolds, reveals him to have been a man of great courage and vitality and a good shepherd so long as he could resist the temptation of being a ram in the women's fold.

On June 5, 1632, the *William & Francis,* after a voyage of eighty-eight days, landed Rev. Stephen Batchiler, together with six of his followers, "mostly daughters and sons-in-law." He was seventy-one years of age, a tall, white-haired, stalwart warrior who, having brought the displeasure of the English bishops upon himself, was forced to seek sanctuary in Holland, whence he sailed for New England. During the long voyage, he "found it necessary to have 'spiritual understandings' with almost every woman on board." It was not to be unexpected, then, that before he disembarked upon the New England shore, a young woman should kiss him fervently and he return the kiss.

His hope in coming to New England was to found a church, a "Holy House without ceremonies," completely freed from control or influence of the state. As church and state in the Massachusetts Bay Colony at that time were inseparable, he found himself thwarted from the first. In the next nineteen years he lived a busy and turbulent life.

First he went to Saugus, the present Lynn, and formed a little congregation. Women flocked to hear him pray and preach. Four months later he was arraigned before court at Boston and forbidden to exercise his calling "until some scandles be removed." Driven from Lynn, he went to Ipswich, and once again women flocked to his church. That Spring, 1636, he started out to found a congregation and community of state-free people in the wilderness on Cape Cod between Sandwich and Eastham. Without money or other resources, he led forth his rebellious followers. While they were building homes, Stephen lived in an Indian wigwam as an example to his people. In the same wigwam dwelt a beautiful Indian woman who, he said was "anxious to learn Christian ways." Even his sons-in-law smiled at the old man.

The settlement failed and Stephen led his disillusioned followers on foot to Newburyport. Here the men of the congregation would not receive him because of the "scandles," and so he went on to Hampton, where he remained and apparently prospered for a time. Once again women flocked to him. It was during this Hampton period, in 1641, that he was charged with the aforesaid soliciting the chastity of his neighbor's wife, from which charge, as we have read, he was finally released.

Soon afterwards his house in Hampton burned and he lost all his possessions. He tried preaching in other churches but they would have nothing of him. Troubles began to pile up. His wife died—his second—and he returned to Sandwich, where he took a third, although he was now almost ninety years old. A young woman she was, with starry eyes and "beautiful as the dawn." Scarcely had their first days together ended than Stephen discovered that his wife Mary was an adulteress, she being with child. The poor old fellow applied for a divorce. After considering the circumstances and his previous record, the court decreed that "Mr. Batchiler and his wife shall lye together as man and wife . . . and if either desert one another, then hereby the court doth order that the marshal shall apprehend both the said Mr. B. and Mary his wife, and bring them forthwith to Boston."

What a cruel, cruel sentence! Completely broken, and yet defiant, Mr. Batchiler set out on foot for Boston, where he boarded a ship for England. Just before it sailed, he learned that the court had also ordered his starry-eyed Mary, adulteress though she undoubtedly was, to "receive forty stripes save one, at the first town meeting held at Kittery, 6 weeks after her delivery and be branded with the letter A."

For Stephen that chapter was ended. Once in the old

country, even though he had never been divorced from Mary, he married for the fourth time. She, again, was a young wife, and he lived with her happily until, at the age of 101, his soul "escaped even as a bird out of the snare of the fowler." [29]

## Parson Goes A-wooing

Since we have begun with a wooing parson, let us pass on to another and more pleasant matrimonial event. It concerns Rev. Nathaniel Appleton. From 1717 to 1781 he served as pastor of the church at Cambridge, Mass. He was a fellow of Harvard, an able preacher, a profound theologian, a man of quick wit and ready resourcefulness—indeed, quite a space could be devoted to his accomplishments. For our purposes, however, we shall limit reports on him to the manner of his wooing.

When a young man, just new to the ministry, he fell in love, as do so many fledgling parsons. The only hurdle was another, who was in love with the same young lady. One day, when Appleton rode to her house, he found his rival's horse tied to the fence. He tied his own horse securely, loosened the other, and giving it a sharp cut with his whip, sent it flying down the road. Then he went inside and remarked to his rival that he had just seen a horse, apparently running away, going full speed down the road. Could it, by any chance, be his? The other suitor rushed out. Appleton, now having the field to himself, stayed, pressed his suit, proposed and was accepted.

Had Mr. Appleton lived today and were it a car instead of a horse he sent careering down the road, the police would probably have something to say about the case, even though he might plead that everything's fair in love. As it is, the story has followed him down all these years.[30]

Of parson's wives who caused distress, apart from Mr.

Batchiler's, the obscure annals of Early American history seem to be particularly silent. From the grab-bag of the past we can extract only one: Imagine the blushes, the explanations, the private chastisement inflicted by the Rev. Jans of New Amsterdam when he learned that Annetje, his wife, had been hauled into court charged "with lifting her petticoat too high in crossing the street!" [31]

## Eccentrics in the Pulpit

Then, as now, the parson found his most ardent expression in his sermon. A New England congregation would feel itself cheated if the minister did not preach through two full turns of the hour glass. The labor of preparing these discourses—the study, the meditation that preceded them, the sheer physical effort required to write them down—must have been prodigious. There was the Rev. Joshua Moody of Portsmouth, N. H., who was finally laid to rest at the age of sixty-five in 1697. His ministry covered roughly forty years. In that time he prepared and wrote over 4,000 different sermons. The ninety-third volume of his manuscript sermons, the last of which was numbered 4,070, was dated nine years before his death, so that his total accomplishment may have mounted to 4,500 discourses.[32]

Some parsons were not as conscientious and generous with their outpourings. Now and then a grim ministerial sense of duty would drive a preacher to fantastic repetitions. One New England minister, on being called to a new charge, preached the same sermon three Sundays in succession. After this third delivery, a committee called on him with the pious hope that he "sing unto the Lord a new song." He replied, "I see no evidence that the one sermon I have preached has produced any effect. When the people begin to practice it, I shall be glad to preach another." [33] Just what the congregation did then, history does not tell; at least their soul-driving preacher afforded a lively topic for conversation.

Much of the same sort of harper on one string was the Rev. Samuel Moody of York, Me. A grand old specialist in gloom, for nearly half a century he preached sermons of the fire and brimstone type, such as "The Doleful State of the Damned, especially such as go to Hell from under the Gospel." What's more, he had them printed and people bought them, which must have convinced this preacher that he knew what his congregation wanted.[34] Indeed, no preacher could attain popularity unless he proclaimed the anger of God and the doctrine of terror. The subject naturally produced "a sublime and impressive style of oratory." Congregations relished their language of menace and apparently preferred a spiritual pessimist to a heavenly optimist.

While most of the sermons preached in seventeenth and eighteenth century America were serious in the extreme, occasionally a preacher did permit himself the indulgence of a smile in the pulpit. Such was the New England minister who found his best apples stolen. At the next service he informed the congregation that the Yellow Sweets in the northeast corner of his orchard would be ripe the following week and he begged those who had been in the habit of helping themselves to delay their pilfering. This put an end to that prædial larceny.[35]

Or, in later years, he might indulge in a witty introduction to catch the interest of his hearers, a type of sermon-beginning that even the most laudable of preachers, including Henry Ward Beecher, have found useful. Rev. Matthew Clarke, a rough, burly, independent Scotch-Irishman, had pulpit tricks that would bring him congregations even today. Once he announced his text as from Philippians 4:13 and he began with the words, " 'I can do all things.' Aye, can ye, Paul? I'll bet a dollar on that." Thereupon he produced a

Spanish dollar and placed it beside his pulpit Bible. Then, assuming a surprised look, he continued, "Stop! Let's see what else Paul says: 'I can do all things through Christ which strengthens me.' Aye, sae can I, Paul. I draw my bet." And he pocketed the dollar.[36] After such an introduction, any congregation would be straining its ears.

The congregation at York, Me., on the other hand, had reason for straining its eyes. Rev. Samuel Moody, who for half a century preached the damnation sermons, was followed by his son Joshua, who has come down the ringing grooves of time as "Handkerchief Moody." Midway in his career he fell into a melancholy. Instead of lightening his burden with an occasional nip, as did some of his fellow parsons, he developed a pronounced phobia: he wanted no one to see his face. Whenever he appeared in public he wore a double fold of crêpe knotted above his forehead and hanging down to his chin. He would mount the pulpit and preach with his back to the congregation, and when he turned to give the benediction, his features were covered with the crêpe.[37]

Naturally he grew less and less popular at weddings, christenings and social gatherings. People avoided him on the road and so he kept to his house. He would walk alone at night on the beach or go prowling around the graveyard. Nevertheless, his life was long, kind and useful. He died in 1770. After he was gone the story came out, through a fellow minister who came to give him spiritual consolation at the end. Inadvertently he had shot a friend. The town believed he had been killed by a roving Indian and never for once suspected the minister, who feared the censure of his townsmen and the blame and anguish of the friend's parents. It was then that he vowed never again to look openly upon the face of mankind. . . . Just before his body was committed to the earth, the clergyman lifted the veil: "Handkerchief Moody's" face was serene and majestic.

After considering these eccentric preachers and scores of others equally queer, one wonders which was the more eccentric—the parson or the congregation which, Sunday after Sunday, tolerated such unaccountable quirks. Possibly the people just received them dumbly as part of the Lord's visitation on them for their sins.

Any natural phenomenon, of course, was attributed to the Almighty's wrath or mercy, according to its nature. But it took a grim sense of humor for the congregation of Hamden, Conn., to sit through a two hour sermon by Rev. Abraham Alling on that day when the temperature was close to zero both inside and outside the church. He chose for his text the 17th verse of the 147th Psalm: "Who can stand before His cold?"

In his "Progress of Dulness," John Trumbull pictured the country parson as he had come to be after the Revolution, after the tides of revivals had died down and preaching was a humdrum affair. He

> starves on sixty pounds a year,
> And culls his text and tills his farm,
> Does little good and little harm;
> On Sundays, in his best array,
> Deals forth the dulness of the day;
> And while above he spreads his breath
> The yawning audience nods beneath.

## Clerical Wit

There is probably no drearier wasteland in which an investigator can find himself than those minute and endless chronicles of religions and churches in New England. Only once in a great while does he stumble across a refreshing oasis. That is why, when one does encounter them, they stand out in such startling proportions. That is why it is such a relief to reach the Rev. Mather Byles, the leading wag and wit among the hundreds of New England preachers.

Born in Boston in 1706, Byles was called to the pastorate of the Hollis Street Church when he was twenty-seven years old, and he held that charge for the next forty-three years. A dramatic preacher, he turned a properly serious face to his congregation on Sunday and on the other six days of the week was a chronic wit and practical joker.

His foil and counter-wit was Joseph Green, Byles' exact contemporary. A Harvard graduate, nevertheless he rose to distinction and wealth by distilling rum; and he used his spare moments thinking up jokes and witticisms or writing poems that caricatured the foibles of his fellow townsmen. He is especially remembered by his "Entertainment for a Winter's Evening," a long poem in which he told off the doings in staid Boston. At one time Byles and Green carried on a wit contest that kept Boston on the verge of frantic laughter for several weeks. Their mots and puns ran through Boston's homes and taverns like fire through stubble.

The more grim-visaged clergy looked on Byles with disapproving eyes, as being no compliment to the cloth, but so brilliant a preacher and so erudite a scholar did he prove to be Sunday after Sunday, filling every seat in his church, that we suspect envy may have tinctured the clergy's disapproval. A local rhymster describes Byle as:

> There's punning Byles provokes our smiles,
> A man of stately parts,
> He visits folks to crack his jokes
> Which never mends their hearts.

> With strutting gait and wig so great,
> He walks along the streets,
> And throws out wit or what's like it,
> To everyone he meets.

MATHER BYLES, Sr.
1707-1788    COPLEY

REV. MATHER BYLES, PUNNING PARSON

Byles did finally encounter public disapproval when, at the beginning of the Revolution, he continued praying for King George. The authorities promptly arrested him. He was tried and sentenced, first to prison and then to exile to England. All of this he took with good grace and a steady flow of jokes. After the public temper had cooled down, his sentence was commuted to house arrest and, day after day, the old wag in his great wig and with strutting gait marched up and down before his house, gun on shoulder, guarding himself! [38]

### Belligerent Ministers

Though he was by no means a wit, Byles' Tory counterpart in Virginia, Rev. Jonathan Boucher, managed to keep his congregations thrilled. A clergyman of outstanding abilities, a pastor who never wearied in laboring for his flock, a persistent improver of the countryside, Boucher was loyal to his King. On entering Holy Orders as a clergyman of the Church of England, he had taken an oath of allegiance to the Crown. He held cures in Carolina, Maryland and Virginia.

When the waves of revolutionary sentiment began breaking around him, he stoutly assumed the immovable posture of King Canute on the Southampton sands. Though constantly threatened for his Loyalist preaching and praying, each Sunday for six months he discoursed to his congregation with a pair of loaded pistols lying beside the pulpit cushion. What a merry scene that must have been! Even in the most solemn moments of the service, imagine how the congregation felt at the thought of those pistols! It may have been merely Mr. Boucher's playful interpretation of attempting to take the Kingdom of Heaven by violence.

He warned his congregation that he would repel violence with violence. One Sunday a number of his parishioners prevented him from preaching by the simple ruse of surrounding him, whereupon the doughty parson grabbed the leader by the collar, pushed a pistol in his stomach and, under guard of his enemies, he solemnly marched out of church! [39]

Consider also how amused or scandalized the congregation of the Episcopal Church at Amwell, N. J., must have been when it entered to find a hangman's noose dangling over the pulpit. This was the patriot's warning to the rector, Rev. William Frazer, to cease praying for the royal family. For a time he heeded the warning—by suspending worship in his church—but so prudent was his conduct and lovely his character that, as soon as peace was declared, he re-opened his church and resumed his ministry with generous acceptance. [40]

At Redding, Conn., Rev. John Beach, Anglican minister, was fired at while praying for the King. He calmly rose and preached from the text, "Fear not them which kill the body but are not able to kill the soul." The bullet is now imbedded in a memorial tablet to him placed near the pulpit in Christ Church, where the attempted assassination took place. [41]

Dr. Samuel Peters, rector of Hebron, Conn., was presented with a coat of tar and feathers and permitted to go to England for his health after he persisted in Royalist preaching. However, he took a sweet revenge: on the coming of peace he returned to America and in 1829 published his "History of Connecticut," which is so packed with errors and exaggerations (including a discourse on the Blue Laws) as to require at least a tablespoonful of salt for every page.

Recourse to arms and violence were not confined to Tory parsons. It could be a way of dissolving the clamors of a dissatisfied congregation, as Rev. Johannes Henricus Goetschius discovered. A Swiss, born in 1717, Goetschius came to this country in 1738. As a minister he soon gained a reputation for being an erudite and clear speaker with an objectionable abruptness. This failing developed into a pronounced eccentricity as the years passed. For ten years he held a charge on Long Island, and then went to preach in churches at Hackensack, N. J., where he entered on the stormiest period of his ministry, from which he was to find little or no peace until death released him in 1774. On one occasion, anticipating forcible resistance to his entering the church, he buckled on a sword and, thus armed, marched into the edifice and preached his sermon.

But Goetschius was accustomed to being barred out of church. At the time there was raging a violent argument in the Dutch Reformed body between those who held that the church in America should be autonomous and those who clung to the control of Holland. Once, in Poughkeepsie, he and others of the American Coetus Party came to ordain a preacher. They found that the Conferente, or opposing party, had seized the church and barred the doors. The ceremony had to be held in the open under a tree.[42]

## Convenient Visions

The vision or trance, whereby those who experience it believe that Divine Wisdom is revealed to them, has been a common experience through all ages of religious history. St. Paul on the road to Tarsus, Buddha under the Bo-tree, John Wesley walking through the fields, St. Francis receiving the stigmata—the list could be continued at great length. Since this is so, we would not set down the experience of the young William Tennet as exceptional did it not have an echo that might be called providential.

William Tennet, one of the sons of a father of the same name, studied for the ministry, as did his three brothers, at the "Log College" of Neshaminy, Pa., founded by the elder

Tennet in 1726. During his studies William Jr. fell into a trance. He fainted and apparently was dead. All efforts to revive him having proved unsuccessful, he was pronounced as departed from this world. Neighbors were invited to the funeral. Among them was one who seemed skeptical: he insisted on inspecting the body. Under one arm he felt a faint pulsation. A doctor was called and the body was placed in a warm bed. Three days later signs of life appeared. For six weeks young Tennet remained in a desperately weak state and did not recover full health for over a year. That he should live to become one of Whitefield's most ardent supporters in the Great Awakening and that he held the pastorate of the First Presbyterian Church at Freehold, N. J., for almost forty-four years, until his death in 1777, may seem little short of a miracle.[43]

We can now leave Mr. Tennet and proceed to the confidence man and horse thief *par excellence* of eighteenth century America.

## Tom Bell and the Parson

One day in the first third of the eighteenth century there landed at Newport, R. I., from Barbados, a merry andrew named Tom Bell. A New Englander, he had gone to Harvard for a short time and thereafter chose the easy way. He posed as the son of prominent men in other provinces and managed to gain both hospitality and support by this deceit. For a time he lived in Barbados, where he passed as Gilbert Burnett, son of Governor Burnett. For this the Barbadian authorities laid the lash generously across his bare shoulders, made him sit in the stocks as a public example and would have branded him on the cheeks had not Governor Byng relented enough to give him a reprieve on condition he left the island by the first boat.

He had a quick wit, an ingratiating manner and practi-

JONATHAN BOUCHER, M.A.

REV. JONATHAN BOUCHER, GUN-TOTING PARSON

cally no morals at all. Arrived in New England again, he wandered through those provinces and New York, Pennsylvania and the Jerseys, living by the lucrative profession of horse-stealing. Finally, on his return to Newport *incognito,* where his purpose was to redeem some fine clothes that lay there attached, he was recognized and, while attempting to escape from someone from whom he had gotten money under false pretenses, was arrested. For a time he amused himself in jail writing his reminiscences, which he promised would be of more than ordinary interest, since he had managed to live and prosper under no fewer than five aliases—Winthrop, DeLancey, Jekyl, Wendell and Francis Hutchinson. Eventually he departed from the Newport jail, either by escape or judicial clemency, for we next find him in New Jersey.[44]

It happened that one day he was strolling down the main street of Princeton when he was accosted by John Stockton, prominent citizen, who addressed him as the Rev. Mr. Rowland and said he was so glad to hear he was to preach in such and such a town. Tom's brain worked like greased lightning. In a few days, garbed as a preacher, he approached that town, rode up to the best house and introduced himself as Mr. Rowland, who had come to fill the pulpit the following Sabbath. As they had heard Mr. Rowland was famous for his sermons, the family was immensely flattered that he should choose to stay with them. For the remainder of the week they offered him the most generous hospitality.

Finally Sunday morning came. His host provided Tom with his best horse and the family all started off for church. Midway there, Tom felt in his pocket and was distressed to find that he had left his sermon at home. He would just ride back himself and pick it up. No, they mustn't bother! He knew exactly where he had left it! He would be gone only a few minutes! So the family stopped and waited. And waited.

And meantime Tom, putting spurs to the fine horse, rode directly to the house, rifled it, and made his escape.

When the owner discovered his loss, he swore a warrant out for the real Mr. Rowland, who had to suffer the indignity of being indicted for the theft of the horse. At the trial, Rev. William Tennet and two others swore that Rowland had been with them in Pennsylvania on that Sunday. They, in turn, were charged with perjury. The trial began to take a nasty aspect. Fortunately two reputable citizens appeared. They corroborated Tennet's statement and further explained that the reason for their appearance in court was that each of them had had a vision of Mr. Tennet in trouble, that the Lord directed them to the court—and here they were. The judge accepted their testimony without batting an eyelash.

Tom Bell was always in scrapes and always managed to evade the law. In Philadelphia he was once advertised as having gone aboard a boat at New Castle on the pretext of being a merchant interested in buying some goods, and while there having stolen clothes, including the captain's red breeches! In New Jersey, again, he was apprehended as being one of a gang of counterfeiters. He had successfully passed as parson, doctor, lawyer, merchant and seaman.[45]

The last heard of him was in 1746, when the *New York Weekly Post Boy* for September 15th of that year reported Tom as having enlisted under Captain Stevens in one of the New Jersey companies and having gone with them to Albany to join the Canada expedition.

# II

## FUN AT THE STEEPLE HOUSE

### Black Sabbaths

For many years New England struggled to maintain its three cardinal virtues—thrift, chastity and Sabbath keeping. As the first is practised even in this generation we can pass lightly over it, leave the second to be arrived at in good time and go directly to the third. To what extent was the New England Sunday, or Sunday in any colonial section where Calvinism held sway, an actual "Black Sabbath"?

It has been pictured as twenty-four hours of unremitting penitential gloom, during which congregations, from the oldest member to the youngest, were subjected to endless discourses on theology and the pernicious effects of sin, a long day when all household work was suspended, when games were forbidden, laughter prohibited and the ordinary movements stilled.

We propose to show that in these dark clouds came some bright rifts, that there were moments and cause for laughter, times when a church service was exciting and often amusing. In short, that there was fun at the Steeple House, as the Quakers used to call a church.

### Churches and Pews

Services were first held in private houses and then, as the new village got under way and the people were sheltered, a meeting house was erected. This was probably a primitive affair at first, designed to serve as church, civic and governmental center and school. It was often little more than a clapboarded or shingled barn, or only a log cabin with a window at front and back and one on each side. The builders of these meeting houses took in earnest Calvin's injunction against seeking the church of God in the beauty of buildings.

In some places dirt served for floor. Furnished with the rudest sort of benches, any sort of gathering could be held here. Our forefathers believed in keeping their meeting houses at work: they weren't the refined edifices of today into which people gather only at stated times and in their Sunday best clothes. At first no provision was made for heating and none for lighting. Church-going was a daylight affair and in Winter a chilly one. Samuel Sewall reports a very cold Sunday in Boston when "the Sacramental Bread is frozen pretty hard and rattles sadly as broken into the Plates." [1]

The next step was to add two steeples, one for the "bell-free" and the other for a watch tower. Before the refinement of bells, the village folk were called to worship by the beat of a drum. In 1651 New London, Conn., paid Peter Blatchford "to beat the drum all saboth days, training days and town publique meetings," the sum of £3 to be paid out of the town rates.[2] In another New England village the town drummer was recompensed for his arduous drubbings with pork.

Later came a floor and, as further refinement, box pews. One was first built for the minister's family directly under the pulpit, and then other villagers were allowed to build their own so long as they conformed with the specifications set forth at town meeting. Moreover, people sat where they were placed and there wasn't any argument about it. The New London town fathers held a meeting to seat the congregation and "Mercy Jiggles is by vote seated in the third seat on the woman's side where she is ordered by the town to sit." [3]

As the village grew, the meeting house would be enlarged. A gallery would be erected at one end and steps up to it. Here the benches from below would be set up again as the floor filled with pews.

So much for the day when

> Each man equipped on Sunday morn
> With Psalm book, shot and powder horn,

conducted his family to meeting. Up in the lookout a watchman kept an eye open for Indians who might think to raid the village while the townspeople were at worship.

In the outlying sections of other colonies, to which the Established Church sent missionaries, it was not unusual for the parson to find, at the beginning of the eighteenth century, that "an old broken house is sufficient to keep us from the injuries of the weather" and one reported that he had "no surplice, no Bible and no Communion Table." [4] The first church built at Jamestown before 1608 was a rude hut, "covered with rafts, sedge and earth," and fortunately it burned eight months after being built or it probably would have tumbled down.[5]

In New Netherlands and Dutch New Jersey the first churches were octagonal in form. The men were seated around the wall and the women in orderly rows in the center. Above their heads was a wooden ceiling with large rafters. The walls were plastered and meant to be white. The pulpit stood at the north end, shaped like a wine glass and surmounted by a sounding board.[6] Eventually these gave way to square or approximately square buildings in the English style.

As villages grew larger and farms extended deeper into

the wilderness, going to the morning and afternoon services and coming home consumed most of the day. The congregation brought their own luncheons, and people living near the church and at the tavern kept large fires going in Winter, where members of the congregation could come indoors and get warm and eat their meal before returning to the icy church for the afternoon service. In Summer various respectable villagers were allowed to open food booths near the church. Later, for the accommodation of those who came a great distance, there were erected close to the meeting house little shelters known as Sabaday or Sabbath Houses. They were divided into two rooms, one for men, the other for women, and here fireplaces were kept well stoked in Winter. These were the prototypes of our present-day parish houses.

In New Amsterdam, and also later in British times, pious church-goers took refuge in Winter in taverns between services. In 1648 Dominie Backerus complained that his hearers rushed off to the tap houses as soon as he finished preaching.[7] Perhaps this was a bit cavalier of the dominie for, after all, the first revenue to be relinquished by the Dutch West India Company was the excise on wine, beer and spirits, and Stuyvesant insisted that the salaries of ministers should be paid from it. In Boston it was customary for many families, after sermon-time, to eat their usual Sunday meal at an inn, thereby saving the good housewife from breaking the Sabbath by cooking. At an early date Boston recognized the need for having the tavern close to the meeting house: in 1650 John Vyall was granted "Libertie to keep a house of common entertainment if the Countie Court Consent, provided he keeps it nere the new Meeting House."

### Solemn Saturday and Giddy Sunday Nights

The Sabbath began at sundown on Saturday and ended at sundown on Sunday. Saturday saw the housewife busy cooking supplies for the next twenty-four hours. The Indian meal was put on to simmer. This she served hot as hasty pudding or supawn that night and then it was fried and served with molasses for Sunday breakfast.

At dusk on Saturday night the household settled down and a religious calm was supposed to pervade the family. But even in the grimmest of Calvinistic days human nature could stand only just so much suppression and then it must blow off steam. Sunday night finally arrived. The sun went down. Children rushed out to see if three stars could be distinctly seen—the sign that the Sabbath was ended. Then old and young alike would fairly burst. People tended "to Meet together and to be Merry and Vain." Some were "guilty of more Sin that Night than on any other Night."

At the opening of the eighteenth century Connecticut fathers were so shocked at the way the young people cut up on Sunday nights that they decreed all such should be subject to a fine or two hours in the stocks if they met together on Sabbath evenings either indoors or out, even though they had attended services that had occupied most of the day.[8] New York Friends were shocked at the goings-on and complained that their children lacked the "Primitive Zeal, Piety and Heat found in the Harts of their parents." [9] Still, in spite of decrees and fines and threats and sighings, Sunday night became the gayest night of the week in New England villages and New York towns. Young men and maidens went merry-making and visiting and their elders gossiped in homes and taverns.

Saturday night remained holy for a long time, however. Even as late as Revolutionary days Blanchard, a French officer, reports that "some pleasant dames, rather jolly souls, whom I went to see in Providence, would not even sing on Saturday evening." He does not say what they did on Sunday evening. For some that, too, was holy.

At Norwich, Conn., in 1720, Samuel Sabin, who feared either his conscience or the authorities, presented himself to the justice and "complaineth against himself that on the last Sabbath day at night he and John Olmbis went on to Wawewas hill to visit their relations and were home late, did no harm and he fears may be a transgressor of the law and if it be, he is very sorry for it and don't allow himself in unreasonable night walking." [10]

Every effort was made to enforce strict Sabbath observance. In tolerant New York in 1738 a watchman marched boys off to the guardhouse for playing bat and ball during the time of divine service, but was assaulted by them for his pains. In Boston, as late as 1777, persons found walking on the streets would be advised to head for the nearest church. While the British occupied Boston, officers and men used to ride and play games on the Common, much to the horror of church-going natives [11] and, later, British prisoner officers who attempted to travel on Sunday were taken up and confined.[12]

Blanchard tells of some French officers who started playing cards on a Sunday in Boston. The landlady burst into the room and tried to snatch the cards. On another Sunday a Frenchman who lived with him began playing a flute, whereupon the people gathered around and would have mobbed him had not the landlord made him stop playing.[13] Allies or no allies, Bostonians were going to have their Sabbath Day kept holy! Another French officer stated, "In Boston one meets nobody on the streets on Sundays and if you happen on some one you dare not stop and talk with

him. You cannot go into a house without finding everyone
reading the Bible." [14]

Laws for Sunday observance lasted a long time—on the
books. By 1653 Boston decreed its strict regulation—no person might travel, cook, clean house or make beds. Three
years later constables were required to hail before the authorities any young person or others found "idyling or playing" outside meeting houses during the time of public worship. However, by 1680 the tendency to disregard the Sabbath was increasing.

Charleston, S. C., in 1712 declared that everyone must attend church on Sundays or pay a 5s. fine. All sports and
pastimes were forbidden and taverns open only to lodgers.
Constables and church wardens patrolled the streets and
investigated punch houses during time of divine service to
rout out idle and ungodly drinkers. This must have caused
these idle and ungodly drinkers to break out into even un-
godlier remarks, seeing that Charleston's famous church, St.
Philip's, was originally built by a tax of 2d. per gallon on
all the rum and ardent spirits imported in 1670!

Vermont pursued its Sabbatarian ways up to the threshold of the nineteenth century. The old law still held good
that whosoever was guilty of any rude, profane or unlawful
conduct on the Lord's Day, in word or action, by clamorous
discourses, shouting, hallooing, screaming, running, riding,
dancing or jumping, was to be fined 40s. and whipped upon
the naked back, not to exceed ten stripes.

The most curious of all Sabbath prejudices was the refusal
of some New England ministers to baptize children born on
Sunday, due to the belief that these children were conceived
on Sunday—an obvious and gross infringement of the Sabbath law as regards amusements and enjoyments. A certain
parson especially was insistent in his refusal—used to talk
and preach about it. In the end Fate played him a scurvy

trick: his wife was brought to bed of twins on the Lord's
Day! New England went into convulsions of laughter. He
publicly confessed what he believed to be his error and
eventually baptized both his offspring.[15]

It was the duty of the tithingman in the New England
village to see that all attended church and to watch those
who traveled on the Sabbath. In Milton, Mass., this job of
ecclesiastical constable was once held by a saucy-tongued
Irishman. Late one Sabbath afternoon he found Governor
Hutchinson entering the town and accosted him, "Your Excellence, it is my business when people travel on the Sabbath
to know where they have been and where they are going."
The governor answered, "Friend Smith, I have been to
Boston and attended my own church both parts of the day
and have heard two very fine sermons." To this Smith replied, "Faith, sir, the best thing you can do is to go home
and make use of them." [16]

In spite of these barren meeting houses, in spite of the
lengthy sermons, in spite of the Sabbath day and night re-
strictions, wasn't there anything to relieve the tension?

Evidence aplenty and accumulative could be cited to prove
that the people were as quick to break the Sabbath prohibition as they are to break any sumptuary law today. The
Black Sabbath is part of the New England legend, but it
rarely was as black as it has been painted. Within a few
years after the first fine frenzy of the early settlers had
slowed down to a steady pulsation of habit, and when drib-
bling in of luxury and ease lessened public and private fear,
and when fresh batches of settlers began landing, then the
Sabbath took on less grim and menacing proportions. It
developed amenities and it offered diversions from the strict
routine of church services.

There was, to name one, the pretty ritual of the minister's
entrance into the New England meeting house. The congre-

gation first filed in and took their seats, women on one side, men on the other, for worship in those days was strictly bisexual. When all were seated, the parson entered. The entire congregation rose. He proceeded up the aisle at a slow and stately pace, bowing first to the ladies, who curtsied, then to the men, who returned the bow. New London saw two generations of clerical processions. The parsonage was close to the church. Rev. Gurdon Saltonstall was the minister. When the drum began rolling, the procession started from the parsonage to the meeting house: first Mr. Saltonstall and his wife, "with a slow, majestic step," followed by his children, four sons and four daughters, marshalled in order, with the servants bringing up the rear. His son, who bore his father's name, made a much lengthier procession, since he had fourteen sons and daughters.[17]

## The Scarlet Letter Girls

During the seventeenth century and well into the eighteenth, congregations could not be sure what was going to happen during church services. It was customary in those days to make public confessions of one's sins, especially one's infringement of the Seventh Commandment. These were made either voluntary or at the direction of the court or church fathers and were carried through not unlike the way Oxford Group devotees today reveal their shortcomings *coram populo*. This practice was as common in Friends' Meetings as among the stern Calvanists. It was also customary for the clerk or pastor to make a record of the confessions. Some of these are still preserved.

Samuel Sewall, after he had sat on the witchcraft cases in Salem, had distinct twinges of conscience and caused to be read in church a general confession so stating. But then, Samuel was always feeling twinges of conscience.[18] We do

not find him, however, publicly confessing to sins of the
flesh, though doubtless as he sat at service he listened to
others unburdening their consciences in this respect. As late
as 1750 a Boston group of mechanics, who formed the New
North Church, insisted that any member who fell from
grace (usually sexually) was to stand before the congregation
in a white robe while the minister read his accusation.[19]

Male confessions were less common than female. Often
both the man and the woman stood before the congregation.
Here are two from the records of the Braintree, Mass.,
church:

"January, 1728. Joseph P. and Lydia his wife, made a confession before the Church which was well accepted for the
sin of Fornication committed with each other before marriage."

"September 28, 1729. Elizabeth M—— made a confession
before the whole congregation for the sin of fornication
which was accepted by the Church."

"The offending female stood in the broad aisle by the
partner of her guilt. If they had been married, the declaration of the man was silently assented to by the woman." The
pastor's records of the Braintree Church from March 2, 1683,
to August 22, 1753, show seventeen couples or individuals
publicly confessing fornication before marriage—not too bad
a record when one remembers that human nature was no
different then than it is today and that bundling was a common pre-marriage custom. One wonders how many others
there were who sinned and didn't confess. In the records of
this particular church two sets of couples were Negroes, who
were aping their betters. One sinner, Elizabeth Morse, after
confessing fornication as above, came back seven years later
and added an additional charge against herself of two bastard
children!

Records of the church at Groton, Mass., show that in fourteen years, out of 200 persons owning the baptismal covenant, sixty-six confessed to committing fornication before marriage. In the church at Dedham, the twenty-five years before 1791 brought out one confession a year and, in the ten years following, fourteen made "post-nubial confessions of antemarital relations."

The vivid details of one of these confessions is set down in the handwriting of Rev. Moses Fiske, pastor of Braintree Church, as he wrote it in his records on March 2, 1683:

"Temperance, the daughter of Brother F——, now the wife of John B——, having been guilty of the sin of Fornication with him that is now her husband, was called forth in the open Congregation and presented a paper containing a full acknowledgement of her great sin and wickedness— publically bewayled her disobedience to parents, pride, unprofitableness under the means of grace, as the cause that might provoke God to punish her with sin and warning all to take heed of such sin, begging the Church's prayers that God would humble her and give a sound repentance. Which confession being read, after some debate, the brethren did generally if not unanimously judge that she out to be admonished; and accordingly she was solemnly admonished of her great sin, which was spread before her in diverse particulars and charged to search her own heart wayes and to make a thorough work in her Repentance."

Nothing is said as to what happened to John B——. Did poor little Temperance have to take all the blame for their intimacy? Even the lurid pages of the Inquisition can furnish no more revolting scene than this torture of a young girl.

By no means was this custom confined to New England churches: as late as 1797 the records of a Pennsylvania Friends' Meeting reveal a wife acknowledging fornication [20] and at the church in Paxton, Pa., several public confessions of this same breach were made in which both the man and the woman appeared before the congregation.[21]

Illegitimacy so worried the church fathers of New England (and the young parents, too) that they made the famous seven months' ruling. At Groton on June 1, 1765—and by this time the effect of Whitefield's Great Awakening had long since been spent, so that the condition could not be attributed to sexual excitation accompanying religious ecstasy—"the church voted with regard to baptizing children of persons newly married, that those parents that have not a child till seven yearly months after marriage, are subjects of our Christian Charity (if in a judgement of Charity otherwise qualified) and shall have the privilege of Baptism for their infants without being questioned as to their honesty." This rule prevailed in Groton Church until 1803.

There were other types of public confession—theft, drunkenness (for which the culprit was suspended from the Lord's Supper), false and abusive language against the minister, "unchristian carriage towards a wife" and non-attendance at church services. One of the last type of offenders proved to be a hardened sinner, according to the Braintree accounts:

"Samuel Tomson, a prodigie of pride, malice and arrogance, being called before the church in the meeting house 28 July, 1697, for his absenting himself from the Publicke Worship, unless when any stranger preached; his carriage being before the church proud and insolent, reviling and vilifying their Pastor at an horrible rate and stiling him their priest and them a nest of wasps." And yet, after a time, the church relented and voted him absolution.[22]

## Penance in Church

In addition to these voluntary displays of contrition, it was customary for criminals to do public penance in church. In

October, 1631, in the church at Jamestown, Va., three men were laid "neck and heels" during divine service "for abusing men and their wives and for night walking." [23] Robert Wyard, who had stolen a pair of breeches, was sentenced to appear in church during the entire service for three Sundays "with a pair of breeches tied around his neck and with the word 'Thief' written upon his back." [24] The same Robert seems to have had an evil tongue. He was arrested for slandering a lady, Mrs. Alice Trevellor, "insomuch as that he liked to have taken away the reputation of the said Alice." He was sentenced to appear in a white sheet with a white wand in his hand three several Sabbath days and to ask Mrs. Trevellor's forgiveness. We rather suspect that Robert had something on his side or that the aforesaid Alice was a very fascinating woman, as she married four times and in each instance a prominent colonist. She evidently believed the way to wealth was to marry and bury husbands. She herself was finally buried in 1660.[25]

In 1646 Richard Buckland was also punished for the favorite Colonial tort of defamation. He wrote a vitriolic poem about one Ann Smyth and was made to stand at the church door between the lessons with a paper on his hat and on it, written in capital letters, "Inimrius Libellos," desiring forgiveness of God and also the aforesaid defamed.[26]

For abusing her aunt, Mary White had to ask Goody Hait's forgiveness three times in church "in ye face of ye congregation." [27] In 1626, for fornication, Jane Hill was required to stand up in the church in James City during service wrapped in a "White Sheete." Her paramour had no such easy sentence: he was given eighty "strypes of ye whippe."

Sometimes the scales of justice were balanced evenly. Joan Butler said terrible things about the wife of another man, for which she had to confess publicly in church and ask forgiveness between the first and second lessons. And the following Sunday the accuser had to do the same for the same sort of language!

These "personal appearances" of pronounced sinners in church, although calculated to deter sin, also would afford no little excitement. Who could stay away from divine service when they knew that some such penal divergence from the liturgy might be offered? When self-condemned sinners would be apt to rise up and spread their failing upon the record, no one could tell. Thereby was added to churchgoing those precious qualities known to all vendors of amusement—suspense and dramatic entrance.

### Sermons, Grisly and Dramatic

Occasionally the congregation was treated to a grisly sermon. Those condemned to execution were subjected, with the hope of arousing proper contrition, to special sermons on the Sunday or Thursday before being put to death. The condemned was brought into the church or meeting house heavily shackled and under guard, placed before the congregation, and for two full turns of the hour glass the preacher poured out the best of his forensic efforts.

Blaming the contemporary foibles of clothes for the wickedness in the world has been the preacher's standby ever since the first of them lifted up his voice. When the congregation sitting under John Elliot, apostle to the Indians, heard him rant and pray against men wearing wigs and fervently state that all the calamities in the country, even Indian wars, might be traced to this absurd fashion, they either smiled indulgently or gave his utterances their stiff-necked nod of approval. Alas, Rev. John lived to see practically every orthodox minister wearing a great white wig.[28] As we have read, Nathaniel Ward, parson at Ipswich and author of the "Simple Cobler of Aggawam," railed equally hard against the vanity of women's clothes. These two preachers are perhaps the earliest on record in America for blaming the sinner's sin on what the sinner wore. They are the ecclesiastical ancestors of those who blamed short skirts, open blouses and silk stockings in our own generation.

Mr. Endicott of Salem followed a close second by embracing the doctrine of veils for women in church. Completely ignoring St. Paul's theory that women should cover their heads in church lest the angels get into their hair, Mr. Endicott claimed that if he worshipped the Lord in the beauty of holiness he was determined that human beauty should form no part of his pleasure.[29] Hence, while they were in church, women should cover their faces with veils.

Election sermons must have been exciting, too. The preacher didn't hesitate to speak right out in the pulpit for or against a candidate. The voting men of his congregation, according to their political lights, must have wanted to shout down or applaud this political ballyhoo.

Occasionally came the ordination sermon, when a tyro parson was either preached at by an older minister (and the congregation could rest comfortably, realizing that all these instructions, injunctions and holy counsels weren't for them) or else the fledgling took to his forensic wings and the congregation sat there solemnly as an audience of critics.

Then there were the titters that must have run through congregations when the parson "made a break" or was snared in his own words. One New England minister, on baptizing a child whose father was a backslider, added to the ritual, "I baptize this child wholly on the woman's account." In a New York church Rev. Martinus Schoonmaker, whose English was a little uncertain, conducted a marriage. He thought it fitting to conclude the service with the English phrase, "I pronounce you man and wife and one flesh." Instead, he came out with the words, "I pronounce you one beef."

### Variations on Prayer Themes

The manner of praying both by the minister and the deacon could surely afford relief from the ordinary burdens of the Sabbath. Elder Brewster of Weymouth, Mass., has come down to us as having possessed "a singular good gift in prayer, both public and private, in ripping up the hart and conscience before God." [30] Rev. Benjamin Lord of Norwich, Conn., used his prayer for a weekly newspaper, sometimes praying the hour-glass through. This must have been diverting: first he would announce the news item and then give editorial comment on it.[31]

Often the prayers left no doubt in the minds of the congregation just what the minister expected a bountiful Providence to furnish. Listen to Minister Miles giving his pious directions for rain: "O Lord, thou knowest we do not want Thee to send a rain which shall pour down in fury and swell our streams and sweep away our haycocks and fences and bridges; but, Lord, we want it to come drizzle-drozzle, drizzle-drozzle for about a week. Amen." [32]

The War of Independence was especially rich in producing picturesque prayers. Most of them would shock our present-day pacifist dominies. Consider this straight-from-the-shoulder, man-to-God orison spoken before the Battle of Monmouth by Rev. Israel Evans, chaplain of General Enoch Poor's brigade: "O Lord of Hosts, lead forth thy servants of the American Army to battle and give them victory; or, if this be not according to Thy sovereign will, then, we pray Thee, stand neutral and let flesh and blood decide the issue."

When Cornwallis was about to land, Rev. Judah Champion of Litchfield, Conn., lifted up his voice before the congregation, which included several members of Col. Benjamin Tallmadge's regiment, and addressed Divinity as follows: "O Lord, we view with terror and dismay the approach of

the enemies of Thy holy religion. Wilt Thou send a storm
and tempest and scatter them to the uttermost parts of the
earth. But, peradventure, should any escape Thy vengeance,
collect them together again, O Lord, as in the hollow of Thy
hand, and let Thy lightnings play upon them."

Rev. Nathaniel Roberts of Torrington was evidently ex-
pecting the Lord to work an election miracle when he
prayed across the bowed heads of his faithful followers,
"Great God, we pray Thee remove Lord North from office,
by death or otherwise." [33] Since prayers of this character are
still uttered on both sides in any war, religion keeps living
up to its name of the Church Militant and history grimly
repeats itself.

Rhode Island, before the days when New England turned
Abolitionist and developed its famous conscience, was a
lively center of slave traffic, Newport being one of the most
active ports of entry. One of the respectable elders in Newport, who prospered through the traffic in black ivory, used
to edify the congregation of his church on the Sunday following the arrival of a slaver. Invariably he arose to lead his
neighbors in a thanksgiving "that an over-ruling Providence
has been pleased to bring to this land of freedom another
cargo of benighted heathen to enjoy the blessings of a gospel
dispensation." [34]

## Patriot in the Pulpit

The patriot in the pulpit can always be counted on to
thrill a congregation. During the Revolution, so numerous
were the clerical patriots that Sunday services must have
been a constant succession of thrills and flutters. Rev. James
Madison, distinguished Professor of Natural Philosophy at
William and Mary, never spoke of the Kingdom of Heaven
in any sermons he delivered during the war, but always of

"that Great Republic, where there is no distinction of rank, where all men are free and equal." [35]

In the Spring of 1776, when Pennsylvania was being called on for her quota of troops to defend New York, Rev. John Carmichael, pastor of the Presbyterian Church of Brandywine Manor, spoke with such vigor and eloquence that every man in his congregation enlisted. The same parson once announced from his pulpit that he had just returned from army headquarters where he found a great shortage of linen for bandages. "You women can spare this much from your shifts," he said, indicating the proper width. On Monday, when he rode back to Valley Forge, he carried a supply of little rolls that had come in from all quarters.[36] Perhaps the ladies of Brandywine Manor, as they felt the wind about their ankles, had a marked sympathy for the troops at Valley Forge.

The oft-cited classic of pulpit patriotism was the valedictory sermon of Rev. John Peter Gabriel Muhlenberg before his crowded congregation of German farmers and their wives at Woodstock, Va. After begging their support in the struggle for liberty, he bade them follow him. Laying aside his gown, he stood before them in uniform and buckled on his sword. The congregation rose to sing Luther's stirring "Eine feste Burg ist unser Gott." Outside, the church drums rolled. In half an hour, 162 men had enlisted.[37]

Muhlenberg's enlistment sermon was echoed in the pointed remark made from the pulpit of the Third Presbyterian Church in Philadelphia by the pastor, George Duffield. He rose and stated, "There are too many men here this morning. I am going to the front." He became chaplain of the Pennsylvania militia.

Still another patriot minister was the Methodist William Percy, chaplain to the third battalion of Philadelphia militia. In June, 1776, the weather being very warm, he bor-

rowed the servant of his commanding general and had him
stand behind him in the pulpit, "fanning him with a degree
of vehemence proportioned to his inflammatory address."
The servant was a very black and remarkably ugly Negro.
Percy spent much of his time during the war preaching to
the American troops and became so obnoxious to the Tories
that one of their versifiers, Joseph Stansbury, wrote this
jingle about him apropos of the above sermon:

> To preach up, friend Percy, at this critical season,
> Resistance to Britain is not very civil.
> Yet what can we look for but Faction and Treason
> From a flaming Enthusiast fanned by the Devil? [38]

A patriotic parson might even relax the insistent routine
of Sabbath church-going to further his country's purposes.
In Litchfield, Conn., Rev. Judah Champion once instructed
his women not to attend afternoon service, as they would be
more acceptable in the sight of God if they stayed home to
weave cloth and sew clothes for the soldiers. [39]

Even after the war, bitter political alignments between
parties continued to produce election sermons and, in one
instance, a situation in a church which surely must have di-
verted the congregation. Rev. John McKean, minister at
Milton, Mass., from 1797 to 1804, wore a black Federal
cockade in his hat. When he entered the pulpit he carefully
placed it so that the congregation could see it. Among the
choir members sitting in the gallery were several Democrats,
who induced one of their members whose hat was decorated
with a white cockade to hang it over the clock in front of
the gallery. This childish parading of political sentiment
went on for several Sabbaths until one day a Federal chorister
reached over and knocked the Democrat's hat to the floor
below, where a Federalist, with proper ceremonial contempt,
kicked it out of the church. [40]

That patriots disagreed with their Tory preachers, we

have seen in the previous chapter. Down South congregations held equally firm views on parsons who might be so
bold as to attack slaveholding. In South Carolina one group
of irate parishioners addressed their minister, "Sir, we pay
you a genteel salary to read us the prayers of the liturgy and
to explain to us such parts of the Gospel as the rule of the
church directs, but we do not want you to teach us what to
do with our blacks." [41]

## Restive Boys

Small boys can be counted on to become restive in church,
causing annoyance or amusement as their pranks turn out.
Very early did the church fathers of New England take
preventive measures against them. The first selectmen of
Springfield, Mass., in 1679 ordered "that all youths or boys
under the age of twelve years sit on the seat under the
deacon's seat and also on that seat against it and on the
stairs." [42] When accompanied by parents, children were allowed to sit with them. Three elders were also ordered to
sit in the gallery to check "disorders in youth and young
men in tyme of Gods worship." When their parents fell
asleep, the tithingman went around with a rod and poked
them into wakefulness.

Mischievous boys, of course, could also provide annoy-
ances. There were the wicked Philadelphia fellows who in
1728 concealed a large sturgeon in the pulpit of a Presbyterian church. The church was closed and the weather warm.
When the congregation assembled the following Sunday, the
sturgeon so scented the air that services had to be abandoned.[43]

Peter Kalm, the Swedish botanist who traveled through
America, tells how the Moravians held services not only
twice or three times on Sundays but also every other night

of the week after dark. In the Winter of 1756 they were
obliged to abandon these evening meetings because of "some
wanton young fellows having several times disturbed the
congregation by an instrument sounding like the note of a
cuckoo; for this noise they made in a dark corner not only
at the end of every stanza but likewise at that of every line
whilst they were singing a hymn." [44]

Even grown-ups could cause disturbance. In 1675 Mary
Wheeler was presented for disorderly carriage in the South
Meeting House at Boston for "hunching Rebecca Bulley in
the publique worship of God." [45] Or they fell sick, as the
case recorded by Samuel Sewall, in 1680 when "a Man
Swoon in our Meeting House and falls down, which makes
much disturbance, yet Mr. Willard breaks not off preaching." [46]

One wonders if Negroes in the Puritan congregations ever
forgot themselves and praised God in too raucous a tone.
New England used to segregate the blacks from the whites
in church. There was a Negro pew or several pews set aside
for them, usually in dark corners, and in some churches these
were even boarded up with only peep-holes for the occupants.[47]

Yet the time was to come when, if one behaved in church,
she could take pride in it. A housemaid, looking for a place
in Philadelphia in 1821, gave as one of her recommendations,
"I can't help laughing sometimes, but I always am sober in
church." [48]

### The Ordeal of Catechism

Once a year children were subjected to the ordeal of recit-
ing the catechism in church. New Jersey set apart three
Summer Sundays for this and a portion was recited each
Sunday at the close of the afternoon service. The children
had been drilled in it week after week at home by their par-

ents until their poor little heads were bursting with theological phrases and their poor little nerves frayed. The recitation in church was limited to children from eight to fifteen years of age. Fortnightly intervals were allowed between catechism Sundays so that the children could perfect their knowledge of the next set of questions and answers.

When finally it came time to start this inquisition, the children were ranged in long facing lines in the broad aisle, boys on one side, girls on the other, with their parents crowding the pews all around. Then the minister mounted the pulpit to give out the questions. In turn each child stepped forth, faced the pulpit and answered.[49]

To be "told," prompted by the minister or another, was a disgrace that the child probably never forgot. However, the ordeal was tempered to these flustered lambs: tots answered the first and easiest questions, the next the second section and the oldest the third and hardest.

While such recitations may appear cruel and difficult to us, we must remember that church-goers in those days were accustomed to feats of memory. Both children and elders tried to pay strict attention to the sermon, because the children would be questioned on it afterwards and their elders would discuss it point by point. Sermon rehash became an intellectual pastime, just as exciting to our forebears as an "Information Please" broadcast is to us.

### Pleasant Country Sundays

As the eighteenth century passed into the nineteenth, we begin having mellow pictures of these churches and meeting houses and the life that centered around them. Black Sabbaths were turning rosy pink. The English traveler John Davis describes Parson Weems' church in Fairfax County, Va., how on Sundays it looked like a race ground, with ladies driving up in carriages and men on horseback. The horses were tied to the trees in the churchyard. Then as the bell, suspended in a tree near the church, began to clatter, they all trooped indoors. After service and good-byes came the rattling of the carriages, the cracking of whips and the shouts of men as they called to their slaves. Finally, when the last of them had gone, the sexton locked the churchyard gate. Then he, too, went home.[50]

In Virginia the church door was the parish bulletin board and its churchyard, before and after service, a place for the exchange of news, opinions and gossip. Often the sermon was pleasing. William Byrd of Westover writes, "Mr. Betty the Parson of the Parish entertain'd us with a good honest sermon, but whether he bought it or borrowed it would have been uncivil in us to enquire. Be that as it will, he is a decent man, with a double chin that fits gracefully over his Band, and his Parish, especially the Female part of it, like him well." [51]

In New Jersey at the end of the eighteenth century people of the Dutch Reformed country congregations and others waited on the church green for the arrival of the pastor and his wife, who were followed by their servants bearing their Bibles and hymn books. Many of the congregation, if it was Summer, had walked there barefoot and were now busy putting on their shoes. If it was a hot day the men, mostly farmers uncomfortable in their stiff Sabbath clothes, removed their coats. Then they trailed the parson and his wife into church. They were perfectly composed for whatever compound of dogma and ethics the pastor might deliver in the next three hours.

Luncheon followed in the Sabbath House or, in warm weather, was eaten on the grass of the churchyard under the trees, or they sat in their white-covered farm carts on kitchen chairs which served for seats and with straw at their feet.

From vendors they might buy root and malt beer, buttered rye bread, sugared olekokes and ginger bread. Half an hour was allowed for this refreshment, then the second service began, after which the congregation dispersed, with a clambering into their carts and those who walked taking off their shoes again. Back home, the children were given religious instruction by their parents, asked for Bible stories and made to repeat the pastor's two texts for the day.[52]

In South Carolina church-going was also a social event. Every Sabbath saw numerous canoes and periaguas bringing people from distant points into Charleston for service at St. Philip's.[53]

These later pleasant gatherings of a congregation indicate how the early grim attitude towards the meeting house and church-going had softened into a kindly communal habit. People were welcomed to stand around the church door. And yet only a century before, this might have been frowned on, as it was in Hingham, Mass., where two men were appointed to keep the porch of the meeting-house "from being needlessly encumbered with women on the Sabbath." What these ecclesiastical traffic cops said to the women and what the women replied can only be surmised. There are several pointed Scriptural passages each might have cited with telling effect.

It was not a difficult life now. Church was the center of the few social activities possible for women members of the congregation. What a relief from the long grind of household and farm toil of the other six days! And what a chance to show off new clothes! Robin, the French army chaplain, observed that, "Piety is by no means the only motive that brings crowds of American women to church. Having no theatre or public promenades, the churches are the only places of public resort, where they can show off their new and constantly increasing luxury; there they display themselves arrayed in silks and sometimes shaded with superb head-dresses, their hair piled up on frames in imitation of French fashions of some years ago." [54]

Had this observant Frenchman stayed in the United States longer, he would have seen the day when congregations were set a-flutter by Yankee pedlars. The church was the best place to display new fashions in a small town. When shawls became the mode, Yankee pedlars used to go with packs of them to country villages and, selecting the most prominent woman there, would present her with one on condition that she wear it to church the following Sunday. Her entrance invariably caused a ripple of whispers as she proceeded proudly up the aisle to her front pew. The following week the pedlar had no trouble getting rid of his stocks.[55]

Yes, they had fun at the Steeple House!

## Shocking Music

Any innovation in the routine of service was sure to cause talk, amazement, agreement and disagreement. In some districts and among some of the sects, the introduction of singing by note roused stout protests. Before this time, hymn books being scarce, the lining deacon raised the tune and read the words two lines at a time. Necessarily the singing was disjointed, yet people seemed to prefer it that way.

By the turn of the nineteenth century the lining deacon had well-nigh disappeared, except in churches far on the frontier. Even before the Revolution, Congregationalists and Presbyterians had introduced singing by note. Many of the older conservatives shook their heads at this opening wedge: "Pray by rule, preach by rule—and then comes Popery," they said. Often these old die-hards, when the note singing commenced, rose and stalked out of church, an interruption that must have cause covert smiles among the liberals and the younger set.

On the other hand, others considered better music in churches as a legitimate allure to larger congregations. At the consecration of Gloria Dei Church in Philadelphia, the Wissahickon hermits gave a concert on violas, trumpets and kettledrums, which must have been a noisy affair. Immediately after the service, one of the visiting clergy wrote home for an organ, saying, "If there were music in the church, the young people would consider church-going a recreation." [56]

*Shaking the Dry Bones*

There were other times, even in staid New England, when the power of the preacher in orthodox houses of worship was such that his congregation was moved to strange antics. We shall see more of this in the next chapter. Here we halt to note how Jonathan Edwards' congregations used to swoon from sheer fright as he dangled them over the pit, and how at Eastham on Cape Cod the people were stirred by strange imaginings. Writing in 1802, the local historian of that charming village reports, "Hysterical fits are very common in Orleans, Eastham and the town below, particularly on Sunday in the time of divine service. When one woman is affected, five or six generally sympathize with her and the congregation is thrown into the uttermost confusion." [57] Doubtless the rest of the congregation was thrown into uttermost embarrassment or even amusement.

This shaking of the dry bones, of course, was not new to American congregations. George Whitefield, the Tennets and other revivalists of the Great Awakening, much of whose preaching came under the category of "That which shocks the thinking charms the crowd," were past masters in religious excitation. Scarcely had the nineteenth century

begun than a new revival swept the country and the camp
meeting, a peculiarly American institution, brought quak-
ing and fits throughout the country. Then, indeed, there was
excitement in churches.

## Strange Visitors

It might be possible to cite other reasons for our forebears
enjoying themselves—apart from the commendable practice
of religious worship which brings interior enjoyment—in the
Steeple Houses: local customs and unheralded incidents and
strange interruptions. We have seen how Benjamin Lay, in
sackcloth and ashes, stood throughout a service in an Anglican church to protest against slave-holding and how he
dramatically stabbed that bladder of pokeberry juice, to the
consternation of the Friends' Meeting at Burlington. Even
the seemly Friends were obliged, at times, to rid themselves
of voluntary preachers whose antics and loose tongues obviously disturbed the inflowing of the Spirit. Many others
could be mentioned. But let us stop with three rare visitors
whose presence must have set congregations a-flutter.

In 1737 there came into New Jersey overland from Boston,
where he had arrived from London, a sturdy man of grave
aspect, bewhiskered and wearing a turban. He spoke and
wrote only Arabic and he claimed to be Sheik Sidi Alla-
hazar, Emir of Syria. In churches of New York, New Jersey
and later at Philadelphia, where the letters of recommendation to charity that he carried got him a ready hearing, he
told his remarkable story.

He had suffered for his religion. A native of Beirut, Syria,
he was born and raised an Orthodox Christian, but the
Turkish government taxed his business on this account until
it was extinct, and his life was constantly threatened for his
insistence on clinging to Christianity. Finally he managed

to escape to Russia, where no less a person than the Czarina befriended him. From Russia he went to London and thence came to America.[58]

What congregation wouldn't be moved by such a story, especially when related by a bewhiskered martyr wearing a turban! In New York the Friends' Meeting gave him 100 pistoles. Everywhere he was well-received, and accepted with gracious gestures the bounty of the charitable. In Philadelphia the governor and council paid out £37 for the entertainment of this "Christian nobleman from Syria," who so feelingly exploited the unfailing gullibility of mankind. From Philadelphia he sailed to Barbados, and we hear no more of him.[59]

Twenty-two years later congregations in New Jersey were startled by the appearance of three natives of Greenland, two young men and a young woman who, even though it was Summer, still wore seal skins. With them were two Indians from Surinam. Moravian converts, they had been exhibited in England and on the Continent. Except for the "praying Indians" whom Elliot and other missionaries converted and exhibited, this constitutes the earliest traveling missionary show in this country.[60] They eventually went to the Moravian settlement at Bethlehem, Pa.

Our next visitor sought neither pity nor money nor even curiosity. Imagine the congregation at Plymouth, Mass., in the year 1813. By this time Yankee sea captains had gone to the far ports of the seven seas, so it required something quite out of the ordinary to rouse the natives of this sophisticated town. In that year the Sally, belonging to Boston and owned by Adam Babcock, came into Plymouth Harbor from Canton, China. It was the first vessel that had ever discharged a cargo from beyond the Cape of Good Hope in this port.

On board was a Chinese, Mr. Washey, which makes us suspect the author of this account of being the first of those who called all Chinese "Washies." Mr. Washey came ashore at Plymouth, "habited in the costume of his country. He attended public worship on the Sabbath, and was a young man of mild aspect and pleasing manners." [61] We hope this "Java Head" visitor did not cause the congregation to be so overly curious as to lose *its* pleasing manners.

# III

## A GALAXY OF GOD'S FOOLS

### Gates Ajar Open Wide

INTO WHATEVER COLONY WE TURN THE LIGHT OF INVESTIGA-
tion, it shows that the Gates Ajar, usually reserved for the
elect, were soon pushed wide open for many to enter.

In Pennsylvania, George Keith, once a Quaker, took to
questioning the tenets of Penn's Holy Experiment. Long before the nineteenth century schism between the Orthodox
and the Hicksites, which divided the Friends into two opposing camps, little flakes were dropping off the Quaker
structure as individual zealots expounded their own theories. Theories such as the notion of William Nichols of Delaware, who believed God was displeased with those who wore
clothes that had been dyed. He gathered quite a body of
followers—many of them later to settle in Guilford, N. C.—
whose clothes were made of materials in only the simple
coloring nature gave cotton and wool.[1] Or Philadelphia
Friends, feeling the pressure of political urgency, became
Anglicans. Strictness in dress, in living, even in bearing arms
were subjected to liberal interpretations by the younger generation of Quakers. This profoundly worried their elders,
yes, even the style of coming to meeting—their "galloping
and riding after an airy, flurting manner inconsistent with
the moderation and gravity becoming Friends." [2]

Farther inland from Philadelphia settled the German
sectarians—Amish, Mennonites, Schwenkfelders, Lutherans,

Dutch Reformed and Moravians—making the countryside a patchwork of churches and isms. Beyond them, on the frontier, spread the Scotch-Irish, unyielding in their loyalty to Presbyterianism. By 1750 Pennsylvania was a vivid marble cake of religious thought.

In New Amsterdam the efforts of the Dutch West India Company to make the Dutch Reformed Church the established religion of the colony soon retreated before the coming of Lutherans, Quakers, Anglicans, Congregationalists and Jews.

Maryland's first strict scheme to sustain acceptance of the imperative categories of the Roman Catholic Church met with resistance from lay members of the Assembly as early as 1635; and in 1649 freedom of religious worship was assured by resolve of the St. Mary Assembly: "Noe person or persons whatsoever within this province shall henceforth bee any waies troubled for or in respect to his or her religion . . . professing to believe in Jesus Christ." With this assurance Quakers and Puritans, Baptists and Jews streaked into the colony and the "Maryland asylum for troubled souls" saw the end of religious warfare.[3]

In addition there were the revivalists, from whose preachments new sects sprang up like weeds. They thrust their sickles into other men's harvests and gathered goodly sheaves of converts. As the result of a revival in New London, Conn., for instance, several people withdrew from the church because of the "deadness and legal preaching." They started a society and took a house they called "The Shepherd's Tent," which was intended as an academy to train male and female exhorters, teachers and ministers. Another sect that cropped up in this neighborhood went under the name of Muggletonians!

Was it any wonder that such a conglomeration of orthodoxies and sects should produce odd sticks? Orthodoxy such as that of the funeral-haunting Judge Sewall of Boston, and heterodoxy such as swayed those deluded souls and pious impostors whose accounts follow in this chapter. Ranging from the earliest times up to the middle of the past century, they make a colorful galaxy of God's fools. Some who burned with undiminished zeal and were thought mad, now, through the passage of time, have earned an aura of holiness and respect. Others were Gospel-glutted men and women on whose vagaries we can smile with charity. Still others were unmitigated scamps.

### The Sinless, Street Preachers and Soul-Sellers

In the earliest days anyone making extraordinary claims in respect to his soul was a subject for investigation by the authorities. Hugh Bennett of Massachusetts Bay Colony in 1640 maintained that he was free from original sin and from actual sin for half a year. The magistrates ordered him banished and if he returned he was to be put to death.[4] In February, 1675, the authorities of New York swore out a warrant against Peter Ellet "who doth pretend and hath reported to have seen sights or visions in this city and fort, which tend to the disquiet and disturbance of His Majesty's subjects in those parts." [5]

On many occasions the Philadelphia Friends had to suffer fools gladly. There was Leah, the tall, thin, half-crazed, spectre-looking old maid, nevertheless a Friend, who had a dread of doctors and thought to chase them away by passing the nights wrapped in a blanket between the graves in a local burying ground.[6]

Idlers in the streets of Philadelphia used to gather to hear the rantings of Michael Welfare, the "Conestoga Philosopher," as he spoke from the balcony of the old court house. He wore a linen hat and a full beard and carried a pilgrim's staff. He claimed to hail from the region of Conestoga where, some years before, John Conrad Beissel had lived as a hermit with three others of like mind, preparing for that assault on the Kingdom of Heaven which was to culminate in the founding of religious orders at Ephrata. To all and sundry Michael declared himself sent to announce the vengeance of the Almighty. An earnest, vehement preacher, he sounded his warning voice in 1736 and augmented it with a pamphlet which he sold for 4d.[7]

Philadelphia and most of the Atlantic seaboard, for that matter, were soon to become accustomed to strangely-garbed and violently-acting preachers. When Gilbert Tennet, one of Whitefield's most vociferous assistants in the Great Awakening, went forth to rouse backsliding souls, he wore his hair long, a mighty mane that swept his shoulders, and bundled his huge figure into a greatcoat bound with a leather thong like a monk's. Whitefield himself was apparently a monument of pious conceit: he could never get into action unless speaking to a large crowd, before which he would weep, fling his arms around and stamp. If his sermon was a failure, instead of blaming his own weakness, he said the Lord had withdrawn Himself!

Contemporary in Philadelphia with the white-hatted Conestoga Philosopher was the distracted young man who popped up there from the South, took lodgings and told a remarkable story. His distraction was caused by the fact, so he solemnly announced, that he had sold his soul to the Devil and that unless the required sum was forthcoming by a certain date the Devil would most certainly appear and carry him off.

Not only was he ardent in his pleas for help, but his decent appearance and otherwise quiet manners soon assured those who might have harbored doubts about his story. This serious business proposition of spiritual foreclosure soon im-

pressed an incredible number of pious Philadelphians. In
churches prayers were said for him and services held. The
day grew nearer. Purses opened. On the day that the final
settling of this commitment was to be consummated, a great
crowd of the anxious and curious assembled. A table was set
in their midst and on the table was laid the money that had
been collected. The sum was apparently far from adequate.
The condemned young man pleaded for more. Purses opened
wider. Money poured onto the table. There it was, ready for
the Devil to come and take it! The hour approached. Panic
seized the crowd. People quivered, cried and prayed. Someone shouted, "There he comes!" In the confusion the young
man disappeared—and the money went with him.[8]

This was the first of three instances gathered from the annals of Philadelphia in which credulous citizens listened to
talks of the Devil buying souls. In 1749 a Michael H——,
member of a well-known family, stated that he had sold his
soul and would be carried away at a certain time. The gathering that crowded the streets to watch the dénouement was
a cause for public scandal.[9] The third was a Negro who came
to Philadelphia from Maryland with the same story. He, too,
attracted the curious, but by this time citizens of the City of
Brotherly Love had wearied of the traffic in souls and as a
means of raising money the story was a failure. The Negro,
finally given work by a generous clergyman, proved to be
suffering from nothing more than the common complaint of
sheer laziness.[10]

Philadelphia in its long career has seen many kinds of odd
preachers and to some of them we shall eventually arrive.
Here, to round out this little group, let us consider Mr.
George H. Munday. In this age he wouldn't appear odd at
all, crowds would not collect to hear him nor would his
name be recorded in the chronicles of the curious, for his
sole outstanding idiosyncrasy was that he never wore a hat.

In Philadelphia, with its heritage of hat-wearing Quakers, this was unique. So they called him the "Hatless Preacher" and he was set down as erratic by those who gathered to hear the torrent of his words in the first quarter of the nineteenth century.[11]

## Rogerenes

As tolerance was gradually extended towards all religions, the gate opened wider and wider for the entrance of strange sects spawned from some individualistic interpretation of a Scriptural passage or the alleged visions in some addled head or from the cunning of some rogue who was overly endowed with the wisdom of the serpent. Even in the opening quarter of the eighteenth century, that era when luxury began first to flourish, it was demonstrated that one easy way to make a living was to start a new religion. Somewhere in these categories would fall the Rogerenes and the Christ-ians.

For the first account of the Rogerenes, who sprang into prominence in 1720, we turn to the fading pages of Trumbull's "History of Connecticut." Dr. Trumbull, being a good Congregationalist, had his own opinion of both Quakers and this local offshoot.

"The Rogerenes were a sort of Quaker, who had their origin and name from one John Rogers of New London. He was a man of unbounded ambition and wished to be something more than common men. One Case and one Banks, two lewd men, called singing Quakers, coming through the colony singing and dancing, accompanied with a number of women to assist them in their musical exercises, and especially to proclaim how their lips dropped with myrrh and honey, fell in company with John and at once made a convert of him to their religion. He, in a high degree, imbibed their spirit and ever retained it. Notwithstanding, it was not long after before he commenced a Seventh Day Baptist. After

maintaining the opinion of his sect for a short time, he returned again to Quakerism. To gratify his pride, and that
he might appear as the head of a peculiar sect, he differed
in several points from the Quakers. Particularly he maintained that there were three ordinances of religious use: Baptism, the Lord's Supper and imposition of hands. To make
himself more eminent as the head of a new sect, he commenced preaching of his peculiar scheme and, without any
kind of ordination, administered baptism to his followers.

"The madness, immodesty and tumultuous conduct of
Rogers and those who followed him, at this day, is hardly
conceivable. It seemed to be their study and delight to violate the Sabbath, insult magistrates and ministers and to
trample on all law and authority, human and divine. They
would come on the Lord's Day into the most public assemblies, nearly or quite naked, and, in the time of public worship, behave in a wild and tumultuous manner, crying out
and charging the most venerable ministers with lies and
false doctrines. They would labor upon the Lord's Day, drive
carts by places of public worship and from town to town,
apparently on purpose to disturb Christians and Christian
assemblies. They seem to take pains to violate the law in
the presence of officers that they might be complained of,
and have an opportunity to insult the laws, the courts and
all civil authority." [12]

It may have been that this desire to disturb church services was part of the Quaker heritage of John Rogers. Less
than fifty years before Judge Sewall related how, "in Sermon-
time a female Quaker slipt in covered with a canvas frock,
having her hair disheveled and loose and powdered with
ashes resembling a flaxen or white Perriwig, her face as black
as Ink, being led by two Quakers and followed by two more.
It occasioned a great and very amazing uproar." [13]

The reason why the Rogerenes stand out so vividly in

Connecticut history is that they were the "first break in the
unity of worship of New London." The Rogerses were an old
family and well-respected. When John Rogers in the 1670's
broke away from the established Congregational Church to
join the Sabbatarians or Seventh Day Baptists, his choice
distinctly shocked the community. When he further withdrew from them to assume ministerial authority and baptize
and preach and gather followers, the town authorities were
painfully alarmed, especially when it became evident that
the purpose of the founder and his followers was "their determination to be persecuted." [14] It was their aggressiveness
in the pursuit of their beliefs that annoyed the community.
All days were alike in sanctity to them. They considered
themselves free to work after their church services. They had
no church buildings, no ministers, no prayers in public
except when the spirit caused some one of them to become
vocal. They refused to take oaths. They also were active
writers for their faith and spread their tracts far and wide.

John Rogers preached in the streets, disturbing public
worship, and courted persecution to such an extent that one
might think him aspiring to martyrdom. In 1676 he was first
fined for profanation of the Sabbath or neglect of public
worship and, as he persisted, the fines accumulated from 10s.
to £5. In early Connecticut the fine for absence from worship was 5s., for labor on the Sabbath 20s. and, for the performance of church ordinances by any other than a minister,
£5. None of these daunted John Rogers: for many years he
was arraigned at every session of the court. Once he was imprisoned for being implicated in the burning of the New
London meeting house and on another occasion, for blasphemy, sat on the gallows beneath a halter.

While John was being fined and punished, his followers
were charged with a wide assortment of offenses: deliberately
catching eels on Sunday or doing servile work. Or John, like

a Low Church Kensitite in England today who disturbs High Church services, would rush into a church and interrupt the minister, acting "as if possessed with a diabolical spirit," which caused women in the congregation to swoon. Once he noisily trundled a wheelbarrow into the porch of a meeting house during divine service; and his women followers would sit in church and knit and sew and chat audibly. Sunday after Sunday this went on.

Fines, public punishments in the stocks or on the gallows, tar and feathers, jail sentences (John Rogers is said to have spent one-third of his life after conversion in jail for his faith), nothing seemed to deter the Rogerenes.

Once, brought into court for disturbing worship on the Sabbath, John made a prodigious noise, demanding of the court what their business with him was. When the indictment was read he pleaded not guilty and began insulting the clerk. To his shouts were joined those of his followers of both sexes who "tuned their pipes and screamed, roared, shouted and stamped."

While John professed to be a holy man and so entirely guided by the Spirit that he had lived without sin for twenty years, yet the bark of his private life broke up on the reefs of marital unhappiness. His wife, unable to tolerate their way of living, left him and was granted a divorce and the custody of their two children. When she married again, the children promptly left her and became their father's stoutest followers. As John did not recognize the power of the court, he refused to accept the verdict of divorce and once had to be withstrained by the law to prevent him from kidnapping his former wife from the bed and board of the respectable Matthew Beckwith whom she had married. Twenty-five years later, with equal disregard for the courts and marriage laws, he took for wife one Mary Ransford, an indentured servant. One of his followers, she had gained repute by pouring scalding water from a second story window on the head of a constable come to collect the minister's rate. Their married life was a succession of family brawls and on more than one occasion the authorities had to be called in to stop them. In 1703 the court, tired of the scandal, summoned her to appear for living in sin and gave her the choice of 40s. or forty stripes and declared her marriage invalid. Mary sided with the law and eventually married respectably.

These actions demonstrated one of the tenets of the Rogerenes: their complete contempt for the laws concerning marriage. They took wives and husbands where and when they chose without benefit of magistrate or clergy.

They were also sternly against employing physicians and using medicines when sick. The cunning way they got around this tenet and still kept a clear conscience can be illustrated by the time some of them suffered from a visitation of the itch. "A number of these people were afflicted with a certain cutaneous disorder, and their principles forbidding them the use of medicines, they were at a loss what to do. After deliberating upon the subject, they came to the conclusion that this disorder (or whatever else it might be called) could not come under the head of bodily infirmity. It was determined that the itch might be considered as a noxious animal, which they might innocently destroy. They accordingly made use of the usual remedies found efficacious for this disorder." [15] John considered himself proof against infection from disease. He deliberately went to Boston while a smallpox epidemic was raging there and sat beside its sufferers. But his faith failed him in the end, for on October 17, 1721, on his return home, he died of smallpox, and a few days later a daughter-in-law and a grandson followed suit.

An historian of Connecticut, writing in 1838, found a considerable number of the descendants of the Rogerenes still living in Groton, New London and its vicinity. These people had so little faith in other denominations that when a new church was being constructed in New London they forbade their people to work on the job as carpenters or in any other capacity.[16]

## The Christ-ians

Hampton, Conn., may have other claims to distinction but to the searcher for Early American curiosa it remains as the spot where first we encounter a sect that called themselves Christ-ians. To unbelievers they were known as Smithites, from Elias Smith, one of their founders.

This group took upon itself the burden of accomplishing various reforms in the world and the way they conceived best to overcome the Devil was to hold meetings so noisy that his Satanic Majesty's voice would be completely drowned out! Neighbors bore witness that the racket from these services could be heard two miles. Christ-ians also believed that in order to conquer evil (which is an appealing notion) they must become literally as little children, trusting to the Scriptural promise that wisdom is withheld from elders and revealed unto babes and sucklings. In their ecstatic search for this humility and its consequent wisdom, they crawled and crept on the floor and rolled one over another, like little children in a nursery. They also made bland public confession of their sins, however bawdy. They were even childlike in their attitudes toward worldly business and their farmwork, letting cows go unmilked and making such other unrural neglects of their bucolic callings.

Besides Elias Smith, the other leader was one Varnum, who claimed to have special and particular revelations from God. They were special in that he alone knew of them until he apprised his victim, and particular in that the All-Seeing Wisdom directed him to ask a certain person for a particular article or a particular sum of money. To one man Varnum reported it revealed to him that he should give him his horse. As the object of this revelation had been "touched" before, and as the horse was valuable, he made a dicker with Varnum—Varnum should pay at least half its value. Varnum, of course, never kept his share of the bargain. The credulous owner of the horse full well deserves to be classed as one of God's fools.

Later Varnum induced some of his followers to move to Ohio, where he proposed setting up a special Eden for them. This was the day—around 1816—when the rich valleys and plains of Ohio appeared as a promised land to any who had struggled with the rock-strewn New England soil. Those who went with him were sorely disillusioned: the Paradise never materialized. Varnum eventually turned Shaker and took with him to his new and agitating religion all who would go along.[17]

## Visions and Interpretations

In the eighteenth century the vision was still an accepted springboard from which one might launch a new religion or pious cult or give evidence to a fantastic legend. The child visionary always attracts a following among the credulous and devout. So Mary Coombs of Millville, N. J., appears as one of these recurring instances which are found in all ages. Born in 1749, she was converted at ten and began audibly expressing her religious devotion at fourteen, which puts her in the category of the girl and boy revivalist preachers who, even in our own age, find publicity and a following. Mary added an extra attraction: she was given to visions and raptures. On one occasion, so the story goes, 500 people gathered to watch her performance.[18]

Almost three-quarters of a century later another victim of trances rolled up a reputation—Rachel Baker, the Somnambulist. Born at Pelham, Mass., on May 29, 1794, she appeared to have been a contemplative child. Later her family moved to Marcellus, N. Y., where she began to demonstrate a most remarkable habit of devotional somnambulation. She would go to sleep quite naturally and during sleep would preach and pray aloud, her devotional exercises being accompanied by the most distressing ecstasies and paroxysms. Regularly every day she was seized with them and her discourses might last a few minutes or an hour. When she awoke she had no awareness of what she had said or done until witnesses told her; consequently these sleep-preachings were thought to be "genuine fruits of repentance, piety and peace." Except for these daily occurrences she seemed to enjoy normal health.[19]

Then there were those who made realistic interpretations of Scriptural phrases torn from their context. Sometimes these home-made exegeses worked lamentable hurt to those who conceived them. This point again we can illustrate from New Jersey, since the incident was reported as happening at Cohansey, West Jersey, by the reputable *Pennsylvania Gazette* of October 28, 1742: one John Leek, "after twelve months' deliberation, made himself an Eunuch (as it is said) for the Kingdom of Heaven's sake, having made such a construction upon Matthew XIX, 12." The *Gazette* adds the assuring news that, "He is now under Dr. Johnson's hands and in a fair way of doing well." As inhabitants of New Jersey in the 1740's were being beaten into ecstatic religious fervor by Whitefield and his preachers, Mr. Leek's realistic interpretation of Matthew XIX, 12, might possibly be attributed to that source.

The vagaries of religious experience might also have been responsible for the marital decision of Mr. A. of Wethersfield, Conn. We are assured that he was a very religious and conscientious man. He appears also to have had a streak of the ascetic in him, the type of asceticism that leads a man cheerfully to immolate himself on the altar of discomfort

for his soul's sake. He deliberately married an ill-tempered
and troublesome woman, apparently the least desirable of
all the free women in Wethersfield. That she should have
captured a man, especially the strait-laced Mr. A., was a
matter for town comment; and that he should have chosen
her from all the available women thereabouts, a matter of
curiosity. Indeed, one of his friends, who could not long
check his curiosity, flatly asked Mr. A. why he had married
her. He answered that so far his course in the world had
been disturbed with little or no trouble and, fearing that he
might become too much attached to the easy things of this
life, he thought that by experiencing some afflictions he
would be weaned away from his false notions. This excuse
was too good to keep confidential. It ran from doorstep to
doorstep, until the wife in question heard it. Her temper
rose to a mighty vow. She publicly proclaimed that she was
not going to be made a packhorse to carry her husband to
Heaven—and forthwith developed into one of the most
pleasant and dutiful wives in town.[20]

But these are obscure, isolated instances that have been
dragged forth to the light of fresh print merely because they
show how the soul of our forebears, left to its own direction,
was apt to run a wayward course. Let us choose a few more
vivid figures even if they are better known.

### The Universal Friend

The observant and sprightly-penned diarist, Jacob Hiltzheimer of Pennsylvania, happened to be in the neighborhood of Cunningham's tavern near the Schuylkill on May
22, 1780. He had heard that Jemima Wilkinson, the "Universal Friend," was to preach. To him she appeared about
twenty-five years old, "her head-dress like that of a man and
she had the look of one, her shirt is buttoned close under

her chin and sleeves close to the wrist, with a black gown such as Church ministers wear, from her shoulders down to her feet." Then Jacob adds, "I expected to hear something out of the way in doctrine, which was not the case, in fact heard nothing but what is common among preachers and commendable. Her speech was much in the New England accent." [21]

Hiltzheimer's last observation presents a facet of this queer character which makes her difficult to place. To the orthodox believers of her day she was most assuredly an odd stick and, to those who held that women should dress as women and men as men, she presented a hybrid that they, not being able to understand, probably laughed at or would have driven from the sphere of her usefulness.

Jemima Wilkinson was born in Cumberland, R. I., in 1758, of Quaker parents who had been expelled from the local Meeting for refusing to use the "plain language." She must have taken rebellion with her mother's milk. With the other eleven children of this worldly-speaking couple we need not concern ourselves. It will be enough to follow Jemima's career, and we are glad to learn that she was a beautiful child much given to reading poetry; although it also seems that she avoided housework and was an ill-tempered vixen until converted by a traveling evangelist.

As we have seen in the actions of the Rogerenes, a spirit of religious rebellion had long been spreading over this corner of New England. A new sect appeared in Rhode Island, doubtless one of the reactions from the Great Awakening, calling themselves, "New Light Baptists" and known to others as, "Separates." They rejected all church organization and claimed to be directed alone by the unhindered guidance of the Spirit.

Although she attended their meetings, Jemima did not join the Separates. After that encounter with the itinerant preacher, she did take to reading her Bible and began avoiding society. It is reported that her search for spiritual peace ended in the arms of a British major "who left her to fight Yankees but lost her address." [22] Thereafter, when she was convinced that he never would return, the ferment of religiosity began boiling within her. She grew moody, complained of ill-health and, in 1776, when all the world around her was trembling at the alarms of war, she took to her bed. The physician summoned to attend her diagnosed her case as mental and beyond his skill. She began to have visions, which she described vividly to her anxious family. Finally she fell into a trance and while in this state of suspended animation was pronounced dead. Her body was placed in a coffin, carried to the church and the service begun. Scarcely had it started when, to the shock of all present, there came a banging on the coffin lid. People rushed to lift it—and up sat Jemima!

Out of an experience of this sort anything might come. Thirty-six hours after her "death" Jemima preached a funeral sermon on her old self—said that she had died and gone to Heaven, where God had re-animated her body and sent her back to earth to make His will known to man. She spoke then and afterwards with remarkable power and sweetness and exhibited an amazing knowledge of the Bible, quoting whole chapters of it from memory. Henceforth, she became the "Universal Friend." She claimed power to foretell the future, to discover the secrets of hearts and to heal diseases. Renewed and strengthened, she began public preaching. Her fame spread from local repute all over Connecticut and passed the borders into other colonies. Her charitable works were of the most commendable order: she gathered in foundlings and the poor and provided shelter and companionship to those who were homeless and had no friends. Followers, called "Jemimaites," gathered in her train. Churches were erected for her. Purses flew open. Her first converts were men and women of wealth and position, who could not but be moved by her charities. Among them was William Potter, a judge of Rhode Island, in whose home she lived for six years.

In 1778 she and two women companions asked the military authorities for permission to go to England and preach, but she got no farther than Newport where Jemima revealed her doctrine to the British officers there. Thence she went preaching to Philadelphia, where the Friends received her cordially in their Meetings. Near Tioga in northern Pennsylvania she built a model community which for a while appears to have been highly successful. It must have been at this time that she assumed her masculine attire. Her black hair was cut short and sleeked back and she wore a man's waistcoat over a white shirt, a stock and a white silk cravat "tied with affected negligence."

In 1786 Ezekiel Sherman, a disciple, visited the Finger Lake region of the Genesee with a view to selecting a permanent site for a colony of Jemima's followers. As the Indians were a danger, he chose a safer spot on Seneca Lake near the present Dresden, N. Y. In June, 1788, twenty-five of her followers settled there. The next year more of them came from Rhode Island and Connecticut. By 1790 there were 260 living in the colony. Jemima joined them. The community had built a log meeting house, a school house and a home for their leader. The last was a superior structure. Its chimney was so huge that it housed flues enough for nine fireplaces. Her own boudoir was furnished in the style of an aristocrat, with soft comforts and feminine amenities not generally associated with a religious leader. She had a fine mirror, clock, armchair, good bed and on the table, although her meals were frugal, was spread the best of linen. At a town meeting, the Jemimaites voted to call their town Penn Yan because they were part Pennsylvanians and part Yankees, and Penn Yan it remains to this day.

The devotion of her followers was due not alone to the forthrightness of her preaching but also to her willingness to share hardships—she always rode horseback until age forced her to take a coach—and because she seemed to have learned the secret of perpetual youth. When she was forty, she appeared only thirty. Her ruddy complexion, fine teeth and beautiful eyes remained with her to the end.

In the frontier countryside she soon became a power. After listening to her sermons, the warring Indians assembled at Canandaigua and signed a treaty of peace in 1794. All this time Jemima continued to aid the poor and struggled vainly to keep peace among her followers. Judge Potter, who had been her stalwart support for many years and who had supplied the financial backing for the community, seceded and sued her for blasphemy. She was arrested but in court defended herself successfully. Then Potter began litigation over the land. Now Jemima's devoted friend and constant companion was one Rachel Miller. All land that Jemima bought was in Rachel's name. Potter lost his case.

The Duc de Liancourt describes dining at Jemima's house, how she and Rachel dined privately in a separate room, after which the company was given dinner. Jemima then spoke to them through the doorway.

This "build-up" of her personality—not unlike that of a well-known contemporary woman evangelist on the west coast—was aided by the community's religious services. The congregation remained in silence until she appeared dramatically in their midst. Her mannish costume, her sleek black hair and black eyes, her musical expressive voice and graceful gestures never lost their charm. There was no distracting element in the service—no singing. Just Jemima as preacher and leader in prayer. When she finished, she began

shaking hands with those near her and the others did likewise. So the service ended.

Jemima was never at a loss to snatch at the dramatic moment. Once she claimed that, like our Lord, she could walk
on the water, and a day was appointed for her to demonstrate this Scriptural prowess. A platform was built on the
shore of Seneca Lake. Jemima's devoted followers strewed
white handkerchiefs where she would tread, and at the exact
peak of their fervor, she drove up in her coach. A stately
progress over the handkerchief-strewn platform and she
dabbled her foot in the water, turned to the multitude and
demanded did they believe that she could walk on the water.
They shouted their faith. Since there was no question of
their belief, she said, there would then be no necessity for
her to prove it.[23]

Except for the legal battles with Potter, her community
pursued a quiet, industrious pace. Many led celibate lives.
Her followers were early workers in the crusade for temperance.

When Jemima died on July 1, 1819, at the age of 61, it
could be said of her that she had "led an earnest, moral, con-
sistent life." That division eventually arose in the ranks and
that young people were lured away from it or not attracted
by its advantages was to be expected. But the erstwhile
Quaker maiden who died and went to Heaven and returned
to earth again not only proved herself a truly Universal
Friend, but she wrote "one of the most important chapters
in the religious and pioneer history of western New York." [24]

## Mother Ann

Chastellux, who traveled here in 1780-2, reported, "A very
comely young woman is, or pretends to be, impressed with
the belief that she is in her own person the Saviour of the

world revived, and travels from place to place attended by twelve young men, whom she calls her apostles; and who, if the general assertion be credited, have literally followed the precept of 'making eunuchs of themselves for Christ's sake.' General Gates told me that he heard her preach at Rhode Island, and I made an attempt to hear her at Philadelphia in October 1782, but the crowd was so turbulent (very common in America) that it was impossible to get near the place of worship." Later accounts say that she bore a child, but this may have only been a canard perpetrated by some evil-minded and envious gossip.

The subject of this report was Ann Lee, in her time one of the vivid personalities among the piously deluded. A native of Manchester, England, being born in February 1736, she married when very young, bore and lost four children, and in 1774 came to America. Here Abram Stanley, her husband, tiring of Ann's religious insistence, found consolation in the arms of another woman. Ann was now free to pursue her course as a "Shaking Quaker." She chose the wilderness around Watervliet, N. Y., as the scene for her activities. Thereafter she was given to strange pietistic extravagances among which she claimed to have a divine revelation that she was the reincarnation of Christ. One of her pet points of attack was marriage. She carried on such a loud and persistent warfare against the connubial state her ex-husband might have had cause for rejoicing.

From time to time she was variously accused: of witchcraft, of being a spy for the British (for which she was held in jail for a year); but by 1780 she had acquired quite a following among those who flocked to hear revival preachers and ranters. She founded a religious group, "The United Society of Believers," for the support and spread of which she started on an extensive preaching mission, accompanied by her "apostles," in 1781. That she was given a hearing in these years when the country was harried by war may seem odd, or perhaps the suffering from war was accountable for the attention common people gave Ann Lee and her fellow ranters.[25] Before she died in 1784 she had founded several Shaker communities. To her followers she was known as "Mother Ann." One of her devotees wrote this apostrophe to her—

> All hail! blessed Mother, the pearl of creation,
> The daughter of Zion, loved child of I AM;
> That ever dear Mother of peace and salvation,
> The Queen of fair Zion, the Bride of the Lamb.

## Vociferous Revivalists

The religious fervor of the common people in cities, towns and countryside rose and fell with a marked pulsation as it was whipped to fever heat by revivals or cooled off after them. Following the Revolutionary War, a stirring, with its storm center at Yale College, began to make itself felt in New England. Scarcely had the new century begun than through Kentucky, Tennessee and the Carolinas rolled another which not alone spawned a new race of picturesque and pious amateur Johns the Baptist but also gave birth to that colorful American phenomenon, the camp meeting. The open field and occasionally the city curb were pulpit enough for these vociferous preachers of the word and to them flocked the Gospel-haunted population.

In this era we see the rise of such rare figures as Lorenzo Dow, the tall, disheveled Connecticut Yankee, self-educated and self-ordained, whose first evangelistic tour took him 4,000 miles in eight months, during which he preached ten to fifteen times a week—a prodigious accomplishment in itself. In spite of the opposition of church ministers, who would gladly have applied the gag rule to all those who unsettled the minds of the simple-hearted people, Dow rolled up large congregations. And having come they were content to sit for hours under the ceaseless spray of his religious verbosity and his shriek-voiced exhorting. Truly the patience of these saints knew no end and not the least of them was Peggy, Dow's meek and pretty little wife, who traveled with him wherever he went. Eventually every state in the Union heard his voice and England and Ireland as well. Little wonder he was dubbed the "Eccentric Cosmopolite"!

Then there was Rev. Moses Crume, a mighty exhorter, whose wife used to shock his congregations by insisting on smoking a pipe. Matthias the Impostor was another. Robert Matthews was his name and Albany his birthplace and carpentry his trade. But he proved a better exhorter than carpenter, so he let his beard grow, put on a grotesque Peter-the-Hermit costume, took the name of Matthias, assumed fierce looks and acquired violent gestures and turned prophet and preacher. He was especially well-known in the western states and the lower South, where he suffered the well-publicized martyrdom of a jail sentence for stirring up the Cherokee Indians.[26]

Powerful of voice and long of wind, these Gospel hawkers who "sucked fire out of their texts" rolled up some mighty records in the annals of revival preaching. One of them had so powerful a voice that, so his congregation averred, they could hear his words pass through their heads and strike the trees behind them. Rev. Benjamin Abbott was so moving an exhorter to repentance that, according to his own modest testament, when women in his congregations wept over their sins, their tears lay in puddles around their feet![27]

These thousands of calls to repentance were supported by the preaching of a Second Advent. Without warning, in the night, He would come. The ears of those who gathered in country meadow and frontier street were constantly strained to catch the toot of the Seventh Angel's trumpet. And to such as could read were given or sold pamphlets that made sure the time was nigh. One of these modest but certain prophecies appeared in Philadelphia in 1814. A little book, much smaller than our present-day midget magazines, it bore the staggering title, "A View of the Last Dispensation of Light that will be in the World, Taking into Consideration its Certainty, Its Effects upon Mankind and the Time When this Light will be Dispensed." Its author was Theophilus R. Gates.

## "Theophilus the Battle-Axe"

In the annals of strange religions the palm will doubtless go to Theophilus R. Gates as the founder of the first sect designed to cheer unhappily married women and brighten the drab hours of hen-pecked husbands. This attainment was the apex of a long, crowded and colorful career.

Theophilus R. Gates was born at Hartland, Conn., on January 12, 1787. His forebears had been patriotic fighters and no less enthusiastic church deacons, while his immediate sire was a man given to spells of mental vagrancy that amounted to derangement. Book learning came naturally to the farm boy who, it seems, had not inherited a very strong constitution. He chose to be a schoolmaster. Early in life he came to "dread pleasures as an offense to God." The hunger in his soul, or it may have been merely an inherited tendency to wander, caused him to leave home. He headed south. "The simple, hapless sincerity of the bedraggled youth" won him kindly welcomes or harsh refusals on the doorsteps at which he halted for food and bed. It was in the South that doors opened more quickly to him. He happened to be in Virginia and heard a Baptist preacher whose words so moved him that he retired to a woods for a rough-and-tumble battle with the Devil. The next day he staggered into the home of the preacher and related his torment through the night. He was given shelter and the following Sunday stood before the congregation to tell how the angels fought for him as they had for Israel against Sisera.

This was the start of a long preaching career that never ceased till death. Theophilus wandered from town to town, lifting up his voice to all who would listen to him. He also spoke in almshouses, in hospitals and jails, carrying his message to those who could not gather in field or on city curb. At no time did he link up with any church or sect: as he himself expressed it in the little book mentioned above, "I have myself been several years without restraint from any society and under the discipline of no one." [28]

En route he found time to write and have printed (Heaven alone knows where the money came from to pay for these pamphlets) the record of his spiritual Odyssey, "The Trials, Exercises, Mind and First Travels of Theophilus R. Gates," which, considering everything, was not too modest a title, seeing that he was only twenty-three and youth can never be expected to excel in modesty. In 1813 he settled down in Philadelphia and published "An Additional Account" and a pamphlet called "Truth Advocated."

Among the friends he made during these early Gospel perambulations was Lorenzo Dow, the "Eccentric Cosmopolite." Like many a dreamer before him and since, Dow planned to found his own City of God. In 1816 he bought 200,000 acres of land in the Western Reserve, for which he laid out $50,000. Here he planned to build "Cosmopolite's Mount Sinai Domain," an asylum for the oppressed of all races. Its capital, "Loren, the City of Peace," was to be laid out in the systematic gridiron pattern of Philadelphia. The Domain even included a "Beulah Ethiopia," a special section for Negroes where they could work and live without masters or the embarrassment of Jim Crow laws.

Caught by the magnificence of this lofty dream, Theophilus managed to scrape together $500, with which he bought 30,000 acres adjoining Dow's Mount Sinai and where he planned to found his own center of freedom and righteous living. He would call this Theophilus Town. In 1825 both these Holy Experiments went up in smoke when Congress decreed that the original purchase from the Indians was invalid. However, in 1817, before this decision was handed down, Theophilus managed to sell 19,000 acres of his land for $275, which left him only $125 out of pocket from his "flyer" in holy real estate.

Meantime he had kept his pen busy. In 1814 appeared the "View of the Last Dispensation of Light" mentioned above, a prophetic work on the day when the lion would lie down with the lamb and all love each other as brothers are supposed to. In this little book his native glibness with Scripture is evident on every page, but it is rather disconcerting to find this untutored revivalist quoting with equal glibness from the Post-Nicene Fathers!

Six years later Theophilus took to crusading in earnest: he published in Philadelphia a magazine called *The Reformer*, devoted to religious views and especially to a campaign against the absurd Sabbath laws which were even proposed to stop the mail coaches on Sundays. Evidently the magazine enjoyed a vogue, for in 1830 he began another, *The Christian*, devoted to religious comment and to attacks on theologians, theological schools and the clergy in general. It was all quite in keeping with his refusal to join any especial sect; he was a free agent. Also he had an eye to journalistic advancement. At the time Miller was beginning to preach his final cataclysm of the world, Gates also became prophetic in his pages, searched for signs of the final end of things and sounded the trumpet of warning. Especially he seems to have been one of the early pacifists. The 1830's were

years of revolutionary unheavals all over the world and in
this distress Theophilus read the immediate forthcoming
wrath of God.

Since the final accounting was about to come, an increasing number of people, whipped into a frenzy of fear, began
worrying about the state of their souls and "sinners came
home like doves to their windows." The year 1831 saw the
countryside pulsating with revivals. Several men were busy-
ing themselves trying to prepare for the Kingdom of Heaven
on earth. Of these various preachers, two ardent workers
were Theophilus R. Gates and John Humphrey Noyes.
Noyes, the young Dartmouth law student, had caught religion and had his eye fixed on the millennium, due to come
in 1880 according to his calculations. On February 20, 1834,
he blandly declared he was free from sin. He soon gathered
followers who, calling themselves "Perfectionists," rose above
all laws human and Biblical. Of these two they fortunately
chose Noyes for their leader. He had a sense of business
administration, as his successful communities at Oneida and
Wallingford later were to demonstrate.

His propaganda, of course, required a mouthpiece, and at
New Haven he began his magazine, *The Perfectionist*. Evidently things were not going so well with Gates' two Philadelphia publications, for he soon closed them down and we
next find him chief contributor to Noyes' journal. But
Theophilus was not a man to be tied to any sect. He soon
showed himself out of step with Noyes' policy and principles
and the collaboration ended. Meantime, also, Theophilus
had married.

Now it may have been that his views on marriage induced
the next step or that his disillusionment with the marital
state drove him to conceive a war against it. In any event,
the year 1837 saw him editing a most inflammatory sheet
called *Battle-Axe and Weapons of War*. In his first number

he proposed that no wife should lack an attentive husband
and no husband an attentive wife. If, in the old phraseology,
neither of them was "buxom at bed and at board," then
something should be done about it. Moreover, children
should not be brought into the world unless parents were
prepared to receive them, which comes surprisingly near our
present scheme of "planned parenthood," showing that
Theophilus was a good century before his time. All worldly
goods were to be shared in a free and holy spirit of brother-
hood. This new religion, which he termed "Onanism," was
calculated to appeal to hen-pecked husbands and unhappy
wives.

At the time he revealed this unusual religion to respectable
Philadelphia, Gates was fifty, a lugubrious, watery-eyed man
by whom no woman could conceivably be attracted. He used
to go about the streets peddling his *Battle-Axe* for 5 cents
a copy. Even Noyes was angered, saying that Gates had stolen
his ideas. Plagiarism in free love was a new charge, so the
public was much confused. Although both believed in no
Sabbath, no baptism, no preaching and no marriage ties,
Noyes felt that free love was his own invention and rushed
into print with a new magazine, *The Witness,* to defend it
and his other Perfectionist tenets.

Nevertheless, Theophilus made his first convert, Hannah
Williamson, a young woman of "aspiring piety and unsteady
virtue." Although Hannah came of good Welsh Quaker
stock, she had been so suppressed as a child that when she
revolted, she went the whole and easiest way. One suspects
that when Theophilus first met up with her on a Philadelphia street, his new religion fitted in perfectly with the style
of life she had been living.

Together with her sister Lydia, of whose morals we know
nothing, Theophilus began his Battle-Axe religion. It was
all so simple that one wonders why somebody hadn't thought

of it before. If a lady Battle-Axe should find that a gentleman Battle-Axe was unhappily married, she conveniently
was vouchsafed an order from God in a dream to go to that
brother and offer herself as a solution to his problems. The
pair might live together a day, a couple of weeks and, in one
instance, it lasted for thirty years. The offending wife or
husband, if he or she was of the faith, could find no fault
with this new arrangement. Or, if they were not of the faith,
he or she was conveniently put aside and the new one took
his or her place. Hannah was a willing sacrifice to Theophilus
Gates' new faith, indeed she took it up rather strenuously.
On two occasions, when she discovered that she was about
to increase the race as the result of her immolations on the
altar of marital distress, she blandly announced that she expected another Christ to be born.

The first experiment of the new religion was tried on
Aaron Taylor Morton, a substantial farmer and veteran of
the War of 1812, who had a wife and ten children. Although
Aaron was a Battle-Axe and subscribed to all its doctrines,
when Hannah rode up with her vision and her blandish-
ments, he begged for a week to think it over. At the end of
the week he committed suicide, and Hannah and Theophilus
were unceremoniously chased out of town by the enraged
inhabitants.

The convenient doctrines of this new sect seemed to appeal especially to Dutch farmers in the neighborhood of
Pottstown, Pa. Here Gates founded a community called the
Free Love Valley. People there took to promiscuous sex
relations and were properly fined for adultery by the authorities. Gates was also an early nudist and part of his
ritual for his followers was to disrobe, male and female
alike, and march in single file down the village street to a
pool, where they all bathed together.

The prize convert in Free Love Valley was a farmer who

had a wife and six children. A Battle-Axe named Magdalene
came to his house one day and informed him that God had
chosen her to be his consort. So he deposed his wife, gave her
back her marriage portion, parcelled out the children among
relatives, and he and Magdalene settled down to an unholy
bliss that lasted for the next thirty years.

Theophilus the Battle-Axe died on October 13, 1846, and
his religion died shortly afterwards. It was not to be expected
that such an easy expression of piety could long outlast the
man who conceived it.[29]

Leaving Theophilus to whatever past deserts were dealt
out to him, we can now cease talking of grandfathers who
were queer. We have recounted tales of enough of them (for
the tales of a host more could have been told) to substantiate
the theory first expressed when this book began: that our
present generation of wags and eccentrics came by their
qualities naturally. May their sons and daughters, in turn, be
worthy of this fantastic heritage!

# NOTES AND REFERENCES

*Note:* Abbreviations are:

*Pa. Mag.*—Pennsylvania Magazine of History and Biography.
*Va. Mag.*—Virginia Magazine of History and Biography.
Mass. His. Coll.—Massachusetts Historical Society Collections.

## INTRODUCTION

1. ENGLISH THOUGHT IN THE EIGHTEENTH CENTURY, by Leslie
   Stephen, Vol. II, pp. 383-4.
2. SCOTCH IRISH PIONEERS, by Charles Knowles Bolton, p. 296.
3. DIARY IN AMERICA, by Captain Marryat, Vol. I, pp. 6-7.

## PART I. THREE CENTERS OF WAGGERY

### 1. THE GENERAL STORE

1. TRAVELS IN FOUR YEARS AND A HALF IN THE UNITED STATES
   OF AMERICA: DURING 1798, 1799, 1800, 1801 AND 1802, by
   John Davis, pp. 384-6.
2. MR. HIGGINBOTHAM'S CATASTROPHE, by Nathaniel Hawthorne.
3. That the pedlar was an easy mark for highwaymen and other
   evil persons is attested by many a local history. Dutchess
   County, New York, reports a pedlar murdered and his body
   thrown down a well. A heart-rending broadside poem of 1828
   relates how a country woman murdered a pedlar and then
   burned her own child by him to death. These examples can
   easily be increased.

4. *New York Gazette,* March 31, 1740.
5. Ibid., May 25, 1772.
6. *Pennsylvania Gazette,* August 5, 1762.
7. AMERICAN NOTE BOOK, by Nathaniel Hawthorne, pp. 187-8.
8. HAWKERS AND WALKERS IN EARLY AMERICA, by Richardson Wright. In these paragraphs on the Yankee pedlar I have helped myself liberally from my own book, now joined the great majority—"Out of Print."
9. AMERICAN NOTES, pp. 145-6.
10. SOME ADVENTURES OF CAPTAIN SIMON SUGGS, by Johnson J. Hooper, p. 12.
11. Hamilton's ITINERARIUM, edited by Albert Bushnell Hart, p. 196.
12. Norfolk Repository, Dedham, 1805.
13. JEROME: A POOR MAN, by Mary Wilkins Freeman, pp. 40-41.
14. THE GRAYSONS, by Edward Eggleston, p. 18.
15. SKETCHES AND ECCENTRICITIES OF COL. DAVID CROCKETT, Chapter 13.
16. HISTORY OF BURLINGTON, N. J., by W. E. Schermerhorn.
17. HISTORY OF MILTON, MASS., 1640-1887, by A. K. Teele.
18. Salem, Mass., *Mercury,* November 7, 1788.
19. *New York Gazette,* December 18, 1752.
20. Ibid., December 31, 1753.
21. Ibid., July 11, 1765.
22. *New York Journal,* January 25, 1770.
23. SKETCHES ON THE LIFE OF WILLIAM STUART, THE FIRST AND MOST CELEBRATED COUNTERFEITER OF CONNECTICUT, 1854, p. 9.

## 2. THE TAVERN

1. OLDTOWN FOLKS, by Harriet Beecher Stowe, p. 29. Courts in Maine clamped down on the idle at an early date. The Grand Jury reports, "We present Charles Potum for living an idle, lazy life; followed no settled employments." He was put under family government, being evidently a young man. Another, who, on being reproved for idleness gave a re-

proachful answer, was sentenced to twenty lashes. Mass. His. Coll., Vol. I, pp. 103-4.

2. ECONOMIC AND SOCIAL HISTORY OF NEW ENGLAND, by W. B. Welden; CITIES IN THE WILDERNESS, 1938, by Carl Bridenbaugh; and THE ECONOMICAL HISTORY OF VIRGINIA IN THE SEVENTEENTH CENTURY, by R. A. Bruce.

3. THE CHARLESTON STAGE IN THE XVIIITH CENTURY, by Eola Willis, p. 20.

4. A FRENCHMAN IN VIRGINIA. BEING THE MEMOIRS OF A HUGUENOT REFUGEE IN 1686, by Fairfax Harrison, pp. 66-8.

5. RETROSPECTION OF AMERICA, by John Bernard.

6. TRAVELS THROUGH THE INTERIOR PARTS OF AMERICA, 1776-1781, by Thomas Ansburey, Vol. II, p. 42.

7. Ibid., Vol. II, p. 33.

8. ROMANCE OF NORWALK, CONNECTICUT, p. 186.

9. Davis's TRAVELS, p. 70.

10. Hamilton's ITINERARIUM, p. 291.

11. REVOLUTIONARY NEW ENGLAND, by James Truslow Adams, p. 276.

12. PROVINCIAL SOCIETY, by James Truslow Adams, p. 75.

13. THE PROGRESS OF DULNESS, by John Trumbull, Part I, 1772.

14. *Philadelphia Mercury*, February 3, 1736.

15. *Pennsylvania Gazette*, September 5, 1737.

16. EARLY CLOCKMAKING IN CONNECTICUT, by Penrose R. Hooper, 1934, p. 8.

17. Diary of the Hon. William Ellery, *Pa. Mag.*, Vol. 2, p. 323.

18. FRENCH MEMORIES OF 18TH CENTURY AMERICA, by C. H. Sherill, pp. 237-8.

19. AMERICAN NOTE BOOKS, by Nathaniel Hawthorne, p. 244.

20. *Charleston City Gazette* or *Daily Advertiser*, February 19, 1790.

21. MANY MINDS, by Carl Van Doren, pp. 34-5.

22. *New York Gazette*, March 20, 1749.

23. Letter of Alexander Mackraby to Sir Philip Francis, *Pa. Mag.*, Vol. 2, p. 28.

24. THE SKETCH BOOK, by Washington Irving.

25. SUT LOVINGOOD: YARNS SPUN BY A NAT'RAL BORN DURN'D FOOL, WARPED AND WOVE FOR THE PUBLIC WEAR, by George Washington Harris.

26. MAJOR JONES' SCENES IN GEORGIA, by William Tappan Thompson.

### 3. THE BARBER SHOP

1. Pennsylvania Archives, 2nd Series, Vol. 5, p. 216.
2. *New England Courant,* November 30-December 7, 1724.
3. The Connecticut Sabbath in the American Museum, February, 1787.
4. *Boston Gazette,* May 7-14, 1739.
5. *New England Weekly Jouurnal,* July 15, 1740.
6. *New York Gazette,* May 21, 1780.
7. Ibid., January 5, 1758.
8. Huggins's title page reads:

Hugginsiana
or
Huggins's Fantasy
being
a collection of the most esteemed modern
Literary Productions
Exposing the Art of making "noise in the world without
beating a drum or crying oysters: and showing how
like Whittington of old, who rose from nothing
to be Lord Mayor of London, a mere *Barber*
may become an Emperor, if he has but
spirit enough to assume, and talents
enough to support the title

9. HISTORY OF AMERICAN GRAPHIC HUMOR, 1747-1865, by William Murrell, p. 55.
10. CAMBRIDGE THIRTY YEARS AGO, by James Russell Lowell, pp. 61-3.
11. *Boston Gazette,* December 18, 1755.
12. *Pa. Mag.,* Vol. XVI, pp. 7: 75.

13. Annals of Philadelphia, by J. F. Watson, Vol. I, p. 185. The abolition of queues in the army was not so easy. In April, 1801, General James Wilkinson, commander, issued an order prescribing the mode of wearing hair for both officers and privates. It was known in the army as the "Roundhead Order." Some older men refused to obey it, saying it was impertinent, arbitrary and illegal. Colonel Thomas Butler, an old queue die-hard, was arrested, court-martialed and sentenced to be reprimanded, but he continued to defy the order. He was arrested a second time on charge of mutinous conduct. He died of yellow fever at New Orleans in 1805—with his pigtail intact! *Pa. Mag.*, Vol. XVII, pp. 501-2.

14. A Sketch of the Life of John M. Todd (Sixty-two Years in a Barber Shop and Reminiscences of His Customers). Written by Himself, 1906, pp. 300-301.

15. House of the Seven Gables, by Nathaniel Hawthorne.

16. American Notes, by Nathaniel Hawthorne, p. 102.

17. Temple Bar, 1861.

18. William Marshe's Journal, Mass. His. Coll., Vol. VII, p. 173.

19. *The Tonsorial Art Pamphlet*, by M. J. Vieira.

20. Todd, p. 110.

21. *Boston Post*, May 18, 1880.

## PART II. WAGS AND ECCENTRICS

### 1. DREAMERS OF GRANDEUR

1. New England History, Elliott, Vol. II, p. 462.

2. The Hartford Wits, by Annie Russell Marble, p. 11.

3. Dudley's Letter.

4. Winthrop's Journal.

5. I am indebted to H. D. Eberlein and Courtlandt Van Dyke

Hubbard, authors of PORTRAIT OF A COLONIAL CITY, for information on van Braam-Hauckgeest.

6. It is easy enough to laugh at Stiegel's easy acceptance of the title of "Baron," but we had another American worthy who was even more anxious for a title—William Alexander (1726-1783), a Revolutionary general of outstanding accomplishments, and a mathematician and astronomer of note; nevertheless he was determined to have his place in the peerage. In 1762 he attempted to establish his claim as Sixth Earl of Sterling, claiming descent from Sir William Alexander, court poet and favorite of James I, who was later created Earl of Sterling. It was refused by the House of Lords. On his return to America, willynilly, he assumed the title Lord Sterling.

7. *Pa. Mag.*, Vol. XV, p. 495.

8. STIEGEL GLASS, by W. C. Hunter, p. 113.

9. Stiegel's Prayer written in prison reads as follows:

"Honored and truthful God, Thou hast by Thy Laws earnestly forbidden lying and false witness and hast commanded on the contrary that the truth shall be spoken.

"I pray Thee with all my heart that Thou woulds't prevent my enemies who like snakes are sharpening their tongues and who, although I am innocent, seek assassin like, to harm and ridicule me, and defend my cause and abide faithfully with me. Save me from false mouths and lying tongues, who make my heart ache and who are a horror. Save me from stumbling stones and traps of the wicked which they have prepared for me. Let me not fall among the wicked and perish among them.

"Turn from me disgrace and contempt; and hide me from the poison of their tongues.

"Deliver me from the bad people and the misfortune they utter about me may it recoil on them. Smite the slanderers and let all lying mouths be stopped of those who delight in our misfortunes and when we are caught in snares so they may repent and return to Thee.

"Take notice of my condition, Oh, Almighty Lord, and let

my innocence come to light. Oh, woe unto me that I am a stranger and live under the huts of others. I am afraid to live among those who hate friends. I keep the peace.

"My lord, come to my assistance in my distress and fright amongst my enemies, who hate me without a cause and who are unjustly hostile, even the one who dips with me in the same dish is a traitor to me.

"Merciful God, who canst forgive transgressions and sin, lay not this sin to their charge. Forgive them for they know not what they do. Forbear with me so that I may not scold again as I have been scolded and not reward the wicked with wickedness but that I may have patience in tribulation and place my only hope on Thee, O Jesus and Thy Holy Will.

"Almighty God if thereby I shall be arraigned and tried for godliness then will I gladly submit for Thou wilt make all well. Grant unto me strength and patience that I may through disgrace or honor, evil or good, remain in the good, that I may follow in the footsteps of Thy dearly-beloved Son, my Lord and Saviour who had to suffer so much for my sake.

"Let me willingly suffer all wrongs that I may not attempt to attain my crown with impatience, but rather to trust in Thee, my Lord and God, who seest into the hearts of all men and who canst save from all disgrace. Yet Lord hear me and grant my petition so that all may turn to the best for mine and my soul's salvation for Thine eternal wills sake. Amen."

10. *Pa. Mag.*, Vol. XXII, p. 380.
11. Mass. His. Coll., 2nd Series, Vol. IV, p. 194.
12. LIFE OF JOHN PATTERSON, by Thomas Egleston, pp. 142-3.
13. In addition to jumping, mighty pedestrianism was occasionally found. Thus the Annals of Albany record, as worthy of note that there arrived, on July 28, 1791, the famous English walker, John Stewart, en route from New York City to Canada. He had already walked Europe, Asia and Africa. A middle-aged man, he stood over six feet.
14. While Plummer was, doubtless, the first and only laureate, some early American poets may have had patrons. William

Sattentwhite, eccentric poet of Philadelphia, successively taught school, was dogged by poverty and tormented by an ill-tempered wife. He finally found a patron in Jeremiah Langhorne, who succeeded James Logan as chief justice, and for whom he wrote a eulogy. *Pa. Mag.*, Vol. VII, p. 83. The WRITINGS OF JONATHAN PLUMMER has been accorded a place in the Proceedings of the American Antiquarian Society, 1933.

15. Lord Timothy Dexter, a delightfully satirical presentation of that worthy by J. P. Marquand is the latest and most comprehensive study and has been used extensively in this short sketch.

## 2. *QUEER CONSCIENCE AND STRANGE VOCATIONS*

1. *Pa. Mag.*, Vol. II, pp. 243-4. A recent governor of Massachusetts displayed the same rectitude towards government stationery: at the bottom of the paper he used for private and political correspondence, he had printed, "This paper was bought and paid for by ——."
2. Elliott's NEW ENGLAND, Vol. I, p. 462.
3. Ibid.
4. Ibid., p. 473.
5. JOURNAL OF MADAM KNIGHT, p. 63.
6. Orcutt, p. 262.
7. *New York Gazette,* Decembes 24, 1734.
8. *Pa. Mag.*, Vol. LV, p. 45.
9. RECOLLECTIONS OF JOSHUA FRANCIS FISHER, by Sophie Cadwalader.
10. *Pa. Mag.*, Vol. LVIII, p. 157.
11. *Va. Mag.*, Vol. X, p. 30.
12. William Marshe's Journal from Virginia to Lancester, Pennsylvania, Mass. His. Coll., 1st Series, Vol. VII, p. 192.
13. HOME REMINISCENCES OF JOHN RANDOLPH OF ROANOKE, by Powhatan Bouldin of Danville, Virginia.
14. JAMES JOHNS, VERMONT PEN-PRINTER, by Robert W. G. Vail

in Papers of the Bibliographical Society of America, Vol. XXVII, Part 2, 1933.

15. *Pa. Mag.*, Vol. LII, pp. 162-7.
16. *Va. Mag.*, Vol. II, p. 100.
17. S. P. O. Colonial Entry Book, No. 92, Section 10, p. 279.
18. *Pennsylvania Gazette*, June 5, 1766.
19. *Pa. Mag.*, Vol. II, p. 266.
20. LIFE AND ADVENTURES OF BAMPFYLDE-MORE CAREW, p. 293. Carew was really a grand old faker. He never had any connection with gypsies. He took his gypsy words from the Canting Dictionary, published at London in 1725.
21. Watson's PHILADELPHIA, Vol. I, p. 271.
22. CONSIDER THE LILIES HOW THEY GROW, by John Joseph Stoudt, pp. 169-171.
23. Ibid.
24. *Pa. Mag.*, Vol. XIII, p. 450.
25. *Pennsylvania Gazette*, March 7, 1737.
26. ANBUREY, Vol. II, p. 252.
27. *Va. Mag.*, Vol. IV, p. 341.

## 3. *A BAGFUL OF ODD STICKS*

1. *Pa. Mag.*, Vol. XXXV, p. 51.
2. Washington's Household Account Books.
3. ENCYCLOPEDIA OF AMERICAN BIOGRAPHY.
4. Culpepper's THE ENGLISH PHYSICIAN first appeared in 1652. Few books touching on the garden have enjoyed so many editions; in fact, within the past few years it has again been revived and reprinted.
5. THE DESCRIPTION OF PENNSYLVANIA, by Thomas Makin. He died at Philadelphia, November 29, 1733.
6. *Pa. Mag.*, Vol. VIII, pp. 285-6.
7. Watson's PHILADELPHIA, Vol. II, p. 381 and *Pa. Mag.*, Vol. XXVII, p. 270.
8. Davis's TRAVELS, p. 95.
9. Letter of Breintnall to Collinson, February 10, 1746. *Pa. Mag.*, Vol. LIX, p. 54.

342    GRANDFATHER WAS QUEER

10. *Pa. Mag.*, Vol. XXVIII, p. 27.
11. *Va. Mag.*, Vol. XIV, p. 237.
12. Spark's FRANKLIN, Vol. I, p. 31-2.
13. *Pennsylvania Gazette*, June 18, 1767.
14. *Pennsylvania Chronicle*, June 6-13, 1768.
15. *American Weekly Mercury*, October 2-9, 1735.
16. Proceedings American Antiquarian Society, 1933.
17. *Virginia Gazette*, August 6, 1767.
18. *Pa. Mag.*, Vol. XXX, p. 4.
19. *Pa. Mag.*, Vol. XXXIII, p. 367.
20. *Va. Mag.*, Vol. VI, p. 241.
21. Broadside in John Carter Brown Library.
22. WILLIAM COOK OF SALEM, by Laurence W. Jenkins in Proceedings American Antiquarian Society, 1925.
23. Watson's PHILADELPHIA, Vol. II, p. 65.
24. *Pa. Mag.*, Vol. XXIV, p. 35.
25. ENCYCLOPEDIA OF AMERICAN BIOGRAPHY.
26. FORGOTTEN LADIES, by Richardson Wright, pp. 93-120.
27. WOMEN OF THE AMERICAN REVOLUTION, by Mrs. Ellet, Vol. II, p. 251.
28. *Va. Mag.*, Vol. X, p. 256-7.
29. THE LIFE AND SUFFERINGS OF MISS EMMA COLE. BEING A FAITHFUL NARRATIVE OF HER LIFE. WRITTEN BY HERSELF. By 1844 this noble biography had reached its fifth edition.
30. Barber's NEW JERSEY, p. 407.
31. Random Notes on the History of the Early American Circus, by R. W. G. Vail. Proceedings American Antiquarian Society, 1933.
32. PICKINGS FROM THE PICAYUNE, by Felix O. C. Darley.
33. Barber's CONNECTICUT, p. 116.
34. Mass. Bay Coll., p. 160.
35. HISTORY OF AMERICAN GRAPHIC HUMOR, 1747 TO 1865, by William Murrell, pp. 51-52.
36. OLD PATHS AND LEGENDS OF NEW ENGLAND, by Katherine M. Abbott, p. 94.

## PART III. CAVE DWELLERS AND SOLITARIES

### 1. CATACOMB ARISTOCRACY

1. Letter by Pastorius, 1683.
2. The Delaware Bank cave dwellers are spoken of in Watson's ANNALS OF PHILADELPHIA, Vol. I, p. 71; and more extensively in John Frederick Lewis's HISTORY OF AN OLD PHILADELPHIA LAND TITLE, Philadelphia, 1934, pp. 32-33.
3. The report from Woburn, Mass., is quoted in George Francis Dow's EVERYDAY LIFE IN THE MASSACHUSETTS BAY COLONY, Boston, 1905, p. 17.
4. Pennsylvania Archives: Series II, Vol. V, pp. 182-3.
5. A wilful adaptation of two lines from Pope's "Epistle to Dr. Arbuthnot."
6. Accounts of Benjamin Lay can be found in various sources: Watson's ANNALS, Vol. I, p. 23; Whittier in the introduction to the Journal of John Woolman and a purported list of his possessions in Amelia M. Gummere's THE QUAKER, A STUDY IN COSTUME. The last word on him has been written from English sources by C. Brightwen Rowntree in the Journal of the Friends' Historical Society, London, 1937, Vol. XXXIV, pp. 3-21.
7. Diary of Hannah Callender. *Pa. Mag.*, Vol. XII, p. 456.
8. Diary of Surgeon Albigence Waldo. *Pa. Mag.*, Vol. XXI, pp. 301-302.
9. Phyle's death is reported in the *Pennsylvania Evening Post* of January 31, 1778, and later in Barber and Howe's HISTORICAL COLLECTIONS OF NEW JERSEY. The pamphlet which revealed his history was titled:

The Hermit
Or an account of Francis Adam Joseph Phyle
A native of Switzerland
Who lived without the use of fire for upwards
Of twenty-two years, in a small cave in the
Midst of a wood, near Mount Holly in

Burlington County, New Jersey; and was found
Dead therein in the year 1788. In a series of letters
From
Batlus Hiltzhimer to Melchior Miller
Interspersed with some
Observations of the Author and
Sentiments of celebrated men of New Jersey
Published by John Atkinson
Printed by John Bioren, No. 88 Chestnut Street
Philadelphia, 1811.

It ran to 102 pages. A second edition appeared the same year.

10. MEMOIRS OF AN AMERICAN LADY, by Mrs. Anne Grant, p. 78.

11. HISTORICAL COLLECTIONS OF CONNECTICUT, by John W. Barber, pp. 150-7. Apropos of the hiding of the regicides in this cave, it is an interesting coincidence that John Bigg, clerk to Simon Mapie, another of the judges of Charles I, also became a recluse. On the restoration of Charles II, he made a cave at Dinton in Buckinghamshire and lived there the rest of his life. He lived mostly in tatters, but had three bottles slung from a belt round his waist, one for strong beer, one for small beer and the third for milk. He died in 1696 at the age of 97. Vide *The Wonderful New Magazine*, Vol. I, p. 88.

12. Barber's CONNECTICUT reports the hermitess of Ridgefield, pp. 400-1. Sarah Bishop may have been the daughter of David Bishop (died September 13, 1781), a refugee to Connecticut. Vide REFUGEES OF 1776 FROM LONG ISLAND TO CONNECTICUT, by Frederic Gregory Mather, p. 271. Her story is also told, without the Long Island beginning, in Kirby's WONDERFUL AND ECCENTRIC MUSEUM, Vol. III, p. 131.

13. NEW HAMPSHIRE COLLECTIONS, Vol. III, p. 214. However, authorities at the Pilgrim Society in Plymouth, Mass., disclaim any knowledge of Rachel and her curse!

14. SECRET HISTORY OF THE DIVIDING LINE, by William Byrd.

## 2. SOLITARIES ABOVE AND BELOW GROUND

1. The title of John Taylor's book, published in 1635, offers an elaborate and comprehensive description of its contents. "The Old, Old, Very Old Man; or, the Age and Long Life of Thomas Par, the son of John Parr of Winnington in the Parish of Alberbury; in the County of Salop (or Shropshire) who was borne in the Raigne of King Edward the fourth, in the yeare 1483. Hee lived 152 yeares, nine monthes and odd dayes, and departed this Life at Westminster the 15. of Novem. 1635, and is now buried in the Abby at Westminster. His Manner of Life and Conversation in so long a Pilgrimage; his Marriages and his bringing up to London, about the end of September last, 1635. Whereunto is added a Postscript, shewing the many remarkable Accidents that hapned in the Life of this Old Man (in Verse)."

2. Broadside in possession of H. T. Everett.

3. Broadside in possession of H. T. Everett.

4. Doubtless when Keats was writing on contemporary women he did not expect these lines would be applied to such as Bathsheba Bower.

5. *Pa. Mag.,* Vol. III, pp. 111-12.

6. HISTORICAL COLLECTIONS OF CONNECTICUT, by John W. Barber, p. 484.

7. Mass. His. Coll., Vol. IX, pp. 137-8.

8. Accounts of Robert the Hermit are found both in the pamphlet mentioned, a choice human document which its author turned into an abolitionist tract; and in the History of Rehoboth by Leonard Bliss, Jr., Boston, 1836, p. 249. Another interesting slave-sailor character was Venture Smith, of Haddam Neck, Conn., who though born a royal African was brought to this country as a slave, worked until he had bought his freedom, developing an interest in boats. Before he died he had acquired three houses, 100 acres of land and twenty ships engaged in river trade. His story as a slave and ship-magnate is told in the AUTOBIOGRAPHY OF VENTURE

SMITH, which went into several printings. He died in 1805 at the age of 77.

9. Watson's PHILADELPHIA, Vol. I, p. 20; and *Pa. Mag.,* Vol. LVI, p. 76.
10. Watson's PHILADELPHIA, Vol. II, p. 22.
11. CHRONICON EPHRATENSE, by "Lamech and Agrippa," translated from the original German by J. Max Hark, D.D., p. 89, and *Va. Mag.,* Vol. XII, p. 316.
12. The pious enthusiasm for conventual life as established by Conrad Beissel caused three women to "dissolve all associations and relations save those entered into directly under the cross of Jesus." One was Maria Christiana, wife of Christopher Saur, famous Germantown printer, who deserted him in 1730 and lived alone in the wilderness to prove by her example that "a man's spirit could dwell in a woman's form." Afterwards she held the position of under-prioress in the sister's convent. Finally, in her old age, she was induced by her son to return to her husband. (CHRONICON, p. 56.) Another was the wife of Philip Hanselmann, who, under the conventual name of Eunice, ended her days at a great age at the convent. (Ibid., p. 56.) On another occasion an irate husband demanded that his wife return to him, attacked the Superintendent and was finally given her back. It is said that thereafter this man always smelt of brimstone! (Ibid., p. 60.)

The most romantic of these pious women was Bernice Heydt of Oley. When merely a young bride, the Superintendent came to her house. So overcome was she by his preaching that, without her bridegroom's knowledge, she followed the visitor and in the settlement took her vow of eternal virginity. "Under the name of Bernice, she finished her course, which is recorded in Heaven, because, for her future glory's sake, she denied herself her carnal bridal couch here below." (Ibid., p. 69.)
13. Chronicon, pp. 71-7.
14. *Pa. Mag.,* Vol. LVI, pp. 266, 269.

### 3. GUILTY MEN AND INNOCENT WANDERERS

1. These three broadsides are in the John Carter Brown Library.
2. Newgate Calendar. London, 1932, pp. 261-276.
3. SKETCHES OF THE LIFE OF WILLIAM STUART. Bridgeport, 1854.
4. UNDERGROUND NEW ENGLAND, by Clay Perry, 1939, p. 23.
5. A NARRATIVE OF THE CONDUCT AND ADVENTURES OF HENRY FREDERIC MOON, ETC., by Walter Bates. London, 1817.
6. Ibid., pp. 48, 55, 72, 73.
7. *New Canaan (Conn.) Advertiser*, May 1, 1934.
8. WESTERLY, R. I., AND ITS WITNESSES, 1626-1876, by F. D. Denison.
9. THEY FOUND A WAY, by I. H. Sterry and W. H. Garrigus, 1938.
10. HAWKERS AND WALKERS IN EARLY AMERICA, pp. 214-15.
11. The data and quotations are from THE STORY OF THE LEATHER MAN, by Mary Louise Hall, in the *New Canaan (Conn.) Gazette*, May 1, 1934. He has also been a subject for study by the Westchester Historical Society. The facts regarding his early life were not furnished by Jules Bourlay himself, but are known from some documents he lost several years before his death, and from the examination of the contents of his bag.

Just as Francis Adam Joseph Phyle, hermit of Burlington, N. J., had his counterpart in an Albany hermit, so did Jules Bourlay have a "twin" in Maine. The town of Exeter gave shelter to an old hermit known as "Leather French." He, too, always wore leather clothes and he lived in "an old hut on the hurricane lands." After his death, David Barker, local poet, wrote a whimsical poem to his memory.

## PART IV. THE GOSPEL-GLUTTED

### 1. ECCENTRICS IN PARSONAGE AND PULPIT

1. EVERYDAY LIFE IN THE MASSACHUSETTS BAY COLONY, by George Francis Dow, p. 175. SEWALL PAPERS, Vol. II, p. 175. Rev. Michael Wigglesworth was an extraordinary character. Born in New England in 1631, he was taken by his family to Connecticut. He was graduated from Harvard in 1631, served as tutor and fellow of the college, and when offered its presidency, declined it on account of ill health. In fact, he was a life-long invalid, suffering from a mysterious disease, which compelled him for a time to suspend his ministry and live in the West Indies. Besides being Malden's physician, he served as its pastor for nearly fifty years. While ill, he wrote poetry. He is especially remembered for THE DAY OF DOOM, first published in 1642, which for many years was taught to children and properly terrified them.
2. Cuthbertson's Diary. *Pa. Mag.,* Vol. LVII, p. 126.
3. Barber's HISTORICAL COLLECTIONS OF CONNECTICUT, p. 508.
4. HISTORY OF ELIZABETH, N. J., by Edwin F. Hatfield, pp. 281-9.
5. Mass. His. Coll., 2nd Series, Vol. II, p. 117.
6. *History of Milton, Mass.* Edited by A. K. Teele, p. 242.
7. HISTORY OF ANCIENT WOODBURY, by William Cothren, Vol. I, p. 32.
8. Mass. His. Coll., 2nd Series, Vol. III, p. 188.
9. CITIES IN THE WILDERNESS, by Carl Bridenbaugh, p. 38.
10. THE OLD SOUTH, by William E. Dodd, p. 138.
11. *Va. Mag.,* Vol. XV, p. 405.
12. Abridgement of Laws of Virginia, *Va. Mag.,* Vol. IX, p. 372.
13. Council and General Court Records, 1641-1659, *Va. Mag.,* Vol. IX, p. 97. Henry Charlton's wrath against the clergy is tame, however, compared with the gross misbehavior of Henry Ayscough, who came into a Virginia Church in 1687 very drunk. He unbuttoned his coat and offered to fight any two persons there. He also tried to ride his horse into the

church. The authorities dealt with him according to his misdeeds and the case is set down in the Henrica County Minute Book, p. 185.

14. CITIES, Bridenbaugh, p. 264.
15. FOUNDING OF AMERICAN CIVILIZATION, by J. J. Wertenbacher, p. 190. These figures reveal how lightly the Dutch West India Company kept its pledge to send over and support "good and suitable preachers, school-masters and comforters of the sick." During the whole Dutch period only thirteen ministers were sent over. The pay was so small that it was difficult to induce ministers to leave home. Later in the seventeenth century the parson was selected by vote of the freeholders in each town and supported by taxes levied upon all alike.
16. EVERYDAY, Dow, pp. 95-6.
17. THE STORY OF AN OLD FARM, by Andrew D. Mellick, Jr., p. 618.
18. ROMANCE OF NORWALK, by Elsie Nicholas Danenberg, p. 98. Alas, this happened to Mr. Buckingham after serving thirty years in the ministry.
19. Barber's CONNECTICUT, p. 492.
20. *Va. Mag.*, Vol. XV, p. 377.
21. Mellick's OLD FARM, p. 447.
22. SOME PHASES OF SEXUAL MORALITY AND CHURCH DISCIPLINE IN COLONIAL NEW ENGLAND, by Charles Francis Adams. Mass. His. Soc., Series II, Vol. VI, pp. 417-516.
23. HISTORY OF THE FIRST CHURCH OF HARTFORD, by George Leon Walker.
24. Mellick's OLD FARM, p. 619.
25. Sewall's Diary, Vol. II, p. 15.
26. ANNALS OF PHILADELPHIA, Watson, Vol. I, pp. 334-5.
27. *Pa. Mag.*, Vol. III, p. 146.
28. Mass. His. Coll., 2nd Series, Vol. VI, p. 420-1.
29. The story of "The Amorous Mr. Batchiler" is told with great tenderness, by Elizabeth Reynard in THE NARROW LAND, pp. 190-98.
30. New Jersey Archives, 1st Series, Vol. XII, p. 75.

31. CITIES, Bridenbaugh, p. 73.

32. Mass. His. Coll., 2nd Series, Vol. X, p. 46.

33. THE NEW ENGLAND HISTORY, by Charles W. Elliott, Vol. II, p. 147.

34. EVERYDAY, Dow, p. 103.

35. Elliott's NEW ENGLAND, Vol. II, p. 147.

36. SCOTCH IRISH PIONEERS, by Charles Knowles Bolton, p. 302.

37. In THE MINISTER'S BLACK VEIL, Hawthorne tells of Parson Hooper who also kept his face covered. It stems from "Handkerchief Moody."

38. Apropos the Byles-Green wit contest, in 1756 there was a duel of wits between Jonathan Gowen of Lynn and Joseph Emerson of Reading, Mass. It was held out of doors and attended by large crowds. Gowen won.

39. MEMOIRS OF A ROYALIST PREACHER, by Rev. Jonathan Boucher, p. 123. Portrait courtesy Houghton Mifflin Co.

40. New Jersey Archives, 1st Series, Vol. XXVI, pp. 213-5.

41. WOODBURY, Cothren, p. 83.

42. AMERICAN CIVILIZATION, Wertenbacker, p. 97.

43. NEW JERSEY, Barber, p. 42.

44. *New York Weekly Journal,* February 15, 1742.

45. Watson's PHILADELPHIA, Vol. I, p. 553.

## 2. *FUN AT THE STEEPLE HOUSE*

1. Sewall's Diary, Vol. I, p. 118.

2. HISTORY OF NEW LONDON, by Frances M. Caulkins, p. 4.

3. Ibid., p. 379.

4. Mellick's OLD FARM, p. 197.

5. *Va. Mag.,* Vol. XII, p. 36.

6. HISTORY OF REFORMED CHURCH OF CLAVERACK, by F. N. Zabriskie, Jr.

7. CITIES, Bridenbaugh, pp. 107, 112.

8. REVOLUTIONARY NEW ENGLAND, by James Truslow Adams, pp. 38-9.

9. DOCUMENTARY HISTORY OF NEW YORK, Vol. I, p. 186.

10. Records of the Arts and Grants of the Town of Norwich, Connecticut.
11. CLERGY AND CHAPLAINS OF THE REVOLUTION, by J. T. Headley, p. 17.
12. TRAVELS THROUGH THE INTERIOR PARTS OF AMERICA, by Thomas Anburey.
13. FRENCH MEMOIRS OF 18TH CENTURY AMERICA, by Charles H. Sherrill, p. 260.
14. Ibid.
15. SEX MORALITY, Adams.
16. MILTON, Teele, p. 136.
17. NEW LONDON, Caulkins, p. 198.
18. Sewall's Diary, Vol. I, p. 445.
19. SEX MORALITY, Adams.
20. *Pa. Mag.,* Vol. XIX, p. 346.
21. Watson's PHILADELPHIA, Vol. II, p. 121.
22. SEX MORALITY, Adams.
23. *Va. Mag.,* Vol. XIII, p. 389.
24. Ibid., Vol. XIX, p. 96.
25. Ibid., Vol. VIII, p. 77.
26. Ibid., Vol. IV, p. 407.
27. Ibid., Vol. VI, p. 103.
28. Mass. His. Coll., 2nd Series, Vol. VIII, p. 24.
29. Ibid., Vol. VI, p. 826.
30. HISTORY OF WEYMOUTH, MASSACHUSETTS, Vol. II, p. 826.
31. THE CLERGY OF CONNECTICUT IN REVOLUTIONARY DAYS, by Alice M. Baldwin, p. 24.
32. Elliott's NEW ENGLAND, Vol. I, p. 157.
33. Baldwin's CLERGY OF CONNECTICUT, p. 24.
34. AN HISTORICAL ACCOUNT OF THE FIRST SETTLEMENT OF SALEM IN WEST JERSEY, by John Fenwick, pp. 97-8.
35. AFRICAN SLAVE TRADE IN COLONIAL TIMES, by G. C. Mason in American Historical Record, Vol. I, 1872.
36. VIRGINIA'S CONTRIBUTION TO SCIENCE, by L. G. Tyler. Proceedings American Antiquarian Society, 1915, p. 367.
37. *Pa. Mag.,* Vol. IV, p. 85.
38. *Va. Mag.,* Vol. X, pp. 128-9.

352 GRANDFATHER WAS QUEER

39. THE LOYAL VERSES OF JOSEPH STANSBURY AND DR. JONATHAN ODELL RELATING TO THE AMERICAN REVOLUTION. Edited by Winthrop Sargent, p. 6.
40. Headley's CLERGY AND CHAPLAINS, p. 20.
41. HISTORY OF MILTON, MASSACHUSETTS, by Teele, p. 262.
42. THE AMERICAN FARMER, by Crèvecœur, p. 234.
43. THE FIRST CENTURY OF THE HISTORY OF SPRINGFIELD, MASSASETTS, by Henry M. Bart, p. 429.
44. Watson's PHILADELPHIA, Vol. II, p. 417.
45. PETER KALM'S TRAVELS IN NORTH AMERICA, edited by Adolf R. Benson, Vol. I, p. 24.
46. Bridenbaugh's CITIES, p. 105.
47. Sewall's Diary, Vol. I, p. 155.
48. THE NEGRO PEW: Being an Inquiry concerning the Propriety of Distinction in the House of God, on Account of Color.
49. THE HERMIT IN PHILADELPHIA, by Peter Atall, Esq. (Robert Waln, Jr.), p. 34.
50. OLD TIME SCHOOLS AND SCHOOL BOOKS, by Clifton Johnson, p. 98.
51. Davis's TRAVELS, p. 332.
52. WRITINGS OF COLONEL WILLIAM BYRD OF WESTOVER IN VIRGINIA, ESQ. Edited by J. S. Bassett, p. 323.
53. Mellick's OLD FARM, p. 436.
54. CHARLESTON, HISTORIC AND ROMANTIC, by Harriette K. Leiding, p. 42.
55. FRENCH MEMOIRS, Sherrill, p. 58.
56. HAWKERS AND WALKERS IN EARLY AMERICA, Wright.
57. Bridenbaugh's CITIES, p. 149.
58. Mass. His. Coll., 2nd Series, Vol. VIII, p. 159.
59. NEW JERSEY, Barber, pp. 49-50. Watson's PHILADELPHIA, Vol. I, p. 551.
60. Mass. His. Coll., 2nd Series, Vol. III, p. 197.

## 3. A GALAXY OF GOD'S FOOLS

1. HISTORICAL SKETCHES OF NORTH CAROLINA, p. 170.
2. Pa. Mag., Vol. VII, p. 354.

3. THE OLD SOUTH, Dodd, p. 160.
4. Elliott's NEW ENGLAND, Vol. II, p. 391.
5. New York Council Minutes.
6. Watson's PHILADELPHIA, Vol. I, p. 406.
7. Ibid., p. 372.
8. Ibid., p. 271.
9. *Pennsylvania Gazette*, 1749.
10. Watson's PHILADELPHIA, Vol. II, p. 271.
11. *Pa. Mag.*, Vol. XXXVII, p. 56.
12. COMPLETE HISTORY OF CONNECTICUT, by Benjamin Trumbull, Vol. II, pp. 19-20.
13. Sewall's Diary, Vol. II, p. 15.
14. Caulkins' NEW LONDON, pp. 201-21.
15. Barber's CONNECTICUT, p. 280.
16. Ibid., p. 286.
17. Ibid., pp. 425-6.
18. Barber's NEW JERSEY, pp. 150-1.
19. Barber's NEW YORK, pp. 390-2.
20. Barber's CONNECTICUT, p. 116.
21. Diary of Jacob Hiltzheimer, *Pa. Mag.*, Vol. XVI, p. 176.
22. THEY FOUND A WAY, by J. H. Hine and W. H. Gurrius, p. 264.
23. Barber's NEW YORK, p. 368.
24. Rev. John Quincy Adams in *American Historical Review*.
25. HAWKERS AND WALKERS IN EARLY AMERICA, p. 224.
26. Ibid., pp. 220-3.
27. Ibid., p. 160.
28. A VIEW, ETC., p. 59.
29. THEOPHILUS, THE BATTLE-AXE, by Charles Coleman Sellers.

# INDEX

355

Lawson, Sam, 47
Lay, Benjamin: Quaker, 178-184
Leather Man, 236-239
Leek, John: eunuch, 316
Link, Mike: cave-dweller, 205
Livezy, Thomas: rhymster, 154
Log Cabin Clubs, 90
Loiterers, 47, 48, 49
Loren, City of Peace, 327
Lotteries, 53

Maelzl, John Nepomuk: showman, 159
Magdalene, Battle-Axe, 332
Mansion in Chinese style, 101
Masonic Lodges, 53
Masqueraders, 107
Matthews, Conrad: Pietist, 212
Matthias the Impostor, 325
Maypoles, 96
McQuain, David: hermit farmer, 205, 206
Medicine hawkers, 31
Meeting houses, 276
*Mehitabel:* merchant ship, 117
Mifflin, Walter: Quaker, 127
Miller, Rachel: Jemimaite, 321
Ministerial threatenings, 300
Mole, Human, 202-204
Moody, Rev. Joshua: sermonizer, 265
Moody, Rev. Samuel: exhorter, 265
Moon, Henry Frederic: puppeteer, 227-232
Moon hoax, 148
Morris, Captain Staats: 101; Governor, 154
Morton, Aaron Taylor: suicide, 331
Morton of Merry-Mount, 96
Mother Ann, 322
Mount Holly's hermit, 184-186
Mount Sinai Domain, 327
Muggletonians, 305
Munchausens, Local, 40, 41
Muskingum fertility, 41

Necromancy, 141
Negro nobility, 109, 110
Negro pews in churches, 295
Noyes, John Humphrey: revivalist, 329

Ordinaries, 50, 51, 52

Panharmonicon, 159
Parr, Thomas: solitary, 196, 197

Patch, Sam: jumper, 111, 112
Pedlar doctors, 33
Pedlars' carts, 29, 35
Pedlars' church advertising, 299
Pedlars' license fees, 25
Pedlars' packs, 25, 26, 27, 28, 32
Pedlars' homemade remedies, 150
Pedlars' tricks, 30, 31, 32
Pedlars, Yankee, 25-35
Penance in public, 284, 285, 287
Penn Yan, 320
Perfectionists, 329
Perkins, Josephine Amelia: horse thief, 221-224
"Personals," 164-166
Phyle, Francis Adam Joseph, 187
Pietists of the Schuylkill, 211, 212
"Pig and Whistle" Inn, 49
Plummer, Jonathan: poet laureate, 119, 132
Poetical advertising, 78, 79
Poisoning, 143, 144
Politics in church service, 293
Pomades and powders, 75
Prayers for conquest in battle, 290; for rain, 290; upon elections, 293; upon the news, 290
Preachers, Street, 306
Preaching, Competitive, 247
Preaching with gymnastics, 307
Prince Grippy, 108-110

Quack doctors, 151, 152
Quack medicines, 149, 150
Quaker cave-dwellers, 172
Quaker stock, 316, 322
Queues in style, 83

Rachel, Aunt, 193, 194
Randolph, John, of Roanoke, 130: as Congressman, 131; minister to Russia, 131; peculiarities, 132, 133
Rattlesnake bites cured, 151
Rauchner: barber-artist, 78
Redheifer: gambler and hoaxer, 158
Regicides, of West Rock, Conn., 188-190
"Regulators," 42
Repentant wife, 317
Restaurant hoaxes, 167
Revelry, Sunday night, 279
Revivalist preachers, 251, 252, 324-326
Revivals in religion, 251, 252
Rhymsters, 153, 154